METACOGNITION, STRATEGY USE, AND INSTRUCTION

METACOGNITION, STRATEGY USE, AND INSTRUCTION

Edited by
HARRIET SALATAS WATERS
WOLFGANG SCHNEIDER

Foreword by John G. Borkowski

THE GUILFORD PRESS
NEW YORK   LONDON

© 2010 The Guilford Press
A Division of Guilford Publications, Inc.
72 Spring Street, New York, NY 10012
www.guilford.com

Printed in the United States of America

This book is printed on acid-free paper.

Last digit is print number: 9 8 7 6 5 4 3 2 1

Library of Congress Cataloging-in-Publication Data

Metacognition, strategy use, and instruction/Harriet Salatas Waters
and Wolfgang Schneider, editors.
    p. cm.
  Includes bibliographical references and index.
  ISBN 978-1-60623-334-4 (hardcover: alk. paper)
   1. Cognitive learning.   2. Creative thinking.   3. Metacognition in
children.   4. Cognitive styles in children.   I. Waters, Harriet Salatas.
II. Schneider, Wolfgang.
  LB1062.M48 2010
  370.15'23—dc22
                                                            2009025319

About the Editors

Harriet Salatas Waters, PhD, is Professor of Psychology at Stony Brook University, Stony Brook, New York. She received her MA in experimental psychology from the University of Colorado at Boulder in 1973 and her PhD from the University of Minnesota's Institute of Child Development in 1976. Her research interests include memory development, the development of prose production skills, strategy use, and the structure and social co-construction of mental representations of early social experience.

Wolfgang Schneider, PhD, is University Vice-President and Professor of Psychology at the University of Würzburg, Germany. He earned his PhD in psychology from the University of Heidelberg in 1979. He is Past President of the German Psychological Society and President-Elect of the International Society for the Study of Behavioral Development. His research interests include the development of memory and metacognition, giftedness and expertise, and reading and spelling, as well as the prevention of reading and math difficulties.

Contributors

Peter Afflerbach, PhD, Department of Curriculum and Instruction, University of Maryland, College Park, Maryland

Martha Carr, PhD, Department of Educational Psychology, University of Georgia, Athens, Georgia

Byeong-Young Cho, MEd, Department of Curriculum and Instruction, University of Maryland, College Park, Maryland

Jennifer L. Coffman, PhD, Center for Developmental Science, University of North Carolina at Chapel Hill, Chapel Hill, North Carolina

Cesare Cornoldi, Professor, Department of Psychology, University of Padua, Padua, Italy

Steve Graham, EdD, Department of Special Education, Vanderbilt University, Nashville, Tennessee

Jennie K. Grammer, BA, Department of Psychology, University of North Carolina at Chapel Hill, Chapel Hill, North Carolina

Karen R. Harris, EdD, Department of Special Education, Vanderbilt University, Nashville, Tennessee

Deanna Kuhn, PhD, Teachers College, Columbia University, New York, New York

Thomas W. Kunnmann, MA, Department of Psychology, Stony Brook University, Stony Brook, New York

Xiaodong Lin, PhD, Teachers College, Columbia University, New York, New York

Richard E. Mayer, PhD, Department of Psychology, University of California at Santa Barbara, Santa Barbara, California

Peter A. Ornstein, PhD, Department of Psychology, University of North Carolina at Chapel Hill, Chapel Hill, North Carolina

Maria Pease, PhD, Teachers College, Columbia University, New York, New York

Tanya Santangelo, PhD, Department of Education, Arcadia University, Glenside, Pennsylvania

Wolfgang Schneider, PhD, Department of Psychology, University of Würzburg, Würzburg, Germany

Robert S. Siegler, PhD, Department of Psychology, Carnegie Mellon University, Pittsburgh, Pennsylvania

Harriet Salatas Waters, PhD, Department of Psychology, Stony Brook University, Stony Brook, New York

Theodore E. A. Waters, BS, Department of Psychology, Emory University, Atlanta, Georgia

In Memory of Michael Pressley

Throughout his remarkable career in developmental and educational psychology Michael Pressley explored the interplay between metacognition, strategy use, and performance, and applications of that knowledge to the classroom. Michael was convinced of Kurt Lewin's maxim "There is nothing so practical as a good theory"—or, better yet, a good theorist—and his laboratory always encompassed and impacted real children in real schools. His legacy includes a sophisticated developmental framework for understanding metacognition and strategy development. Always alert to new possibilities and applications, his recent chapter for the *Handbook of Child Psychology*, 6th edition (2006) heralded a new generation of research on strategy development. Where many of his colleagues saw a mature field, Michael argued that we are only at the threshold of understanding how strategy discovery, cognitive growth, and metacognition interact and play out in classroom settings. Many in the field now agree with that assessment. The current book brings together leading contributors to the study of metacognition, strategy development, and instruction to celebrate Michael's contributions and frame the key questions in the field for a new generation of researchers.

The chapters address different issues about how metacognition and strategy use relationships are best conceived, always with an emphasis on the implications for instruction. They are organized into three areas of investigation: (1) skilled memory; (2) math and science; and (3) reading, writing, and academic performance. These areas reflect the broadening investigation of metacognition and strategy development over the years into diverse cognitive domains beyond their early roots in memory. The different contributors highlight common threads in their investigations based on their interests in metacognition, strategy development, and instruction, in spite of the differing skill domains in which they work. This book provides a single source for researchers who want to better understand metacognition and strategy use commonalities across cognitive domains.

Michael had an unbridled enthusiasm for the field of metacognition and strategy development, and we think that he would be particularly pleased with this volume. He always had time to talk to anyone who was interested, whether it was at a conference or in a chance encounter, and was equally open to conversing with students as well as with colleagues. He understood the importance of sharing ideas and maintaining open lines of communication across different cognitive domains. The present volume honors that insight by bringing researchers together to share ideas about metacognition and strategy use, and we hope in doing so to frame future investigations on strategy growth through discovery and instruction.

HARRIET SALATAS WATERS
WOLFGANG SCHNEIDER

Foreword

Hidden in the 2004 version of his vita, Michael Pressley provided a unique and fascinating self-portrait: "Mr. Pressley does not align consistently with the political perspectives of either major political party with respect to literacy (or any other issue for that matter). He is not a registered member of either party, but rather prefers to be fiercely independent in his political affairs, sometimes characterized as moderate, but always advocating for the rights of children and families, especially their educational rights. He is a career supporter of foreign policy initiatives that are more likely to bring lasting peace to the world rather than proliferate conflict."

"Mr. Pressley" was indeed an iconoclast. Rarely do scholars include such personal reflections in their vita, and generally for good reasons. Yet, I believe Michael penned these comments for a good reason—a reason, in retrospect, related to the themes, scope, and importance of *Metacognition, Strategy Use, and Instruction*.

As in his political life, Michael did not align himself in his professional life to a single methodological perspective. His award-winning work on children's strategic learning in controlled settings used experimental designs, while his last empirical paper (published in the *Journal of Educational Psychology*) on the reasons for the striking educational successes at Chicago's Providence St. Mel school used a comprehensive, ethnographic approach. He was not a registered member of any particular theoretical camp, although he found the good information-processing model reasonably comfortable. He accepted this framework so as to focus on the nature of competent teaching to improve children's literacy and classroom achievements, using knowledge tested in diverse methodological paradigms.

If Michael sometimes saw himself as a political moderate, he was not a moderate in his search for sound answers to complex educational problems. As an editor and critic, he pushed friends and colleagues hard—as well as the field at large—to improve the preciseness of their thinking and the soundness of their methodological approaches. While there was for Michael—as for all of us—a deeply personal factor in his scholarship and its subsequent recognition by many professional organizations, he maintained an overwhelming desire to influence children's lives through quality education and, thus, to improve the world's chances for peace by elevating literacy and making "best teaching practice" available to all, rich and poor. Perhaps this is why he put so much time and energy into editorial assignments and tutoring young scholars, knowing full well his own limited time to effect sweeping changes in strategy-based teaching and learning in classrooms here and around the world.

Michael would be pleased with *Metacognition, Strategy Use, and Instruction*. His friends Harriet Salatas Waters and Wolfgang Schneider have assembled a group of colleagues who represent methodological diversity, theoretical richness, and innovative insights in their scholarly work. Their collective scholarship summarizes much of what we know about the meaning of skilled memory, how mathematical and scientific reasoning can be advanced through strategic learning, and how to improve academic performance in a variety of domains and settings. What is unique about this book is the integration of laboratory and classroom research. Michael Pressley was equally passionate about studying cognition in the classroom and in the laboratory and was convinced that research on cognitive development was of profound relevance for understanding children's progress in school.

The individual threads of Michael's scholarship over nearly four decades can be woven into a set of five interrelated themes: (1) understanding children's development of cognitive and metacognitive strategies; (2) designing interventions that promote complex strategy use, especially in early reading readiness; (3) classifying how motivation affects strategy use and self-regulated learning; (4) searching for strategy use in classrooms led by expert teachers; and (5) translating all of this knowledge—derived from controlled and naturalistic research settings—so as to improve teacher training. This is how Michael hoped to shape the lives of children and, in turn, to prod the world toward peace and prosperity.

This book reflects the major themes of Michael's research agenda. The first set of chapters—Waters and Kunnmann on strategy discovery in early childhood (Chapter 1); Ornstein, Grammer, and Coffman on teacher's mnemonic styles and children's development of skilled memory (Chapter 2); and Schneider on metacognition and memory development (Chapter 3)—emphasize the complexity involved in the development of skilled memory. In contrast to the first phase of memory research (around 1975 to 1995), the new wave explores the precise conditions under which goal-directed strategy use develops in young children, the role of strategic teachers in prompting children's enduring use of strategies in classroom contexts, and the process through which a child's knowledge of mental verbs (e.g., knowing or forgetting) and acquisition of a "theory of mind" become precursors to metamemory, and, subsequently, to enhanced recall performance. These three chapters reflect more complex theory, more intense data gathering, and greater respect for individual differences in background, talent, and motivation than the first wave of memory research.

The second set of chapters analyze the role of cognitive and metacognitive processing for success in math and science as well as the importance of contextual supports sometimes provided by peers. Siegler and Lin begin by focusing on how self-explanations promote children's learning (Chapter 4); Waters and Waters study how children and adult bird experts differ in knowledge utilization and self-monitoring (Chapter 5); Kuhn and Pease analyze how production and inhibition are key components in developing an effective use of strategies (Chapter 6); Mayer shows how multimedia instruction fosters scientific reasoning (Chapter 7); and Carr reports on how metacognition influences conceptual changes underlying children's math strategies (Chapter 8). These five chapters are noteworthy for their emphases on microgenetic designs in which variability among children—measured intensively over time—becomes the venue for observing stability and instability in strategy use. The field is indebted to Siegler, Kuhn, and other researchers for developing this methodological approach, whose impact is seen in many of the chapters in this section. Parenthetically, Michael's own use of the ethnographic method in classrooms at Providence St. Mel and at Benchmark School in Media, Pennsylvania, bears similarities to the microgenetic approach. Given the typical variability observed in individual behavior, even over short time spans, "single-shot, one-look" approaches to studying complex cognitive processing yields confusion and chaos rather than reliable, profound insights.

The third and final set of chapters—on reading, writing, and academic performance—mirror Michael's main concerns during the final phase of his illustrious career. Afflerbach and Cho demonstrate the potential role of the Internet in fostering reading strategies (Chapter 9); Harris, Santangelo, and Graham show the power of strategy instruction on skilled writing (Chapter 10); and Cornoldi develops an integrative model of metacognition, working memory, and intelligence as they conjointly influence academic performance (Chapter 11). These final chapters reflect specific interventions and a working theoretical framework that together point the way to improving classroom performance through the enhanced use of novel strategies in the essential skills of reading and writing. Waters and Schneider provide a summary and analysis of the book and highlight its major themes in the conclusion (Chapter 12).

The last decade of Michael's research career focused on the nature of classroom instruction, with a keen eye toward how expert and novice (or poor) teachers employ a variety of strategies useful to students in carrying out reading and reasoning assignments and how they motivate students to persist in the face of challenging work. In many respects, *Metacognition, Strategy Use, and Instruction* fulfills Michael's dream of using research in controlled and naturalistic settings to influence a new generation of teachers who will inspire their students to become lifelong learners, morally conscious about the world around them, and dedicated to peace and justice. Michael would be happy to read about the diverse, high-quality scholarship that has been assembled in this book—a book that sets the stage for the next generation of research on metacognition and strategy use.

JOHN G. BORKOWSKI, PHD
University of Notre Dame

Contents

Part I

SKILLED MEMORY

1

Metacognition and Strategy Discovery in Early Childhood

Harriet Salatas Waters
Thomas W. Kunnmann

Since the field of the memory development began several decades ago, evidence has accumulated on important age differences in strategy use, metacognition, and the impact of both on memory performance (Schneider & Pressley, 1997; Schneider & Bjorklund, 1998; Pressley & Hilden, 2006). Young children are capable of using strategies, but only if the materials are just right, the processing conditions are right, and instructions are set up to prompt strategy use. It is only as children mature that they broaden their strategy use across different materials and processing conditions. Hand-in-hand with strategy development, there are comparable changes in metacognition, with an increasing awareness of strategy use and its impact on performance (Pressley, Borkowski, & Schneider, 1987; McCormick, 2003).

Thus, we have a general picture of the developmental pattern leading toward more skilled memory, but have learned very little about how individual children make the transition from the more passive, less deliberate strategy use of early childhood toward the more active, goal-directed strategy use typical of older children. Part of the problem has been that early work on memory strategy development relied on adult experimental paradigms adapted for children. These paradigms were primarily used in cross-sectional designs and did not provide information about intra-individual patterns of development. Not surprisingly, researchers continue to bemoan how little we know about factors that propel children toward skilled remembering (e.g., Ornstein & Haden, 2001).

In the most recent decade, however, there has been a movement toward longitudinal and microgenetic investigations that can track individual performances across several years in the case of longitudinal designs and several sessions in the case of microgenetic designs (Schneider & Weinert, 1995; Schneider, Kron-Sperl, & Hunnerkopf, 2009; Siegler, 2006). This change in methods gives us an opportunity to answer a range of questions concerning intraindividual differences in patterns of development. Not too long ago Crowley, Shrager, and Siegler (1997) noted the interplay between both associative and metacognitive mechanisms in strategy discovery, pointing out that both play a significant role. Of particular interest to the current chapter is their discussion of the role of metacognitive awareness in children's ability to adapt and generalize a strategy to new contexts. Although strategy discovery can be accompanied by varying degrees of metacognitive awareness, such awareness often accelerates the generalization process (e.g., Siegler & Jenkins, 1989).

Granting that there is an interplay between associative and metacognitive mechanisms during the typical move toward more sophisticated, goal-directed strategy use, it is worth asking whether we can enhance that progression by intervening on the side of metacognitive processes. The literature on the links between metacognition and strategy use has produced a wealth of information, but has left us with a somewhat unsatisfactory result. Sometimes children will link their behavior to their performance, and sometimes they will not (e.g., Andreassen & Waters, 1989; Fabricius & Hagen, 1984; Pressley, Borkowski, & O'Sullivan, 1985). Particularly disconcerting is the fact that researchers can prompt strategy use that appears "strategic" but may not generalize or result in metacognitive awareness.

In light of the importance of enhancing children's memory skills as they proceed through the education system, the current investigation takes a closer look at the on-again, off-again pattern of early strategy use along with the unevenness of metacognitive awareness that accompanies that strategy use. The goal is to better understand "the forces that propel the development of skilled remembering" (Ornstein & Haden, 2001, p. 202). In turn, this understanding should provide some direction in how our society can produce students who are well equipped to meet the cognitive challenges of our information-rich age.

TRANSITION TO ACTIVE, GOAL-DIRECTED STRATEGY USE

On the surface, it is obvious that older children are more goal-directed than younger children in their use of strategies like rehearsal, organization during study, and elaboration. They are more likely to report what they are doing during study and can evaluate the effects of their strategy use (Schneider & Pressley, 1997). But there are degrees of "doing something" during study, some more obviously going beyond the task instructions and materials and some less. When an older elementary school child groups unrelated words together to form subjective clusters, there is little doubt he or she is organizing the materials for recall. But what about a younger child who is given a categorizable list of words comprising familiar categories and typical examples of those categories? If the child's recall should be grouped by semantic category, how confident can we be that he or she is being strategic? After all, the materials almost "shout out" to be grouped by category. Thus, we are still left with the key developmental question "How do we know when we have active, goal-directed strategy use?"

Some promise in answering this question more fully has come with an expansion of methods. Not only have researchers adopted longitudinal designs, but they are relying more on detailed analyses of ongoing study behavior within and across experimental sessions that come with microgenetic designs (Siegler, 2006). These designs open up the possibility of a more fine-grained examination of ongoing strategy behavior, ranging from timing characteristics, variations on strategy implementation, and strategy choices. And with these developments, there is the opportunity to reexamine the question about what constitutes active, goal-directed strategy use.

For example, Lehmann and Hasselhorn (2007) tracked the use of different rehearsal strategies, from simple labeling to single-item rehearsal to cumulative rehearsal, within and across sessions (with repeated assessments every 6 months for 2 years). The movement toward the more active, cumulative rehearsal across sessions was not unexpected, but closer analyses within sessions revealed list position effects and the coexistence of several strategies within single sessions. A more recent analysis of this study by Lehmann and Hasselhorn (in press) also showed differences in recall inter-response times between items rehearsed together compared with items that had not been rehearsed together. In sum, research indicates that movement toward active, goal-directed rehearsal involves more than just an increasing rehearsal set, and that there are important details in the study and recall dynamics of strategy use that are only revealed with detailed within-session analyses.

Earlier analyses available for organization during recall also reported some interesting details on the recall dynamics of that strategy (Hasselhorn, 1992). Children from second to fourth grade showed greater differences between within-category and between-category latencies under circumstances where they were more likely to engage in goal-directed strategy use (i.e., in a sort-recall situation with materials comprised of typical examples of familiar semantic categories). In addition, the size of organization chunks during recall has been associated with deliberate organization during recall (Bjorklund & Buchanan, 1989). With these findings, it becomes evident that researchers can take advantage of online strategy features to determine whether children are engaging in deliberate, goal-directed strategy use.

In the present investigation, we examine one of the classic paradigms that first tackled the question of strategy use, metacognitive awareness, and generalization of strategy use (Salatas & Flavell, 1976; Andreassen & Waters, 1989). Children in all three of our studies were asked to study and remember categorizable picture sets placed on a lectern-like apparatus that provides rows for picture placement that map onto the category structure of the picture sets. Both organization during study and organization during recall can be assessed in this paradigm. Our first goal was to pinpoint key processing features of goal-directed strategy use by using detailed assessments of strategy implementation. Once these were identified, our goal shifted onto how to best prompt strategy discovery. Specifically, the aim was not to simply prompt strategy use in a particular context, but also to prompt metacognitive awareness of strategy use in a manner that leads to transfer to more difficult variants of the memory task. In addition, the current investigation focused on early elementary school children who are rarely credited with deliberate, goal-directed strategy use.

STUDY 1: CHARACTERISTICS OF GOAL-DIRECTED STRATEGY USE

In order to highlight key features of goal-directed strategy use, this first study manipulated cognitive load during the memory task at two different ages in early childhood (first and third grades). By manipulating information-processing demands, the hope was to manipulate the relations between important aspects of strategy implementation, recall performance, and metacognition, and thereby identify features of recall dynamics that are tied to deliberate strategy use. In the light cognitive load condition, children were asked to study and recall a categorizable set of eight pictures, two from each of four familiar semantic categories. In the heavy cognitive load condition, children were asked to study 16 categorizable pictures, four from each of the four semantic categories. Two different picture sets were constructed from which both 8-item and 16-item sets were selected (see Figure 1.1 for one of the picture sets). Category organization was chosen as the strategy under investigation because objective and independent measures of both organization during study and recall are available.

In addition to the standard measures of organization during study and recall, aspects of strategy implementation were more closely monitored by including several additional measures. First, the number of items per category chunk was also assessed. In the heavy cognitive load condition in particular, it would be more efficient to recall all *four* items from a category before moving on to the next category. Although associative processes might produce some two-item clusters and give the appearance of strategy use, consistent three to four items in a cluster more strongly

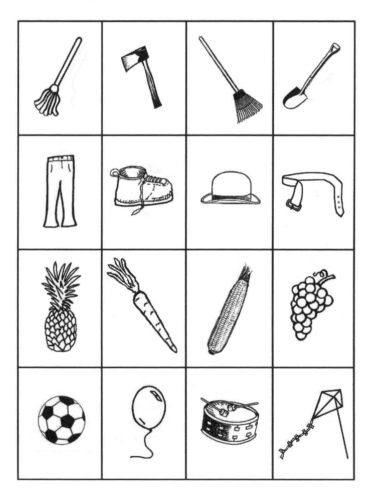

FIGURE 1.1. One of the two categorizable picture sets used in the present series of studies.

suggest deliberate organization in recall. Second, all of the memory sessions were tape-recorded and recall time between items within and across category boundaries was measured. Both adult and child studies of category clustering have reported faster times for items within category boundaries, suggesting that efficient implementation of category clustering during recall entails greater speed in moving through items within a category cluster (Hasselhorn, 1992; Pollio, Richards, & Lucas, 1969). Third, correlations between organization during study and recall were examined in order to determine whether organizational processes at the time of study were coordinated with organizational processes at the time of recall, a mark not only of strategy effectiveness, but of goal-directed strategy use (Lange, Guttentag, & Nida, 1990).

Procedure

Once again, 40 first-grade and 40 third-grade children were given an opportunity to place categorizable pictures on rows on a lectern-like apparatus, with the number of rows matching the number of semantic categories in the picture set. The children were shown their picture set and asked to name each picture. The pictures were presented in a blocked format with the category names mentioned in passing, without calling undo attention to them. After the children named all of the pictures, the experimenter placed the pictures randomly on the table in front of the children such that no two same-category pictures were contiguous. The children were then free to place the pictures on the rows of the lectern-like apparatus any way they thought would help them remember. After the children had studied the pictures for 1 minute, they were covered by an opaque cover and the children were asked to recall as many as they could in any order they wanted.

Findings

Organization during study was determined by first counting the number of picture pairs on the lectern rows that represented the same category. Perfect clustering for an 8-picture set would be a score of 4, and for a 16-picture set it would be a score of 12. Each child received a percentage score, that is, how many clustered pairs out of the possible maximum for each picture set. Organization during recall was assessed using the Adjusted Ratio of Clustering (ARC) measure (Roenker, Thompson, & Brown, 1971). Table 1.1 presents the means on all of the performance measures across age and experimental conditions. Percent recall was used because of the different sizes of the picture sets used in the two cognitive load conditions.

Two (age) by two (cognitive load) analyses of variance were conducted for each of the performance measures. Not surprisingly, third graders showed better recall performance, and recall rates were higher for the 8-picture set, $F(1,76) = 28.92$, $p < .001$, and $F(1,76) = 70.13$, $p < .001$, respectively. In addition there was a significant interaction between age and cognitive load, $F(1,76) = 4.11$, $p < .05$. Although both ages show a clear decrement in recall performance with the more cognitively demanding 16-picture set, the effect was more pronounced for the first-grade children. For the organization during study and recall measures, the 2 × 2 analyses of variance only produced an age effect in both cases, $F(1,76) = 4.39$, $p < .05$, and $F(1,76) = 6.04$, $p < .05$, respectively.

More interesting patterns regarding organization emerged when we examined the additional measures for monitoring recall dynamics. Beginning with the size of the category clusters during recall, main effects were accompanied by a significant interaction, $F(1,76) = 8.79$, $p < .01$. Mean differences across picture sets are not surprising since there is a maximum of two per cluster for the 8-picture set and a maximum of four per cluster for the 16-picture set. The key question was really whether the children at either age adapted the size of their recall clusters to better map onto the category structure of the different picture sets, an indication of intentional strategic behavior. The significant interaction indicated that first

TABLE 1.1. Mean Scores on Strategy and Performance Measures across Cognitive Load and Age—Study 1

	8 pictures	16 pictures
First grade		
% recall	86%	49%
% pairs clustered during study	64%	50%
Recall clustering (ARC)	.54	.33
Number of items per category cluster	1.55	1.56
Number of categories recalled	3.70	3.60
Within-category times	2.88 sec	7.06 sec
Across-category times	6.16 sec	8.88 sec
Third grade		
% recall	98%	76%
% pairs clustered during study	76%	70%
Recall clustering (ARC)	.73	.64
Number of items per category cluster	1.70	2.46
Number of categories recalled	4.00	3.85
Within-category times	2.05 sec	4.16 sec
Across-category times	4.18 sec	7.90 sec

graders failed to increase their category cluster size as they went from the 8- to the 16-picture set, whereas third graders showed a significant increase, $p < .001$, post-hoc Newman–Keuls analysis.

Further evidence of differences in intentional behavior across conditions and age was found in the analyses of time latencies within and across category boundaries. In these analyses we made specific comparisons within groups in order to test the hypothesis that within-category times should be faster than across-category times whenever children engage in deliberate category clustering during recall, a pattern consistent with adult strategic behavior (Pollio et al., 1969). Although unintentional associative processes can also produce some level of category clustering, these processes should not have as pronounced an effect on within- versus across-category times. Only four children who did not have both within- and across-category times were omitted from the analyses. Individual within-subject t-tests produced significant results for three of the four comparisons. Within-category times were faster than across-category times for the first-grade/light cognitive load condition, $t(18) = 3.12$, $p < .01$; for the third-grade/light cognitive load condition, $t(19) = 2.71$, $p < .01$; and for the third-grade/heavy cognitive load condition, $t(18) = 3.02$, $p < .01$, two-tailed tests. The comparison between within- and across-category times in the first-grade/heavy cognitive load condition, however, was not significant, $t(17) = .88$. It appears that first graders under the more demanding cognitive load were not engaging in deliberate, goal-directed strategy use.

One final set of analyses included correlations among measures of recall, organization during study, and organization during recall (see Table 1.2). Time parameters were omitted because they are primarily relevant in terms of the relation within and across categories, not in terms of absolute means. Correlations from the third-grade, 8-picture-set group were also omitted because of ceiling effects. The patterns of significant correlations among measures in Table 1.2 identify under which conditions we have deliberate, goal-directed strategy use. Starting with the third-grade children with the more demanding 16-picture set, we see that all measures are correlated. Organization during study predicts organization during recall and organization during recall in turn predicts overall recall performance. In addition, organization during study is significantly correlated with the size of the category clusters, suggesting that the children are recalling all items from one category before they move on to the next. With all this evidence we can reasonably be certain that the third graders under these circumstances are engaging in deliberate strategy use.

Using the third-grade pattern of correlations as our metric, we can then move on to the question of whether the first graders are engaging in goal-directed strategy use in either the light or the heavy cognitive

TABLE 1.2. Intercorrelations among Performance Measures across Cognitive Load and Age—Study 1

	Recall clustering	Items per cluster	% recall
First grade—8 pictures			
Organization during study	.79**	.84**	.45*
Recall clustering (ARC)	—	.90**	.30
Items per cluster	—	—	.42*
First grade—16 pictures			
Organization during study	–.04	.32	.48*
Recall clustering (ARC)	—	.84**	–.29
Items per cluster	—	—	–.20
Third grade—16 pictures			
Organization during study	.78**	.79**	.65**
Recall clustering (ARC)	—	.82**	.65**
Items per cluster	—	—	.79**

*$p < .05$, **$p < .01$, one-tailed tests.

load conditions. First, in the light cognitive load condition, correlations between organization during study and the two measures of recall clustering (ARC scores and number of items per cluster) are highly significant, .79 and .84, respectively. The correlations between the two measures of recall clustering and percent recall are weaker, with only the correlation between cluster size and percent recall being significant, .42. But when you consider the small picture set, and that category clustering is not necessary to be able to remember quite a number of the pictures, these weaker correlations may not surprising. Overall these results point to deliberate, goal-directed strategy use in this condition. In contrast, the results from the heavy cognitive load condition tell a very different story. Not only is there no difference in the time latencies within and across category clusters in that condition, the correlations between organization during study and the measures of organization during recall are not significant. Nor are the measures of recall clustering related to percent recall. In sum, there is no evidence that first graders are engaging in deliberate, goal-directed strategy use in the more cognitively demanding 16-picture set.

STUDY 2: PRIMING STRATEGY DISCOVERY

Study 1 produced the standard developmental pattern of strategy use in which younger children are capable of deliberate strategy use only under circumstances that encourage such use. The more manageable, smaller 8-picture set enabled the first-grade children to engage in deliberate organization during study and recall. This kind of developmental pattern lends itself to the typical interpretation that with time and practice in strategy use, children will eventually be able to implement the strategy in question under more cognitively demanding circumstances. The purpose of this investigation is to challenge this interpretation. Do we really have to wait for strategy use to become more practiced before children can use the strategy under more demanding circumstances? In Study 2 we explore two different options to prompt immediate broad-based strategy generalization. One possible approach is to double our efforts to prompt strategy use under the more demanding circumstances, anticipating that these efforts will lead to genuine strategy discovery. If so, there will be evidence in measures linked to goal-directed use and in transfer. A second approach relies on the importance of metacognitive awareness of strategy use and its links to performance. Here the hypothesis is that once a strategy is "discovered," children will be able to generalize the strategy to the more demanding cognitive circumstances. In other words, metacognition trumps the more incremental, steady progress associated with practice and automaticity.

In order to evaluate these two approaches, the present study manipulated cognitive load in a memory situation in which the children are prompted (by task circumstances) to implement an organization strategy, that is, category clustering. The same procedure and materials of Study 1 were used. Forty first-grade children were introduced to the materials by asking them to name the pictures as the experimenter presented them in a blocked format, with the experimenter mentioning the category labels in passing. In Study 2, however, the experimenter placed the pictures in both the light and the heavy load conditions on the lectern by category, guaranteeing that all of the children would study the materials by category. After the children had 1 minute to study their pictures, they were asked to remember as many of the pictures as they could in any order they wanted. We anticipated high rates of category clustering in both cognitive load conditions.

The children then returned in 1 week for a second session in which everyone was given a new 16-picture set. The purpose of the second session was to evaluate whether the children continued to use the strategy after their initial "discovery" of the category-clustering strategy during Session 1. Once again pictures were presented by category, but this time the experimenter randomly arranged the pictures next to the lectern after the naming procedure. Thus the children were given an opportunity to place them on the lectern by category or not. After recall they were also asked whether they had done anything to help themselves remember in order to assess their metacognitive awareness of strategy use. If practice in using the strategy under cognitive demanding circumstances enhances strategy implementation, then children assigned to the heavy cognitive load condition in Session 1 would be more likely to generalize to Session 2. If the key is metacognitive awareness of strategy use, then the light cognitive load condition would give the children an opportunity to reflect on what they were doing during recall and prompt generalization to the more demanding 16-picture set in Session 2.

Findings

The key question for the first session was whether the children would encode the category structure of the pictures during study and therefore use category clustering to help themselves to remember regardless of the cognitive load condition. Table 1.3 presents mean scores across the two conditions on all of the strategy and performance measures. For Session 1, there were no differences across the two cognitive load conditions (*t*-test comparisons) for any of the organization measures (ARC scores, number of categories, number of items per category chunk). Children in both groups also showed faster times for within-category items compared with across-category times, even though the children in the 16-picture condition were overall slower in recalling items ($p < .05$). In sum, children in both conditions appeared to be engaging in deliberate, goal-directed strategy use, based on key markers regarding recall dynamics.

With comparable levels of organization established in Session 1, the next step was to compare changes in performance in Session 2. In order to test for differences relative to Session 1, 2 (cognitive load training) × 2 (session) analyses of variance were conducted on all measures except for organization during study (only Session 2 data available). The first and most important question was whether children in both cognitive load groups, having experienced the value of category-clustering in recall, would initiate a category clustering strategy during study. The results were quite dramatic. Out of a possible 12 clustered pairs on the lectern (perfect organization) the mean scores were 8.60 versus 1.90 (light vs. heavy cognitive load training), producing a highly significant difference, $t(38) = 7.25, p < .001$. Other organization measures followed suit, with both ARC scores and number of items per category chunk greater in the light (vs. heavy) cognitive load training groups in Session 2 compared with no differences in session one, $F(1,38) = 4.88, p < .05$, and $F(1,38) = 29.38, p < .001$, respectively. Experiencing the value of category clustering under light cognitive demands led to transfer to a more difficult memory task (16 pictures in the second session), but not so if the experi-

TABLE 1.3. Mean Scores on Strategy and Performance Measures across Sessions—Study 2 (First Graders)

	8 pictures	16 pictures
Session 1		
% pairs clustered during study	—[a]	—
Recall clustering (ARC)	.76	.70
Number of items per category cluster	1.69	1.97
Number of categories recalled	3.70	3.60
Within-category times	2.08 sec	5.14 sec
Across-category times	5.27 sec	10.35 sec
% recall	85%	55%
Session 2 (all children receive 16 pictures to study)		
Number of pairs clustered during study (maximum = 12)	8.60	1.90
Recall clustering (ARC)	.72	.24
Number of items per category cluster	2.32	1.32
Number of categories recalled	3.50	3.75
Within-category times	4.00 sec	4.87 sec
Across-category times	7.82 sec	7.13 sec
% recall	62%	47%
Metacognition score (0–3)	2.00	0.50

[a]Since the experimenter placed the pictures on the lectern-like apparatus, the number of clustered pairs during the study was the maximum for both the 8-picture and 16-picture-set groups.

ence occurred under more demanding circumstances. Post-hoc Newman–Keuls analyses support all interpretations of the reported interactions. With regard to times and percent recall, the only differences were faster times and greater percent recall in the light cognitive load group in Session 1, probably due to the easy picture set.

Our last question was whether performance on the metacognition question at the end of Session 2 reflected the differences in strategy use between the two groups. Two raters scored the children's responses on a 4-point scale representing a range from no statement of category structure use (0) to an explicit and complete statement of using categories, naming at least three of the categories (3). Initial agreement between scorers was 90% on the children's responses, with disagreements resolved by discussion. Mean metacognition scores are presented in Table 1.3 and examples from the full range of the metacognition scale are presented in Table 1.4. The light cognitive load training group articulated a clear-cut and explicit understanding of how they had used category clustering to help themselves remember in the second session. In contrast, the heavy cognitive load group had little to say about using organization as a strategy, not surprising since they did not organize their study or retrieval efforts (2.00 vs 0.50, $t(38) = 4.81$, $p < .001$).

In sum, the results of Study 2 support the hypothesis that strategy discovery is more likely under lighter cognitive demands. Particularly striking is the fact that both groups in the initial session showed high rates of category clustering during recall. Nonetheless, only the children under the light cognitive load condition transferred an organization strategy to the second session where they had an opportunity to group their pictures for study. It appears that the lighter cognitive load condition enabled the children to recognize their own organization efforts during recall and facilitated the integration of category clustering into a goal scheme for the memory task. The implications for educational practices are quite significant. Strategy discovery is more likely under "easy" learning conditions where in fact the strategic behavior is not that crucial.

TABLE 1.4. Sample Metacognition Responses across Scale Points

Scale point zero: No reference to use of categorization; may indicate an idiosyncratic or illogical plan for recall or have no recognition of having done anything.

"Easy, because B starts with ball and that's for my last name and D for drum, I remember the words, different words for the different pictures."

"Because I memorized them by saying them."

"I don't know."

Scale point 1: Child refers to one of the categories, but the rest of the explanation refers to idiosyncratic groupings.

"These are animals. I don't know. So I could remember them better."

"By thinking of them. Um, I, um remembered, I think for some animals and I said the ducky and the squirrel ... and the snake."

Scale point 2: Child names two of the categories, but the rest are mislabeled or not identified.

"So that the animals were together, the waterfall and mountain are together. The others are mixed up."

"The things that move and the animals are here. I just remembered those."

"Ducks swim in water, you drive these, can and pitcher go together."

Scale point 3: At least three of the four categories are mentioned. Child recognizes having gone group by group in trying to remember items.

"These fly and these you could work with and these two you eat. And you wear."

"These are two vehicles, these are two animals, these are two things in nature."

" They are the same: toys, clothes, food, and tools."

STUDY 3: ROLE OF METACOGNITION
IN STRATEGY DISCOVERY

The interpretation of Study 2 is intriguing, but needs some additional empirical support. We have argued that under cognitively demanding circumstances, even though a strategy (category clustering during recall) is implemented, the child is unlikely to make the strategy–performance connection because of limits on cognitive capacity. If that connection is not made, then the likelihood that the child would use category organization to study as well as to recall materials in subsequent memory tasks would be very low, in fact essentially zero. Although this interpretation matches the results of Study 2, we do not have direct evidence that the strategy–performance connection was actually made in the light cognitive load condition in contrast with the heavy cognitive load condition. None of the children were questioned immediately after the first memory session was completed.

In order to evaluate our hypothesis about enhanced metacognitive awareness in the light cognitive load condition, Study 3 reproduces the first sessions of Study 2 and follows the memory task immediately with the metacognition question. Forty first graders were tested with 20 children each in light and heavy cognitive load conditions. The same instructions and procedures were followed as those of Study 2. Picture sets were presented with the category labels mentioned in passing as the children named the individual pictures. Then the experimenter placed the pictures on the lectern-like apparatus category by category. After the children studied and recalled their pictures, they were asked the metacognition question, that is, Did they do anything to help themselves remember? The pictures on the lectern were available during the questioning.

Findings

Table 1.5 presents mean scores across the two cognitive load conditions on all of the strategy and performance measures including scores on the metacognition question. Once again there were no differences across the two cognitive load conditions (t-test comparisons) for any of the organization measures (ARC scores, number of categories, number of items per category chunk). Both groups also showed faster times for within-category items compared to across-category times, although the times were overall slower in the 16-picture condition, $p < .05$. Thus, recall dynamics were comparable on a number of key features across the two conditions and were consistent with deliberate goal-directed strategy use. With regard to the metacognition results, the mean differences in metacognition scores between conditions (1.95 vs. .85) were in fact

TABLE 1.5. Mean Scores on Strategy and Performance Measures—Study 3 (First Graders)

	8 pictures	16 pictures
Number of words recalled	6.95	8.00
% recall	87%	52%
Recall clustering (ARC)	.85	.86
Number of items per category cluster	1.75	2.33
Number of categories recalled	3.60	3.35
Within-category times	2.67 sec	3.95 sec
Across-category times	4.48 sec	7.73 sec
Metacognition score (0–3)	1.95	0.85

significant, $t(38) = 2.33$, $p < .05$. Children in the light cognitive load condition were able to report on how they helped themselves remember the pictures (i.e., by category). In contrast the children in the heavy cognitive load condition were largely unaware of their own strategic behavior even though they showed very high rates of category clustering (.83 on the ARC clustering measure that ranges from 0 for no clustering to 1.00 for perfect clustering).

In order to better understand the effects of cognitive load, we examined the relationship between time variables and metacognition responses, the only variables effected by the change in cognitive load. There was a strong negative correlation between across-category times and metacognition scores, $r = -.51$, $p < .001$. Children who switched quickly to a new category during recall were more likely to report on their strategic behavior than children who went more slowly. A weaker correlation was also found for within-category times, $r = -.30$, $p < .06$. Thus children who implemented the category-clustering strategy quickly and efficiently were better able to report on their own strategic behavior. In other words, they were prepared to "discover" the strategy. The heavy load condition, by slowing down strategy implementation, apparently precluded strategy awareness for many of the first-grade children in that condition.

In sum, Study 3 demonstrated that strategy discovery (making the strategy–performance connection) was hindered under more cognitively demanding circumstances even though the children were showing comparable levels of strategy use as under less demanding circumstances. In fact, the results indicate that strategy discovery is more likely under circumstances in which the strategic behavior may not actually be necessary due to the simplicity of the task.

METACOGNITION AND STRATEGY DISCOVERY: EDUCATIONAL IMPLICATIONS

The series of studies presented in this chapter paint a different developmental picture about the acquisition of memory strategies over time. On the one hand, the results reflect children's increasing abilities to implement strategies under cognitively demanding circumstances with age (Study 1). That pattern is not surprising and is consistent with a developmental progression in which slowly but surely children become more adept at implementing strategies across a broader range of circumstances.

On the other hand, a closer examination of this developmental pattern suggests that this prototypic pattern of results can be changed. In the current investigation we began with the goal of identifying features of strategy implementation that indicated active, goal-directed strategy use. More standard measures of strategy use like the ARC measure of category clustering during recall can occur at high rates without the children being aware of their own strategic behavior. Particularly noteworthy in our results is the fact that ARC scores were noticeably high, almost perfect in fact, but children under more demanding processing circumstances were still unaware of what they were doing to help themselves remember (Studies 2 and 3).

To identify genuine goal-directed strategy use, additional measures of online strategy implementation were necessary. Children engaging in deliberate strategy use adapt their category clusters to the changing category structure of the materials. Furthermore, they show faster times between items within category clusters than across category borders. Add to this a particularly intriguing result from Study 3 in which ease of implementation increases the likelihood that a young child (first grader) will note the connection between strategy use and performance. There may be limits to noticing one's own strategic behavior even when a child has the cognitive resources to implement the strategy. Instead the child needs both the cognitive resources to implement a strategy and to note its use for acquiring metacognitive knowledge necessary for generalization of strategy use.

How do these results change our understanding of the interplay between metacognitive and associative processes and the discovery of strategies? Up until now researchers have, for the most part, utilized memory tasks that were reasonably challenging, where children might or might not use a strategy to help themselves remember. Researchers then explore the situation in terms of how to prompt strategy use and whether strategy use improves performance (Bjorklund & Coyle, 1995; Schneider & Pressley, 1997; Waters, 2000). The developmental pattern that emerges is one that gives credit to both metacognitive and associative processes in strategy use and generalization (Crowley et al., 1997). We do not argue with that conclusion. There is a wealth of evidence to support it. But we do challenge the inevitableness of the more incremental pattern of slow but steady increasing strategy use across conditions as the only path along which strategy development may proceed.

We'd like to make the case for enhancing the role of metacognition in strategy development. Deanna Kuhn (2000) in particular has emphasized that the "metalevel" is the locus of developmental change. She states, "Strategy training may appear successful, but if nothing has been done to influence the metalevel, the new behavior will quickly disappear once the instructional context is withdrawn and individuals resume metalevel management of their own behavior" (p. 24). Recent research on strategy development (e.g., the chapters in the current volume) in fact supports Kuhn's position. We'd like to take this position one step further and propose that early interventions that bring metacognition to the fore will prompt metacognitive awareness and active, goal-directed strategy use in young children who otherwise might have years to go toward goal-directed strategy use.

The current findings give us a glimpse of the possibilities. First graders rarely undertake deliberate, goal-directed strategy use and often fail to connect what they do to help themselves remember with their actual performance. Although we may be clever in prompting strategic behavior by manipulating materials and instructions, the connection is still often missed. In our studies first graders were prompted to use category clustering to remember by placing pictures on rows by category in front of them. Nonetheless, when they are asked to remember a relatively difficult picture set (16 pictures) for their age, the connection between retrieving items by category during recall and performance is lost to them. Remarkably, it is under conditions where category clustering is not needed to remember well that first graders are able to make that connection. Eight pictures to remember is not a challenging memory task for first graders. Many can remember the majority of the eight pictures whether they organize or not. But it is under these circumstances, in which organization is not a vital strategy for effective performance, that they have the cognitive resources to both implement an organization strategy and to be aware of their strategy use. The conclusion that follows is that goal-directed strategy use is best prompted under easy learning conditions. Other researchers have also noted this same circumstance, that cognitive demands associated with more sophisticated reasoning or strategy use can preclude young children's ability to note and explain their thinking (Bjorklund, Miller, Coyle, & Slawinski, 1997; Tunteler & Resing, 2002).

Furthermore, the current findings indicate that the key to continued strategy use is metacognitive awareness even though it can be rare in young children. Ornstein, Grammer, and Coffman (Chapter 2, this volume) explored the metacognitive context in early elementary school. Of particular interest for our purposes are the strategy results linked to high versus low mnemonic teachers. High mnemonic teachers who provide a metacognitive framework in the classroom prompt strategy development in their students. When first graders from these classrooms are trained in category clustering, they continue to use the strategy not only throughout the first grade, but also into the second grade where their teachers have in fact changed. Young children primed to note the connections between what they do and outcomes will generalize this "metacognitive" mind-set to contexts outside the original classroom with different instructors. This is a remarkable finding because researchers have not given young elementary school children much credit for metacognitive awareness.

Taken together with the findings of the current investigation, there is reason to think that young children's attention can be focused on the metacognitive level. First, we can provide children with teachers who focus on strategy use and encourage their students to think about what they do in their classroom discussions. Second, we can provide strategy training under circumstances where implementation is so easy that even young children have the cognitive resources to note what they are doing and how that is affecting their performance. Strategy training in fact should begin before children actually need be strategic to remember well. To the degree that future research focuses on this two-pronged approach, we will not only have more metacognitive-savvy teachers, but metacognitive-savvy students, and at an early age.

REFERENCES

Andreassen, C., & Waters, H. S. (1989). Organization during study: Relationships between metamemory, strategy use, and performance. *Journal of Educational Psychology, 81,* 190–195.

Bjorklund, D. F., & Buchanan, J. J. (1989). Developmental and knowledge base differences in the acquisition and extension of a memory strategy. *Journal of Experimental Child Psychology, 48,* 451–471.

Bjorklund, D. F., & Coyle, T. R. (1995). Utilization deficiencies in the development of memory strategies. In F. E. Weinert & W. Schneider (Eds.), *Memory development and competencies: Issues in growth and development* (pp. 161–180). Mahwah, NJ: Erlbaum.

Bjorklund, D. F., Miller, P. H., Coyle, T. R., & Slawinski, J. L. (1997). Instructing children to use memory strategies: Evidence of utilization deficiencies in memory training studies. *Developmental Review, 17,* 411–441.

Crowley, K., Shrager, J., & Siegler, R. S. (1997). Strategy discovery as a competitive negotiation between metacognition and associative knowledge. *Developmental Review, 17,* 462–489.

Fabricius, W. V., & Hagen, J. W. (1984). The use of causal attributions about recall performance to assess metamemory and predict strategic memory behavior in young children. *Developmental Psychology, 20,* 975–987.

Hasselhorn, M. (1992). Task dependency and the role of category typicality and metamemory in the development of an organizational strategy. *Child Development, 63,* 202–214.

Kuhn, D. (2000). Does memory development belong to an endangered topic list? *Child Development, 71,* 21–25.

Lange, G., Guttentag, R. E., & Nida, R. E. (1990). Relationships between study organization, retrieval organization, and general strategy-specific memory knowledge in young children. *Journal of Experimental Child Psychology, 49,* 126–146.

Lehmann, M., & Hasselhorn, M. (2007). Variable memory strategy use in children's adaptive intratask learning behavior: Developmental changes and working memory influences in free recall. *Child Development, 78,* 1068–1082.

Lehmann, M., & Hasselhorn. M. (in press). The dynamics of free recall and their relationship to rehearsal between 8 and 10 years of age. *Child Development.*

McCormick, C. B. (2003). Metacognition and learning. In I. B. Weiner (Editor-in-Chief) & W. M. Reynolds & G. E. Miller (Vol. Eds.), *Handbook of psychology: Vol. 7. Educational psychology* (pp. 79–102). New York: Wiley.

Ornstein, P. A., & Haden, C. A. (2001). Memory development or the *development of memory? Current Directions in Psychological Science, 10,* 202–205.

Pollio, H. R., Richards, S., & Lucas, R. (1969). Temporal properties of category recall. *Journal of Verbal Learning and Verbal Behavior, 8,* 284–295.

Pressley, M., Borkowski, J. G., & O'Sullivan, J. T. (1985). Children's metamemory and the teaching of memory strategies. In D. L. Forrest-Pressley, G. E. MacKinnon, & T. G. Waller (Eds.), *Meta-cognition, cognition, and human performance* (pp. 111–153). New York: Academic Press.

Pressley, M., Borkowski, J. G., & Schneider, W. (1987). Cognitive strategies: Good strategy users coordinate metacognition and knowledge. In R. Vasta & G. Whitehurst (Eds.), *Annals of child development* (Vol. 5, pp. 89–129). New York: JAI Press.

Pressley, M., & Hilden, K. (2006). Cognitive strategies. In D. Kuhn & R. S. Siegler (Eds.), *Handbook of child psychology: Vol. 2. Cognition, perception, and language* (6th ed., pp. 511–556). New York: Wiley.

Roenker, D. L., Thompson, C. P., & Brown, S. C. (1971). Comparison of measures for the estimation of clustering in free recall. *Psychological Bulletin, 76,* 45–48.

Salatas, H., & Flavell, J. H. (1976). Behavioral and metamnemonic indicators of strategic behaviors under remember instructions in first grade. *Child Development, 47,* 81–89.

Schneider, W., & Bjorklund, D. F. (1998). Memory. In D. Kuhn & R. S. Siegler (Eds.) *Handbook of child psychology: Vol. 2. Cognition, perception and language* (5th ed., pp. 467–521). New York: Wiley.

Schneider, W., Kron-Sperl, V., & Hünnerkopf, M. (2009). The development of young children's memory strategies: Evidence from the Würzburg Longitudinal Memory Study. *European Journal of Developmental Psychology*, 6, 70–99.

Schneider, W., & Pressley, M. (1997). *Memory development between 2 and 20* (2nd ed.). Hillsdale, NJ: Erlbaum.

Schneider, W., & Weinert, F. E. (1995). Memory development during early and middle childhood: Findings from the Munich Longitudinal Study (LOGIC). In F. E. Weinert & W. Schneider (Eds.), *Memory performance and competencies: Issues in growth and development* (pp. 263–279). Mahwah, NJ: Erlbaum.

Siegler, R. S. (2006). Microgenetic analyses of learning. In D. Kuhn & R. S. Siegler (Eds.), *Handbook of child psychology: Vol. 2. Cognition, perception, and language* (6th ed., pp. 464–510). New York: Wiley.

Siegler, R. S., & Jenkins, E. (1989). *How children discover strategies*. Hillsdale, NJ: Erlbaum.

Tunteler, E., & Resing, W. C. M. (2002). Spontaneous analogical transfer in 4–year-olds: A microgenetic study. *Journal of Experimental Child Psychology*, 83, 149–166.

Waters, H. S. (2000). Memory strategy development: Do we need yet another deficiency? *Child Development*, 71, 1004–1012.

2

Teachers' "Mnemonic Style" and the Development of Skilled Memory

Peter A. Ornstein
Jennie K. Grammer
Jennifer L. Coffman

The work on the development of memory outlined here can be seen as a bridge between studies of children's cognition in the laboratory and explorations of teachers' instruction in the classroom. Reflecting a view of the artificiality of any rigid boundary between "basic" and "applied" research, our research program stems from laboratory-based investigations of children's memory but is also focused squarely on the world of the classroom. Our interest in the classroom is twofold. We are drawn to the classroom context—especially to teachers' memory-relevant "talk"—because of the role that we feel it plays in the emergence and consolidation of children's deliberate memory skills. But we are also attracted to the classroom as a setting for examining experimentally the linkages between teachers' talk and children's skills that we observe in our longitudinal research. Moreover, an eventual goal of ours is to develop interventions that have the potential to improve teaching, and thereby influence children's acquisition and refinement of memory and study skills.

In this chapter, we begin with a brief treatment of the development of deliberate strategies for remembering—such as rehearsal, organization, and elaboration—discussing linkages between the deployment of these techniques and children's success in remembering. This presentation of strategy use and remembering includes a treatment of children's metamnemonic understanding and sets the stage for the developmental question that initiated our "adventure" in the classroom: Where do children's strategies for remembering come from? Our tentative answer to this question is that formal schooling is implicated in the emergence and consolidation of children's strategies, although the plot thickens with the observation that these techniques do not seem to be taught deliberately in school. Given the potential importance of the classroom, we then turn to a discussion of research designed to explore teachers' language as they present lessons in language arts and mathematics. We focus on differences in the language that teachers use in the course of instruction, emphasizing differences between high and low "mnemonic styles" in the classroom and the mnemonic skills of children who are exposed to these two contrasting styles of talk.

THE DEVELOPMENT OF SKILLED REMEMBERING

Over the past 35 years, a rich database concerning age-related changes in the generation of memory strategies has been amassed (Kail & Hagen, 1977; Ornstein, 1978; Schneider & Pressley, 1997). This research has shown convincingly that with increases in age across the elementary school years, children become more proficient in the use of strategies, plans for the storage and retrieval of information. Despite this wealth of information, however, the literature is largely silent with regard to two key developmental issues (Ornstein, Baker-Ward, & Naus, 1988; Ornstein & Haden, 2001). First, what can be said about the course of memory development within individual children? And second, what are the factors that serve to mediate this development? To a considerable extent, these critical gaps in our understanding of memory development stem from problems inherent in the cross-sectional research designs that characterize the overwhelming majority of studies of children's memory. As we see it, cross-sectional research methods—which are so valuable in describing the skills of children of different ages—can provide no information about developmental pathways to mnemonic competence because they are based on parallel samples of children of different ages. Longitudinal and microgenetic studies are clearly necessary to examine developmental changes within individual children, especially those that permit the identification of potential mediators of developmental change (Ornstein & Haden, 2001). In this regard, one very useful hint concerning the sources of developmental changes in children's mnemonic skills can be found in the cultural psychology literature. Indeed, it is now evident that these skills for remembering develop typically in the context of experiences in settings—such as school—in which memory is both expected and valued (Cole, 1992; Rogoff & Mistry, 1990; Wagner, 1981). For this reason, our discussion of the development of deliberate memory strategies is followed directly by our treatment of remembering in the classroom context.

Cross-Sectional Studies of Strategy Use and Recall

Age-related changes in a number of different strategies—rehearsal (e.g., Ornstein & Naus, 1978), organization (e.g., Lange, 1978), and elaboration (e.g., Rohwer, 1973)—have been examined extensively. In the context of tasks that involve the deliberate memorization of sets of words or pictures, across the elementary school years there is a very systematic transition from relatively "passive" to more "active" techniques of remembering. For example, when given a list of words to remember and prompted to "talk aloud" as the items are being presented, younger children tend to rehearse each to-be-remembered item alone as it is displayed, whereas older participants rehearse each one with several previously presented stimuli (Ornstein, Naus, & Liberty, 1975). To illustrate, if the first three items on a list are *table, car,* and *flower,* older children are apt to rehearse *table, table, table,* when *table* is presented; *table, car, table, car,* when *car* is presented; and *table, car, flower,* when *flower* is displayed. In contrast, younger children typically rehearse *table, table, table,* when the first word is shown; *car, car, car,* when *car* is presented; and *flower, flower, flower,* when the third word is shown. Importantly, these differences in rehearsal style are related to marked differences in remembering, such that with increases in age rehearsal becomes more active—with several different items being intermixed—and recall improves dramatically, especially that of the early list items (Ornstein et al., 1975).

Paralleling these changes in the use of a deliberate rehearsal strategy are comparable differences in the deployment of organizational techniques. For example, when presented with relatively unrelated or low-associated items and told to "form groups that will help you remember" third and fourth graders will rarely sort on the basis of semantic relations, but rather tend to form fragmented groupings that are not consistent from trial to trial (Bjorklund, Ornstein, & Haig, 1977; Liberty & Ornstein, 1973). In contrast, older children (sixth grade and above) and adults routinely form semantically constrained groups, even though the instructions only make reference to a memory goal and do not prompt semantic grouping. Thus, older individuals readily translate an instruction to form groups that will facilitate remembering into one that involves a search for some form of meaning-based organization (Ornstein, Trabasso, & Johnson-Laird, 1974), whereas children in the middle elementary school grades approach the recall task in a seemingly astrategic manner. These differences in sorting style are associated with corresponding age differences in recall, but it should be noted that the failure of the younger children to group items in a semantically constrained manner does not indicate a lack of understanding of the semantic linkages among the items. Indeed a number of studies suggest that young children are aware of semantic relations, at least to some extent, both when the items are taxonomically related (Nelson, 1974) and when the organizational structure is less salient (Bjorklund et al., 1977; Liberty & Ornstein, 1973; Worden, 1975). As such, the apparent failure to organize in recall does not stem from a lack of knowledge of organizational structures, but rather from a failure to apply this knowledge strategically.

Although these initial studies of rehearsal and organization were clearly correlational in scope, with age differences noted in both strategy use and remembering, later investigations included manipulations that permitted the establishment of causal linkages. For example, with regard to rehearsal, the provision of minimal instructions to rehearse several items together is sufficient to increase the recall of younger children, and prompts to rehearse each item on a list alone or in relative isolation can reduce the recall of older children (Ornstein & Naus, 1978; Ornstein, Naus, & Stone, 1977). Similarly, given that young children do understand the semantic relations among words that they are asked to remember—but do not spontaneously make use of these associations in a strategic manner—their recall can be affected by a number of manipulations. First, when they are required by a yoking procedure to follow the more semantically constrained sorting pattern of older children or adults, their recall is facilitated; in a similar fashion, when adults are yoked to the sorts of young children, their recall is reduced (Bjorklund et al., 1977; Liberty & Ornstein, 1973). Moreover, children's sorting of low-associated materials can also be manipulated—with corresponding effects on their remembering—by simply instructing them to sort on the basis of meaning; indeed, by telling young children to form groups of words that "go together" or are "similar in some way," as opposed to groups that will "help you remember," we can observe a major change in sorting style and recall performance (Bjorklund et al., 1977; Corsale & Ornstein, 1980). The organized sorting and recall of young children can also be facilitated by exposing them to materials that are highly structured (Best & Ornstein, 1986).

These findings indicate clearly that there are causal linkages between children's strategic efforts and their success at remembering. However, it should also be noted that there are limits to the success of experimental interventions and that these limits provide information on other factors that contribute to effective strategy production. For example, although third graders can benefit from instructions to rehearse several items together, their use of an active rehearsal strategy does not increase their recall to the level of sixth graders (Ornstein et al., 1977). This failure to eliminate age differences in remembering seems to stem from the fact that the use of an active rehearsal strategy requires that young children expend more of their attentional resources than is necessary for older children (Guttentag, 1984). Consistent with Guttentag's analysis of the attentional demands of active rehearsal at different points in development, it certainly is easier for third graders to rehearse several items together when the effort required to carry out the task is reduced (Guttentag, Ornstein, & Siemens, 1987). As such, when instructions to rehearse actively are combined with a procedure in which children have continued visual access to each to-be-remembered item after its initial presentation, striking improvements in strategy use and subsequent recall are noted (Ornstein, Medlin, Stone, & Naus, 1985). Although effort demands are also important in the context of organizational strategies (see Bjorklund & Harnishfeger, 1987), when children of different ages have comparable understanding of the to-be-remembered items and are led by instructions to use this knowledge as a basis for their sorting, recall differences are generally eliminated (Corsale & Ornstein, 1980).

Two comments are in order on this early cross-sectional work on children's use of mnemonic strategies. First, although the research cited thus far has focused on individual memory techniques such as organization or rehearsal, more recent studies have explored the extent to which multiple strategies are deployed when children are asked to remember (e.g., Coyle & Bjorklund, 1997; Cox, Ornstein, Naus, Maxfield, & Zimler, 1989; Lehmann & Hasselhorn, 2007). Coyle and Bjorklund (1997), for example, reported that with increases in age, there were increases in the use of multiple strategies, with corresponding gains in remembering. Moreover, an impetus for some of this research can be found in Siegler's (1996) strategy choice model, reflecting the notion that at any point in time children may have a repertoire of strategies that they can use that may be more or less effective, depending on the task. As children grow older, however, their use of less effective strategies decreases, as they choose to implement more efficient technique (see, e.g., Coyle & Bjorklund, 1997). Second, it seems clear that one of the "problems" faced by the young learner is decidedly metacognitive in nature. Children in the early elementary grades often have information—procedural as well as conceptual—available to them in permanent memory that they do not utilize spontaneously in the service of a memory goal. Granted that young children's use of an active rehearsal technique is moderated by the effort demands of this procedure (Guttentag et al., 1987), when prompted they can rehearse several to-be-remembered items together, with some improvement in remembering. Similarly, when prompted to focus on the organizational structure of to-be-remembered materials through (1) yoking, (2) direct instructions, or (3) exposure to highly salient materials, children are able to do so, with improvements in memory being noted. As such, an enduring question about children's memory remains: What factors are associated with children's acquisition of mnemonic understanding that leads them to apply what they know to the task of remembering?

Longitudinal Studies of Children's Strategy Use and Recall

As suggested earlier, the literature on children's memory is based largely on cross-sectional experiments and, as a result, relatively little can be said about developmental change within individual children. To be sure, cross-sectional work provides us with very important descriptions of the average levels of performance of children of different ages on specified memory tasks and can suggest factors (e.g., attentional resources, metacognitive understanding) that may be involved in the age-related progression that is observed. However, these studies do not enable us to go further to make inferences about the course of development within an individual child or about contrasting patterns of change for different groups of children. Moreover, cross-sectional work does not enable us to search for the origins of a given group of children's rehearsal and organizational strategies in their earlier skills on tasks that require simple procedures such as naming or visual examination, or on autobiographical memory tasks that call for talking about the past (see Ornstein, Haden, & San Souci, 2008). For information of this sort, it is necessary to make use of longitudinal methods in which skill development is tracked over time, with children being assessed on a range of contrasting tasks.

A casual reading of the cross-sectional literature on children's strategy use might suggest a gradual course of skill development across the elementary school years. However, recent longitudinal work suggests that the impression of gradual development may be an artifact of averaging the performance of children who acquire competence in strategy use at different points in time. An illustration of this artifact of averaging can be observed in the findings of the very important Munich Longitudinal Study on Individual Development (the LOGIC study; Weinert & Schneider, 1999). Included in the assessment battery of this large-scale investigation was a measurement of the children's organizational strategies every 2 years between the ages of 4 and 12 (Sodian & Schneider, 1999). Although the data revealed impressive increases in the children's strategic behavior across the 2-year intervals—increases that were quite consistent with the impressions drawn from the cross-sectional literature—test–retest correlations indicated that at the level of individual children organized sorting was quite unstable from one point of measurement to the next. Sodian and Schneider (1999) concluded that this lack of stability reflected underlying variability among the children in their patterns of strategy acquisition and suggested that, for more than 80% of the children in the sample, their findings revealed a pattern of all-or-none transition from the nonuse of an organizational strategy to complete use.

The pattern of a largely abrupt transition from non-strategy use to competence in the use of organized sorting that was obtained by Sodian and Schneider (1999) was also observed by Schagmüller and Schneider (2002) in the context of an 11-week microgenetic study of third and fourth graders. However, two factors—the long intervals between measurement points in the Munich study (2 years) and the small sample size in the microgenetic investigation ($n = 22$)—made it difficult to make definitive statements regarding the course of strategy acquisition. As such, two new longitudinal investigations of strategy acquisition were launched in Würzburg and Göttingen by Schneider, Kron, Hünnerkopf, and Krajewski (2004) and Lehmann and Hasselhorn (2007), respectively. In their parallel studies, Schneider and Hasselhorn and their colleagues (see Kron-Sperl, Schneider, & Hasselhorn, 2008, for an overview) assessed the mnemonic performance of almost 200 children every 6 months across a period of 4 years, so as to better understand the nature of changes over time in children's strategy deployment.

Kron-Sperl et al. (2008) were able to confirm one of the major findings of the Munich study, namely, that for many children the acquisition of a strategic sorting strategy was both less gradual and more rapid than had been implied by the cross-sectional literature. However, with their fine-grained lens and large combined sample, Schneider and Hasselhorn and their colleagues were able to document at least two developmental pathways to skilled remembering. Consistent with the Munich data, a substantial number of children acquired the sorting strategy abruptly between two assessment points, but the numbers were considerably lower (37% of the Würzburg sample and 45% of the Göttingen cohort) than had been observed in the LOGIC study. Moreover, substantial numbers of children (27% in Würzburg and 15% in Göttingen) seemed to acquire the strategy gradually over time. Clearly, the identification of these two subgroups of children (and of smaller groups of children who did not acquire the sorting technique at all) complicates matters, but it also provides us with an interesting opportunity to explore alternative trajectories in the development of generalized cognitive skill (Waters, 2008).

In order to understand these developmental trajectories, it will first be important to explore the extent to which extended experience in tasks that require remembering is associated with the contrasting acquisition patterns. As Kron-Sperl et al. (2008) suggest, amount of experience with the sort-recall task does seem to be associated with differences between the Würzburg and Göttingen samples as well as between these two cohorts, on the one hand, and the Munich study, on the other, thus paralleling the documented effects of microgenetic investigations in the acceleration of cognitive skill (see, e.g., Kuhn, 1995; Schlagmüller & Schneider, 2002). It will also be important to document factors associated with "membership" in these subgroups, such as metacognitive understanding, basic memory capacity, and performance on a range of other mnemonic tasks. Moreover, it is also of interest to document the long-term consequences of group membership by exploring the later performance of the children on more complex tasks, including those encountered in school contexts. Just as Guttentag et al. (1987) identified two groups of third graders—on the basis of their rehearsal strategies under "scaffolded" versus "traditional" modes of presentation—and showed contrasting patterns of growth in skill over the course of a year, the abrupt versus gradual acquisition groups may evidence quite different developmental patterns across the elementary school years. Finally, reflecting the themes to be developed below in our treatment of the classroom, it becomes essential to examine aspects of the classroom context (including teacher instructional style) that may be associated with these different developmental trajectories.

The Role of Metamemory

In addition to the documented changes in children's strategy use and remembering summarized briefly above, with increases in age there are also corresponding changes in metamemory, or children's knowledge of memory processes and the demands of various tasks that require remembering (Cavanaugh & Perlmutter, 1982; Flavell & Wellman, 1977; Schneider, 1999). Understanding the development of this metamnemonic knowledge is certainly interesting in its own right, but much of the research on this topic has been motivated by an assumption—either explicit or implicit—that children's knowledge about memory influences their selection of specific strategies such as rehearsal and organization in tasks that require remembering (e.g., Brown, 1978). Moreover, as children acquire more detailed understanding of the operation of memory, their enhanced metamemory is thought to enable them to monitor the effectiveness of their strategic efforts and, when necessary, to adjust the particular techniques that are used in the service of remembering (see, e.g., Borkowski, Milstead, & Hale, 1988). Unfortunately, as numerous researchers have noted (Schneider & Pressley, 1997), it has proved difficult to find unequivocally strong support for these assumptions about linkages between metamnemonic understanding, strategy use, and remembering.

Somewhat surprisingly, given the theoretical importance of associations between metamemory and strategy use, the results of correlational studies have been quite mixed (Schneider, 1985; Schneider & Pressley, 1997). It certainly is the case that these linkages have been shown to vary somewhat as a function of methods of measurement (Best & Ornstein, 1986) and children's motivation (Schneider & Lockl, 2002), and that their strength increases with age (e.g., Joyner & Kurtz-Costes, 1997; Schneider & Pressley, 1997). Nonetheless, although correlations between metamnemonic understanding and strategic behavior have been identified in both cross-sectional and longitudinal investigations, they have often been relatively small (e.g., Cavanaugh & Perlmutter, 1982) and—when studied longitudinally—somewhat inconsistent across time (Sodian & Schneider, 1999). Additional problems have been noted in cases in which children are able to verbalize knowledge of a specific mnemonic technique but then fail to make use of it (Sodian, Schneider, & Perlmutter, 1986), and also in situations in which children use what might be viewed as a deliberate strategy, but are unable to demonstrate any corresponding metamnemonic awareness (Bjorklund & Zeman, 1982). However, these difficulties notwithstanding, in a meta-analysis of 60 investigations Schneider and Pressley (1997) reported a correlation of 0.41 between the metamemory and strategy use. Nonetheless, it should be noted that these correlations may reflect bidirectional linkages, with metamnemonic understanding influencing strategic behavior, on the one hand, and strategic efforts leading to increases in understanding, on the other (Borkowski, Carr, Rellinger, & Pressley, 1990; Kuhn, 1999; Schneider & Pressley, 1997).

Despite the mixed results of these correlational investigations, evidence consistent with the fundamental assumption of a linkage between children's metamnemonic understanding and their use of strategies for remembering comes from a series of training studies. As indicated above, children can be trained in the use of mnemonic techniques, with improvements in remembering being noted. However, the effectiveness of the training manipulation—particularly in terms of the extent to which transfer is observed in different contexts—has been shown to vary markedly as a function of the degree to which strategy information is supplemented by the provision of metacognitive information. To illustrate, in a review of the literature on strategy acquisition and transfer, Cox, Ornstein, and Valsiner (1991) reported that those studies that were least likely to promote transfer were ones in which children received basic instruction but were given very little additional information. In contrast, they noted that the most effective protocols were those in which a central feature of the instructional regimen was the provision of metacognitively relevant information about the value and effectiveness of the strategies being taught. It thus seems clear that the inclusion of metacognitive information is essential for the successful acquisition and transfer of a range of strategies for remembering (e.g., Paris, Newman, & McVey, 1982; Pressley, Ross, Levin, & Ghatala, 1984; Ringel & Springer, 1980).

One important example of the impact of this technique can be seen in evidence from a microgenetic study of strategy acquisition conducted by Paris et al. (1982). In this investigation, participants in two contrasting groups (control and experimental conditions) were trained over the course of a week in a range of techniques to aid in remembering (i.e., sorting, labeling, cumulative rehearsal, self-testing, and clustering). Importantly, children in the experimental condition were provided with an elaborated demonstration of these strategies that included explanations of why each would be helpful. In addition to this direct instruction, the children in the experimental training condition were provided with metacognitive feedback in the form of elaborated praise regarding their performance on subsequent trials of the memory tasks. In contrast, children in the control condition were trained in the same strategies, but were not provided with any metacognitive information either about the techniques or about their performance. Paris et al.'s findings indicated that even though both groups of children showed improved recall and strategy use on the day on which they were trained, only children in the experimental condition who experienced the elaborated training and feedback maintained the strategies they had learned after a 2-day delay.

The importance of metacognitive information for the maintenance and transfer of mnemonic techniques raises a number of issues concerning development. The bulk of the correlational literature on metamemory discussed above has focused on a search for concurrent linkages between metamnemonic understanding and effective strategy deployment. Indeed, at any given point in developmental time the question being addressed has been that of whether children with enhanced metamemory will exhibit more effective strategy use than their peers with lower levels of metamnemonic understanding. Although this is a very important question, the more significant developmental question concerns the degree to which enhanced metacognitive awareness at time t is associated with enhanced strategy use at time $t + 1$, and the training literature, with its focus on transfer, reinforces this question. In this regard, it is particularly noteworthy that Schlagmüller and Schneider (2002) in their short-term microgenetic study found that children who acquired an organizational strategy over the course of the project evidenced increases in metamemory well ahead of actually exhibiting the technique. In addition, the success of training manipulations, such as that of Paris and his colleagues (1982), encouraged many researchers to think about how these same findings could be applied to general instruction in the classroom setting (e.g., Palincsar & Brown, 1984; Duffy et al., 1987).

SCHOOL AS A CONTEXT FOR DEVELOPMENT

A number of lines of research point to the potential impact of formal schooling on the development of memory strategies. Consider first cross-cultural investigations in which researchers have contrasted the performance of children matched in chronological age but who differed in terms of whether they had or had not participated in Western-style schooling. For example, children in Morocco (e.g., Wagner, 1978) and Liberia (e.g., Scribner & Cole, 1978) who attended school demonstrated superiority in the types of mnemonic skills that have typically been studied by Western anthropologists and psychologists. To illustrate, in a review of cross-cultural studies on memory performance, Rogoff (1981) concluded that non-schooled children generally do not make use of organizational techniques for remembering unrelated items and that school seemed necessary for the acquisition of these skills. These findings, of course, do not in any way imply that "schooled" children outperform their "unschooled" peers on everyday memory tasks that are embedded in activities central to their culture. Nonetheless, they do suggest that some feature of the formal school context most likely is related to the emergence of skills that are important for success on tasks that involve deliberate memorization.

With cross-cultural research indicating that something about formal schooling encourages the development of strategic behavior, the next question might be, When during a child's experience in school does this growth occur? First grade seems to be a strong possibility, as Morrison, Smith, and Dow-Ehrensberger (1995) showed that this grade is very important in terms of the development of memory skills. Morrison and his colleagues studied children who "just made" the mandated date for entry into first grade (a "young" first-grade group) and those who "just missed" the date (an "old" kindergarten group). As such, the children were basically matched in terms of age but nonetheless differed in their school experience, thus allowing for an exploration of the impact of attending kindergarten and the first grade on children's developing skills. To assess memory, Morrison et al. (1995) used a task in which the children were asked to study a set of pictures of common objects. Taking performance at the start of the school year as a baseline, the young first graders evidenced substantial improvement in their memory skills.

In contrast, the performance of the older kindergartners did not change over the year, although improvement was noted the next year, following their experience in the first grade. These findings imply that there is something in the first-grade context that is supportive of the development of children's memory skills.

The potential importance of the first-grade experience is also suggested by the results of a study by Baker-Ward, Ornstein, and Holden (1984) in which age differences in strategic effectiveness were documented. In contrast to their performance on tasks involving rehearsal and organization (e.g., Ornstein & Naus, 1978; Lange, 1978), skills that flower during the elementary school years, Baker-Ward et al. showed that 4-, 5-, and 6-year-olds made use of a set of similar (albeit fairly simple) techniques. These children were placed in a setting in which they could interact with a set of common objects and toys for a 2-minute period. Although all children were told that they could play with the items, some of them received specific memorization instructions as well. The use of an observational coding scheme revealed that even at age 4, the children told to remember behaved differently from those simply instructed to play. For example, spontaneous labeling or naming occurred almost exclusively among the children instructed to remember, who also played less than the other children. The children who received instructions to remember also engaged in more visual inspection and evidenced more of what seemed to be reflection and self-testing. However, even though the memory instructions were associated with a "studious" approach to the task by the 4-, 5-, and 6-year-olds alike, only among the older children were the strategic behaviors associated with the facilitation of recall, suggesting again the importance of experiences in the first grade.

Although the evidence thus identifies the school context as a setting that is important for the development of children's deliberate memory skills, relatively little is known about the specific mechanisms operating in the classroom that underlie the acquisition of strategic competence. However, findings from several areas of research suggest that adult–child social interactions may be important in fostering the emergence and refinement of a range of cognitive skills. Thus, for example, within the domain of memory, studies of mother–child reminiscing about the past (e.g., Reese, Haden, & Fivush, 1993) suggest that elaborative conversational interactions facilitate children's autobiographical memory (see Fivush, Reese, & Haden, 2006). Indeed, differences among parents in the ways in which they talk with their children about past events are clearly associated with variation in children's reports of these experiences, as reflected in their contributions to the conversations. To illustrate, the children of parents who employ a *high elaborative* style in conversations about past experiences—posing many questions, following-in on their children's efforts to contribute to the conversation, adding new information even when the children do not do so—evidence enhanced recall, in contrast to their peers whose parents use a *low elaborative* style in their conversations (Reese et al., 1993). Most important, longitudinal data suggest that differences in reminiscing styles are associated with later differences in children's abilities to recall personally experienced events.

Research on parent–child conversations about past events—as well as an emerging parallel literature on the impact of elaborative conversations as events unfold on subsequent remembering (e.g., Haden, Ornstein, Eckerman, & Didow, 2001)—has been motivated at least in part by Vygotsky's (1978) social constructivist perspective. From this point of view, children's cognitive skills emerge and are honed in the context of social exchanges with caretakers (including parents and teachers) who, in essence, provide scaffolding that supports children's performance on a range of tasks and fosters growth and development (see Brown & Reeve, 1987; Cox et al., 1991). These caretakers, either directly or in the form of educational materials that are culturally sanctioned, provide experiences that help children move beyond their current levels of independent competence. By adjusting the scaffolding as a function of what a child can and cannot do alone, the sensitive caretaker is able to provide a context for the internalization of cognitive skill. Inspection of the transcripts of mother–child reminiscing indicates clearly the ways in which parents adjust the level of scaffolding provided to children of different ages who are able to contribute differentially to these conversations about past events (Fivush et al., 2006).

The Vygotskyan (1978) perspective provides an important framework for thinking about the socialization of cognition, one that also has many implications for instruction in the classroom and for the diagnosis of cognitive skill. As such, the key features of this framework can be seen in Brown and Reeve's (1987) "bandwidths of competence" approach to skill acquisition, with its emphasis on "dynamic assessment," supportive contexts, and the transition from other- to self-regulation. Indeed, as Brown and Reeve indicate, the adult's task in social interactions that foster the internalization of skill—in terms of the "gradual transfer of the executive role" (p. 180)—is to help the child develop an increasingly more sophisticated understanding of the tasks being undertaken, and this assistance often involves providing metacognitive information that serves to support task performance. In this regard, it is important to note that Pressley and his colleagues (e.g., Pressley & Hilden, 2006; Pressley & Harris, 2006) clearly believed that instruction in the classroom that was based on metacognitively rich language was critical for supporting the development of "skilled thinkers" in reading, writing, and problem solving. Moreover, the key role of metacognitive language has been demonstrated in a range of studies designed to provide training in strategies that facilitate reading comprehension (e.g., Brown, Pressley, Van Meter, & Schuder, 1996). Nonetheless, Pressley and his collaborators (e.g., Pressley, Wharton-McDonald, Mistretta, & Eschevarria, 1998) note that without prompting this type of instruction is not observed frequently in the elementary school classroom.

Given the productivity of the Vygotsktyan approach for instruction in the classroom, it might be expected that teacher–child conversation—particularly metacognitively rich instruction in deliberate strategies for remembering—would play a key role in the emergence and refinement of children's mnemonic skills. Nonetheless, even though this is a straightforward extension of the social constructivist perspective, it is not supported fully by detailed observations of teachers' instruction in the elementary school years. Indeed, in their detailed observations in elementary school classrooms, Moely and her colleagues (1989, 1992) found that explicit instruction in mnemonic strategies was rare, but they also observed that when such information was incorporated into teachers' regular instruction, children's independent use of mnemonic techniques was facilitated. We are thus presented with a puzzle: if school is a context that is important for the development of a repertoire of deliberate memory skills, but if teachers do not routinely provide direct instruction, what is it about the classroom setting that enables children to acquire and hone these important skills for remembering? Based on the findings that elaborative adult–child conversational interaction plays an important role in the development of children's autobiographical memory (Fivush et al., 2006), we feel that it is fruitful to address this question by exploring the extent to which teacher–child conversational interchanges in the classroom are of importance for the socialization of children's deliberate memory skills.

THE CLASSROOM MEMORY STUDY

Given the evidence suggesting (1) the importance of school as a context for the development of cognitive skills, (2) the role of adult–child interaction in the development of autobiographical memory, and (3) the salience of metacognitive information in efforts to train children in the use of mnemonic techniques, we have focused our research program on the language that teachers use in the context of their lessons as a possible mechanism underlying the development of memory strategies. Our own naturalistic observations of elementary school classrooms confirm the reports of both Pressley et al. (1998) and Moely et al. (1992) in indicating that explicit instruction in strategies along with the provision of metacognitive information is a rare but nonetheless important feature of the elementary school classroom.

In the remainder of this chapter, we discuss some findings from our recently completed longitudinal investigation of linkages between aspects of teacher "talk" in the classroom and children's mnemonic skills. We focus in particular on the identification of key features of the language used by first-grade teachers in the course of instruction in mathematics and language arts that may be associated with the acquisition and consolidation of strategies such as organization and rehearsal. Importantly, our characterization of the nature of teachers' memory-relevant "talk"—including the memory demands that are expressed by teachers and the specific strategies that are modeled or discussed—is similar in some respects to Pressley's specification of key aspects of instruction and turns out to be associated with children's changes in memory performance over time (Coffman, Ornstein, McCall, & Curran, 2008; Ornstein, Coffman, Grammer, San Souci, & McCall, in press).

Measuring the Classroom Context

The longitudinal study of children's memory and academic achievement described here was launched with the recruitment of a sample of 107 first-grade children from 14 participating classrooms in four elementary schools from two school districts. These children were assessed several times as first graders and then again on multiple occasions when they were in the second, fourth, and fifth grades. In addition to the collection of child-level data, we also made in-depth observations of the children's teachers as they taught lessons in language arts and mathematics. These observations in the individual classrooms were carried out for 60 minutes in each of these two areas, thus enabling us to explore the alternative mnemonic demands that may be embedded in instruction in mathematics and language arts. For example, lessons in language arts often require children to retrieve relevant information from memory and to make knowledge-based inferences, whereas instruction in mathematics frequently carries with it an emphasis on remembering per se (as in the memorization of arithmetic facts) and on providing children with problem-solving strategies.

In an effort to characterize the classroom, we (Coffman et al., 2008) developed a coding system, the *Taxonomy of Teacher Behaviors*, and a set of observational procedures. Our system is based in part on Moely et al.'s (1992) observational instrument, as well as on our extensive pilot work. Following procedures recommended by Cairns, Santoyo, Ferguson, and Cairns (1991), we use two trained observers in the classroom, with these assistants alternating between (1) using the *Taxonomy* to make decisions every 30 seconds about the nature of a teacher's memory-relevant conversation, and (2) writing a detailed contextual narrative of the lesson as it unfolded, including descriptions of the content, the dominant teacher and child activities, and the children's verbal responses. Combined, these two sets of observational reports allow us to make statements about the nature and extent of various instructional strategies and to draw inferences about the memory demands being communicated.

Although these observations provided us with extensive information about a range of commonly occurring instructional techniques implemented by teachers, we were specifically interested in the extent to which teachers supported children's remembering and metacognitive skills. In particular, reflecting our belief in the importance of teachers' use of metacognitive information in the classroom, we focused on five component codes that we felt characterized the *mnemonic orientation* or *style* of the individual teachers. These five component codes drawn from the *Taxonomy* and *Narrative Coding* systems are described in Table 2.1: (1) *strategy suggestions*, (2) *metacognitive questioning*, (3) the co-occurrence of *deliberate memory demands* and *instructional activities*, (4) the co-occurrence

TABLE 2.1. Teacher Relevant "Talk": Component Codes in Teacher Measure

Individual taxonomy codes	Definitions
Strategy Suggestions	Recommending that a child adopt a method or procedure for remembering or processing information
Metacognitive Questions	Requesting that a child provide a potential strategy, a utilized strategy, or a rationale for a strategy he or she has indicated using

Co-occurring codes	Definitions
Deliberate Memory Demands and Instructional Activities	Intervals that contain both requests for information from memory and also the presentation of instructional information by the teacher
Deliberate Memory Demands and Cognitive Structuring Activities	Intervals that contain both requests for information from memory and teacher instruction that could impact the encoding and retrieval of information, such as focusing attention or organizing material
Deliberate Memory Demands and Metacognitive Information	Intervals that contain both requests for information from memory and the provision or solicitation of metacognitive information

of *deliberate memory demands* and *cognitive structuring activities,* and (5) the co-occurrence of *deliberate memory demands* and *metacognitive information.*

From the perspective of linking the teachers' mnemonic orientation with the memory performance of the children in their classrooms, it was fortunate that there was considerable variability in the extent to which teachers made use of the memory-related "talk" that is reflected in the codes described in Table 2.1. Across the 14 classrooms the provision of strategy suggestions varied between 0.8% and 13.8% of the 30-second observational intervals, and the degree to which the teachers posed metacognitive questions ranged from 0.8% to 9.6%. In addition, substantial differences across the classrooms were also seen in the co-occurrence of deliberate memory demands and either instructional activities (25.8% vs. 50%), cognitive structuring activities (10% vs. 35.4%), or metacognitive information, including metacognitive questions and strategy suggestions (1.3% vs. 12.1% of the intervals). This naturally occurring variability in memory-related talk allowed us to form two groups of first-grade teachers, those who were *high* versus *low* in their *mnemonic style* in the classroom, based on a median split of the average of the standard scores that were calculated for each of the codes. As such, the instruction of the *high mnemonic* teachers was characterized by a considerable use of the memory-relevant language, such as asking the children if a word selection makes sense, or eliciting a specific strategy for answering a mathematics problem. Alternatively, the teaching of the *low mnemonic* instructors was characterized by fewer instances of the memory-relevant language. Although these teachers were certainly engaging the students in the topics being discussed, in contrast to the high mnemonic teachers, they posed more basic questions, focused less on strategy use, and did not emphasize understanding why a specific answer might be correct.

Much of what we were able to capture certainly reflected the naturally occurring variation across elementary school classrooms in the provision of metacognitive information and requests for remembering. However, it must be emphasized that even though high mnemonic teachers use more metacognitive language than do low mnemonic teachers, their use of metacognition in the course of instruction does not necessarily take place with regard to memory prompts or requests for remembering. Indeed, most of the metacognitive language that we observed was offered by the teachers in the service of their basic instructional goals in the areas of mathematics and language arts. Consider, for example, the sample intervals described in Table 2.2 that are drawn from our observations in the first-grade classrooms. In this table, we present brief descriptions of lessons in language arts and mathematics, including excerpts of teacher

TABLE 2.2. Description of Sample Observational Intervals in Language Arts and Mathematics

Lesson description	Teacher language	Taxonomy codes
Language arts		
Example 1:		
The students are checking a word chart on the wall in the classroom to help them come up with appropriate words to complete sentences.	The teacher tells the class that that is how she wants them to check to see if their words are correct. She tells the students that when they read, the sentences always have to make sense.	*Strategy Suggestion*—The teacher suggests checking the word wall as a strategy for making sure the students are using the correct words. *Deliberate Memory Demand with a Strategy Suggestion*—The teacher wants the students to remember as they complete their current assignment and future assignments that when they read their sentences, they need to make sense.
Example 2:		
The class went through a writing exercise where together they came up with directions for how to put on a coat. They go back to reread what they just wrote.	The teacher tells the children that when they write, they want to make it make sense, so they should go back and reread. She says, "Remember when you write, you have you go back and read what you wrote out loud."	*Strategy Suggestion*—The teacher suggests rereading what they write as a strategy for making sure that what they write makes sense. *Deliberate Memory Demand with a Strategy Suggestion*—The teacher's use of "remember" implies that the rereading strategy is something they should apply when they write in the future.
Mathematics		
Example 1:		
The class is working on solving different word problems. The current problem is: There are three green fish and two blue fish. How many in all?	The teacher asks the student, "How did you solve the problem?" She tells the student to come up to the board and write the mathematical equation.	*Metacognitive Question*—The teacher is asking the student for the strategy that he or she used to solve the problem. For past examples during this lesson, the students had worked with counters as a way to help them solve these types of problems.

(*continued*)

TABLE 2.2. (*continued*)

Example 2:

The children are working on place value. The teacher gives the class a number and then has them determine how many tens and ones are in the number and then represent the number on the overhead with tally marks. They are currently working on the number 38.

The teacher tells the class to remember to use the strategy of labeling the number since it is a big number. She goes on to say that it is a good strategy and good habit to use because no matter how large the number they are faced with, they will be able to solve it.

Metacognitive Strategy Suggestion—As a strategy for deciding how many tens and ones are in a number, the teacher suggests that they label which number is in the tens place and which number is in the ones place. They can either write out "tens" and "ones" or use "T" and "O."

Metacognitive Information (Strategy Rationale)—The teacher justifies why labeling the place values of the number helps. She says that it will allow them to work with any numbers no matter how big they are.

Deliberate Memory Demand with a Strategy Suggestion—The teacher's use of "remember" implies that the labeling strategy is something they should apply when they are working on place value in the future.

conversation and the relevant codes from our *Taxonomy* that highlight the metacognitive underpinnings of our assessment of mnemonic orientation.

The examples shown in Table 2.2 illustrate the ways in which some of the teachers observed incorporated metacognitively rich and strategy-relevant information into their classroom instruction, which may to some extent reflect their exposure to research findings (e.g., Pressley & Harris, 2006) and professional development materials (e.g., Harvey & Goudvis, 2000) that encourage the presentation of information about strategies in the classroom. Importantly, however, not all teachers employ these techniques regularly, and the variability observed in teacher's mnemonic orientation has provided us with the opportunity to explore the differential impact of varying levels of mnemonic instruction. Thus, in the next section we provide a sample of our findings linking teacher mnemonic style to measures of children's strategy use and recall.

Linking the Classroom Context and Children's Memory Skills

To explore the linkage between teachers' mnemonic style in the classroom and children's developing memory skills we examined the performance of children in our sample who were taught by the high versus low mnemonic teachers (Coffman et al., 2008; Ornstein, Coffman, & McCall, 2005). As described by Coffman et al. (2008), of the 107 first-graders in our sample, 46 were in classes taught by low mnemonic teachers and 61 in classes taught by high mnemonic teachers. Importantly, these two groups of children did not differ on measures of basic memory capacity at the beginning of their year in the first grade. This equivalence notwithstanding, by the end of the year the children in these two groups of classes differed in their use of memory strategies and in the amount of information recalled on a range of tasks.

To illustrate these differences in memory skills as a function of the mnemonic style of the first-grade teachers, consider first the children's performance on the task used initially by Baker-Ward et al. (1984) and now labeled the Object Memory Task. As discussed earlier, with this task the participants were given a 2-minute study period to "work to remember" a set of interesting objects and then asked to recall the items. The study period was videotaped so that we could code for the presence of eight simple behavioral strategies that could be used while attempting to remember the objects: *association, categorization, covert mnemonic activity, manipulation, naming, object talk, pointing,* and *visual examination.* To characterize the children's overall strategic performance, we used a composite measure that reflected the total number of seconds in the study interval in which a child was engaged in any of these eight strategic behaviors. As reported by Coffman et al. (2008) and displayed in Figure 2.1, the children in the high versus low mnemonic classrooms exhibited different patterns of strategy use on the Object Memory Task over time, such that after the first time point the first graders taught by high mnemonic teachers evidenced significantly more time on the use of the strategies than did their peers taught by low mnemonic teachers. Paralleling these differences in strategy use were comparable differences in the children's recall of the to-be-remembered objects, as displayed in Figure 2.2 (see Coffman et al., 2008).

Comparable differences in the performance of children taught by the two groups of teachers were also observed on a Free Recall with Organizational Training Task (Moely et al., 1992). With this task, each child was presented with 16 line drawings (four cards from each of four categories) across a series of baseline, training, and generalization sort-recall trials. The participants each received three trials at the first assessment point

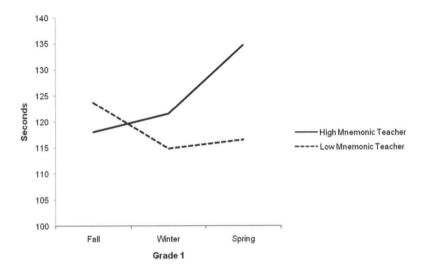

FIGURE 2.1. Number of seconds engaged in strategic behaviors on the Object Memory Task over the first grade as a function of teachers' mnemonic orientation. Adapted from Coffman, Ornstein, McCall, and Curran (2008). Copyright 2008 by the American Psychological Association. Adapted by permission.

in the fall of grade 1, including a baseline, training, and generalization trial. In the training trial, children were given instructions on how to use the category structure in their sorting and to cluster the items in recall, and were also told that these techniques would aid them in remembering. At each subsequent assessment in the winter and spring, noninstructed generalization trials were administered. Similarly, when the children were in grade 2 and thus taught by different teachers, three assessments with noninstructed generalization trials were carried out, one each in the fall, winter, and spring. At all points, performance measures included the children's use of categorical sorting during the sorting (study) phase of each trial, as indexed by adjusted ratio of clustering (ARC) scores (Roenker, Thompson, & Brown, 1971), which range from –1 (below chance organization), to 0 (chance), to 1 (complete categorization), and the number of items recalled.

As reported by Coffman et al. (2008) and displayed in Figure 2.3, we again observed linkages between the classroom context and children's mnemonic skills, such that students in classes taught by high mnemonic teachers sorted on the Free Recall with Organizational Training Task at higher levels than their peers in low mnemonic classes. These patterns of diverging skill emerged in the winter of the first grade and were main-

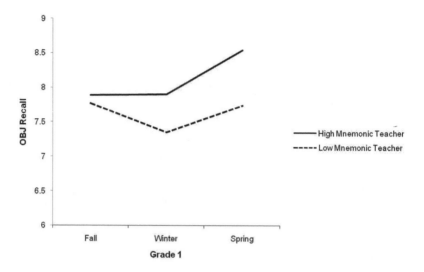

FIGURE 2.2. Number of items recalled on the Object Memory Task over the first grade as a function of teachers' mnemonic orientation. Adapted from Coffman, Ornstein, McCall, and Curran (2008). Copyright 2008 by the American Psychological Association. Adapted by permission.

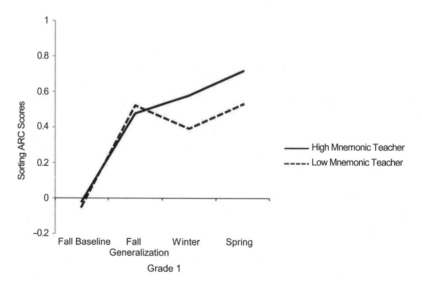

FIGURE 2.3. Sorting ARC scores on the Free Recall with Organizational Training Task over the first grade as a function of teachers' mnemonic orientation. Adapted from Coffman, Ornstein, McCall, and Curran (2008). Copyright 2008 by the American Psychological Association. Adapted by permission.

tained through the spring of that year. Further, paralleling the findings with the Object Memory Task, the data presented in Figure 2.4 indicate differences in the children's recall of the items in the Free Recall with Organizational Training Task, as a function of the mnemonic orientation of their first-grade teachers.

In addition to these demonstrations of associations between teachers' mnemonic style and the children's memory performance in the first grade, the long term impact of the first-grade teachers was observed in the children's sorting in the second grade, when they were taught by other teachers. Indeed, consistent with inspection of Figure 2.5, significant differences are seen at each of the three time points (fall, winter, and spring) of grade 2. Interestingly, associations between the first-grade mnemonic context and the children's memory skills have also been observed as late as the fourth grade, when the children were given a Sort-Recall Task (see Corsale & Ornstein, 1980). In contrast to the Free Recall with Organizational Training Task, with its categorized materials used in grades 1 and 2, only low-associated items were used with this Sort-Recall Task. The participants were presented with a set of 20 cards that contained low-associated nouns and were instructed to form groups with the cards that would facilitate remembering. Each trial was subsequently scored in

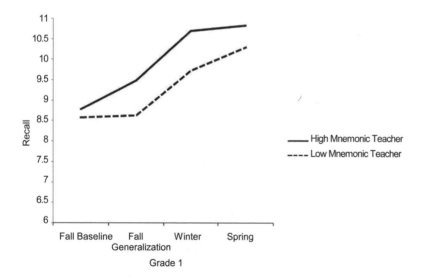

FIGURE 2.4. Number of pictures recalled on the Free Recall with Organizational Training Task over the first grade as a function of teachers' mnemonic orientation. Adapted from Coffman, Ornstein, McCall, and Curran (2008). Copyright 2008 by the American Psychological Association. Adapted by permission.

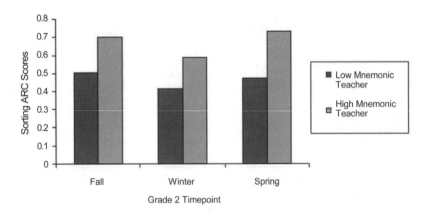

FIGURE 2.5. Sorting ARC scores on the Free Recall with Organizational Training Task over the second grade as a function of first-grade teacher mnemonic
orientation.

terms of the level of semantic organization observed in each sort, with
the scores ranging between 0 and 4 and reflecting a continuum from
random sorting to that based on clear semantic associations. As can be
seen in Figure 2.6, when the sorting scores were examined as a function
of the mnemonic orientation of the first-grade teachers, it was found that
children from high mnemonic first-grade classrooms sorted more semantically than did their peers from low mnemonic classrooms.

Finally, we have also observed relations between teachers' mnemonic style and children's performance in grade 4 on a Study Skills Task
(adapted from Brown & Smiley, 1977, 1978). In this task, each child was
asked to "work" to remember a short passage derived from grade-appro-
priate science and social studies texts. The students were given materials,
including a pencil, highlighter, notepad, and dictionary, to aid in remembering, but they were not encouraged explicitly to use the materials that
were provided. We coded the children's use of study behaviors such as
note taking, *text underlining*, *highlighting*, *rereading*, and *self-testing* on
a scale on which individual scores could range from 0 (very few task-
related behaviors) to 3 (very organized, efficient use of strategies). These
scores were then averaged into a single composite strategy score, and
as can be seen in Figure 2.7, differences in average strategy scores were
observed as a function of the first-grade classroom context. Although
these differences were not statistically significant in the fall of the fourth
grade, by the winter and spring children who had been in high mnemonic
first-grade classrooms significantly outperformed their peers who had
been in low mnemonic classrooms. This surprising yet intriguing linkage

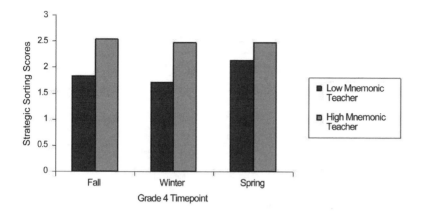

FIGURE 2.6. Fourth-grade strategic sorting scores on the Sort-Recall Task as a function of first-grade teacher mnemonic orientation.

provides additional evidence of the potential lasting importance of the metacognitive milieu of the early educational context.

CONCLUSION

Reflecting the view that any division between basic and applied research is in fact artificial, we have provided an overview of the development of children's deliberate memory skills that incorporates both laboratory- and school-based research. As we see it, this bridge between laboratory assessments of children's mnemonic skills and observations of teaching in the classroom has increased our understanding of children's memory by identifying one set of factors associated with developmental changes in memory performance. Building on the findings of a range of studies that articulate the importance of metacognitive language—both in exper- imental manipulations of mnemonic strategies and in teacher "talk" in the classroom (see, e.g., Moely et al., 1992; Paris et al., 1982; Pressley & Hilden, 2006)—we have been able to establish clear linkages between teachers' mnemonic style and children's memory skills.

The memory-rich language that takes place in high mnemonic first- grade classrooms during naturally occurring lessons in language arts and mathematics appears to have important implications for the development of children's basic memory skills. Not only is the context that is created by these teachers of importance for the first graders in their classes, it also seems to be related to the children's memory performance several years

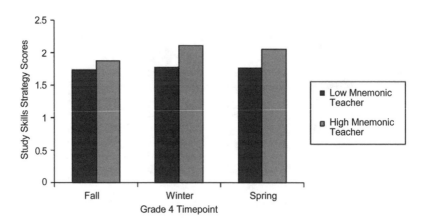

FIGURE 2.7. Fourth-grade strategic studying as a function of first-grade teacher mnemonic orientation.

later, after they have been exposed to different teachers. Thus, the characterization of these important interactions may lead us closer to understanding the mechanisms that underlie children's strategic growth. With the encouraging evidence from our project, we are now poised to implement a series of instructional manipulations and classroom interventions that will allow us to examine further the role of metacognitively rich language during instruction and, we hope, to develop instructional packages for teachers that may facilitate children's skills for remembering.

REFERENCES

Baker Ward, L., Ornstein, P. A., & Holden, D. J. (1984). The expression of memorization in early childhood. *Journal of Experimental Child Psychology, 37,* 555–575.

Best, D. L., & Ornstein, P. A. (1986). Children's generation and communication of mnemonic organizational strategies. *Developmental Psychology, 22,* 845–853.

Bjorklund, D. F., & Harnishfeger, K. K. (1987). Developmental differences in the mental effort requirements for the use of an organizational strategy in free recall. *Journal of Experimental Child Psychology, 44,* 109–125.

Bjorklund, D. F., Ornstein, P. A., & Haig, J. R. (1977). Developmental differences in organization and recall: Training in the use of organizational techniques. *Developmental Psychology, 13,* 175–183.

Bjorklund, D. F., & Zeman, B. R. (1982). Children's organization and metamemory awareness in the recall of familiar information. *Child Development, 53,* 799–810.

Borkowski, J. G., Carr, M., Rellinger, E. A., & Pressley, M. (1990). Self-regulated strategy use: Interdependence of metacognition, attributions, and self-esteem. In B. F. Jones (Ed.), *Dimensions of thinking: Review of research* (pp. 53–92). Hillsdale NJ: Erlbaum.

Borkowski, J. G., Milstead, M., & Hale, C. (1988). Components of children's metamemory: Implications for strategy generalization. In F. E. Weinert & M. Perlmutter (Eds.), *Memory development: Universal changes and individual differences* (pp. 73–100). Hillsdale, NJ: Erlbaum.

Brown, A. L. (1978). Knowing when, where, and how to remember: A problem of metacognition. In R. Glaser (Ed.), *Advances in instructional psychology* (Vol. 4, pp. 77–165). Hillsdale NJ: Erlbaum.

Brown, A. L., & Reeve, R. A. (1987). Bandwidths of competence: The role of supportive contexts in learning and development. In L. S. Liben (Ed.), *Development and learning: Conflict or congruence?* (pp. 173–223). Hillsdale, NJ: Erlbaum.

Brown, A. L., & Smiley, S. S. (1977). Rating the importance of structural units of prose passages: A problem of metacognitive development. *Child Development, 48*, 1–8.

Brown, A. L., & Smiley, S. S. (1978). The development of strategies for studying texts. *Child Development, 49*, 1076–1088.

Brown, R., Pressley, M., Van Meter, P., & Schuder, T. (1996). A quasi-experimental validation of transactional strategies instruction with low-achieving second grade readers. *Journal of Educational Psychology, 88*, 18–37.

Cairns, R. B., Santoyo, V. C., Ferguson, L., & Cairns, B. D. (1991). Integration of interactional and contextual information: The synchronic observations procedure. *Mexican Journal of Behavioral Analysis, 17*, 105–120.

Cavanaugh, J. C., & Perlmutter, M. (1982). Metamemory: A critical examination. *Child Development, 53*, 11–28.

Coffman, J. L., Ornstein, P. A., McCall, L. E., & Curran, P. J. (2008). Linking teachers' memory-relevant language and the development of children's memory skills. *Developmental Psychology, 44*, 1640–1654.

Cole, M. (1992). Cognitive development and formal schooling: The evidence from cross-cultural research. In L. C. Moll (Ed.), *Vygotsky and education: Instructional implications and applications of sociohistorical psychology* (pp. 89–110). New York: Cambridge University Press.

Corsale, K., & Ornstein, P. A. (1980). Developmental changes in children's use of semantic information in recall. *Journal of Experimental Child Psychology, 30*, 231–245.

Cox, B. D., Ornstein, P. A., Naus, M. J., Maxfield, D., & Zimler, J. (1989). Children's concurrent use of rehearsal and organizational strategies. *Developmental Psychology, 25*, 619–627.

Cox, B., Ornstein, P. A., & Valsiner, J. (1991). The role of internalization in the transfer in mnemonic strategies. In L. Oppenheimer & J. Valsiner (Eds.), *The origins of action: Interdisciplinary and international perspectives* (pp. 101–131). New York: Springer-Verlag.

Coyle, T. R., & Bjorklund, D. F. (1997). Age differences in, and consequences of, multiple- and variable-strategy use on a multitrial sort-recall task. *Developmental Psychology, 33,* 372–380.

Duffy, G. G., Roehler, L. R., Sivan, E., Rackliffe, G., Book, C., Meloth, M., et al. (1987). Effects of explaining the reasoning associated with using reading strategies. *Reading Research Quarterly, 22,* 347–368.

Fivush, R., Haden, C. A., & Reese, E. (2006). Elaborating on elaborations: Role of maternal reminiscing style in cognitive and socioemotional development. *Child Development, 77,* 1568–1588.

Flavell, J. H., & Wellman, H. M. (1977). Metamemory. In R. V. Kail & J. W. Hagen (Eds.), *Perspectives on the development of memory and cognition* (pp. 3–33). Hillsdale, NJ: Erlbaum.

Guttentag, R. E. (1984). The mental effort requirements of cumulated rehearsal: A developmental study. *Journal of Experimental Child Psychology, 37,* 92–106.

Guttentag, R. E., Ornstein, P. A., & Siemens, L. (1987). Children's spontaneous rehearsal: Transitions in strategy acquisition. *Cognitive Development, 2,* 307–326.

Haden, C. A., Ornstein, P. A., Eckerman, C. O., & Didow, S. M. (2001). Mother–child conversational interactions as events unfold: Linkages to subsequent remembering. *Child Development, 72,* 1016–1031.

Harvey, S., & Goudvis, A. (2000). *Strategies that work: Teaching comprehension to enhance understanding.* Portland, ME: Stenhouse.

Joyner, M. H., & Kurtz-Costes, B. (1997). Metamemory development. In N. Cowan & C. Hulme (Eds.), *The development of memory in childhood* (pp. 275–300). East Sussex, UK: Psychology Press.

Kail, R. V., & Hagen, J. W. (Eds.). (1977). *Perspectives on the development of memory and cognition.* Hillsdale, NJ: Erlbaum.

Kron-Sperl, V., Schneider, W., & Hasselhorn, M. (2008). The development and effectiveness of memory strategies in kindergarten and elementary school: Findings from the Würzburg and Göttingen longitudinal memory studies. *Cognitive Development, 23,* 79–104.

Kuhn, D. (1995). Microgenetic study of change: What has it told us? *Psychological Science, 6,* 133–139.

Kuhn, D. (1999). Metacognitive development. In L. Balter & C. S. Tamis-LeMonda (Eds.), *Child psychology: A handbook of contemporary issues* (pp. 259–286). New York: Psychology Press.

Lange, G. (1978). Organization-related processes in children's recall. In P. A. Ornstein (Ed.), *Memory development in children* (pp. 101–128). Hillsdale, NJ: Erlbaum.

Lehmann, M., & Hasselhorn, M. (2007). Variable memory strategy use in children's adaptive intratask learning behavior: Developmental changes and working memory influences in free recall. *Child Development, 78,* 1068–1082.

Liberty, C., & Ornstein, P. A. (1973). Age differences in organization and recall: The effects of training in categorization. *Journal of Experimental Child Psychology, 15,* 169–186.

Moely, B. E., Hart, S. S., Leal, L., Santulli, K. A., Rao, N., Johnson, T., et al.

(1992). The teacher's role in facilitating memory and study strategy development in the elementary school classroom. *Child Development, 63,* 653–672.

Moely, B. E., Hart, S. S., Santulli, K. A., Leal, L., Kogut, D. J., McLain, E., et al. (1989, April). *Teacher's cognitions about the memory processes of elementary school children: A developmental perspective.* Poster presented at the biennial meeting of the Society for Research in Child Development, Kansas City, MO.

Morrison, F. J., Smith, L., & Dow-Ehrensberger, M. (1995). Education and cognitive development: A natural experiment. *Developmental Psychology, 31,* 789–799.

Nelson, K. (1974). Concept, word, and sentence: Interrelations in acquisition and development. *Psychological Review, 81,* 267–285.

Ornstein, P. A. (Ed.). (1978). *Memory development in children.* Hillsdale, NJ: Erlbaum.

Ornstein, P. A., Baker-Ward, L., & Naus, M. J. (1988). The development of mnemonic skill. In F. E. Weinert & M. Perlmutter (Eds.), *Memory development: Universal changes and individual differences* (pp. 31–49). Hillsdale, NJ: Erlbaum.

Ornstein, P. A., Coffman, J. L., Grammer, J., San Souci, P., & McCall, L. (in press). Linking the classroom context and the development of children's memory skills. In J. Meece & J. Eccles (Eds.), *Handbook of research on schools, schooling, and human development.* New York: Routledge.

Ornstein, P. A., Coffman, J. L., & McCall, L. E. (2005, April). *Linking teachers' memory-relevant language and children's memory performance.* In F. J. Morrison (Chair), *The socialization of cognition: Environmental influences on developmental change.* Symposium paper presented at the biennial meeting of the Society for Research in Child Development, Atlanta, GA.

Ornstein, P. A., & Haden, C. A. (2001). *Memory* development or the *development of memory? Current Directions in Psychological Science, 10,* 202–205.

Ornstein, P. A., Haden, C. A., & San Souci, P. P. (2008). The development of skilled remembering in children. In J. H. E. Byrne (Ed.) & H. Roediger III (Vol. Ed.), *Learning and memory: A comprehensive reference: Vol. 4. Cognitive psychology of memory* (pp. 715–744). Oxford, UK: Elsevier.

Ornstein, P. A., Medlin, R. G., Stone, B. P., & Naus, M. J. (1985). Retrieving for rehearsal: An analysis of active rehearsal in children's memory. *Developmental Psychology, 21,* 633–641.

Ornstein, P. A., & Naus, M. J. (1978). Rehearsal processes in children's memory. In P. A. Ornstein (Ed.), *Memory development in children* (pp. 69–99). Hillsdale, NJ: Erlbaum.

Ornstein, P. A., Naus, M. J., & Liberty, C. (1975). Rehearsal and organizational processes in children's memory. *Child Development, 46,* 818–830.

Ornstein, P. A., Naus, M. J., & Stone, B. P. (1977). Rehearsal training and developmental differences in memory. *Developmental Psychology, 13,* 15–24.

Ornstein, P. A., Trabasso, T., & Johnson-Laird, P. N. (1974). To organize is to remember: The effects of instructions to organize and to recall. *Journal of Experimental Psychology, 103,* 1014–1018.

Palincsar, A. S., & Brown, A. L. (1984). Reciprocal teaching of comprehension-fostering and monitoring activities. *Cognition and Instruction, 1,* 117–175.

Paris, S. G., Newman, R. S., & McVey, K. A. (1982). Learning the functional significance of mnemonic actions: A microgenetic study of strategy acquisition. *Journal of Experimental Child Psychology, 34,* 490–509.

Pressley, M., & Harris, K. R. (2006). Cognitive strategies instruction: From basic research to classroom instruction. In P. A. Alexander & P. H. Winne (Eds.), *Handbook of educational psychology* (pp. 265–286). Mahwah, NJ: Erlbaum.

Pressley, M., & Hilden, K. (2006). Cognitive strategies. In W. Damon & R. Lerner (Series Editors), & D. Kuhn & R. Siegler (Vol. Eds.), *Handbook of child psychology: Vol. 2. Cognition, perception, and language* (6th ed., pp. 511–556). Hoboken NJ: Wiley.

Pressley, M., Ross, K. A., Levin, J. R., & Ghatala, E. S. (1984). The role of strategy utility knowledge in children's decision making. *Journal of Experimental Child Psychology, 38,* 491–504.

Pressley, M., Wharton-McDonald, R., Mistretta, J., & Echevarria, M. (1998). The nature of literacy instruction in ten grade-4 and -5 classrooms in upstate New York. *Scientific Studies of Reading, 2,* 159–191.

Reese, E., Haden, C., & Fivush, R. (1993). Mother–child conversations about the past: Relationships of style and memory over time. *Cognitive Development, 8,* 403–430.

Ringel, B. A., & Springer, C. J. (1980). On knowing how well one is remembering: The persistence of strategy use during transfer. *Journal of Experimental Child Psychology, 29,* 322–333.

Roenker, D., Thompson, C., & Brown, S. (1971). Comparison of measures for the estimation of clustering in free recall. *Psychological Bulletin, 76,* 45–48.

Rogoff, B. (1981). Schooling and the development of cognitive skills. In H. C. Triandis & A. Heron (Eds.), *Handbook of cross-cultural psychology* (Vol. 4, pp. 233–294). Boston: Allyn & Bacon.

Rogoff, B., & Mistry, J. (1990). The social and functional context of children's remembering. In R. Fivush & J. A. Hudson (Eds.), *Knowing and remembering in young children* (pp. 197–222). New York: Cambridge University Press.

Rohwer, W. D. (1973). Elaboration and learning in childhood and adolescence. In H. W. Reese (Ed.), *Advances in child development and behavior* (Vol. 8, pp. 1–57). New York: Academic Press.

Schlagmüller, M., & Schneider, W. (2002). The development of organizational strategies in children: Evidence from a microgenetic longitudinal study. *Journal of Experimental Child Psychology, 81,* 298–319.

Schneider, W. (1985). Developmental trends in the metamemory–memory behavior relationship: An integrated review. In D. L. Forrest-Pressley, G. E. Mackinnon, & T. G. Waller (Eds.), *Cognition, metacognition, and human performance: Vol. 1. Theoretical perspectives* (pp. 57–109). New York: Academic Press.

Schneider, W. (1999). The development of metamemory in children. In D. Gopher & A. Koriat (Eds.), *Attention and performance XVII: Cognitive regulation* of performance: Interaction of theory and application (pp. 487–513). Cambridge, MA: MIT Press.

Schneider, W., Kron, V., Hünnerkopf, M., & Krajewski, K. (2004). The development of young children's memory strategies: First findings from the Würzburg Longitudinal Memory Study. *Journal of Experimental Child Psychology, 88,* 193–209.

Schneider, W., & Lockl, K. (2002). The development of metacognitive knowledge in children and adolescents. In D. L. Forrest-Pressley, G. E. Mackinnon, & T. G. Waller (Eds.), *Applied metacognition* (pp. 224–257). New York: Cambridge University Press.

Schneider, W., & Pressley, M. (1997). *Memory development between 2 and 20.* New York: Springer-Verlag.

Scribner, S., & Cole, M. (1978). Literacy without schooling: Testing for intellectual effects. *Harvard Educational Review, 48,* 448–461.

Siegler, R. S. (1996). *Emerging minds: The process of change in children's thinking.* New York: Oxford University Press.

Sodian, B., & Schneider, W. (1999). Memory strategy development—Gradual increase, sudden insight, or roller coaster? In F. E. Weinert & W. Schneider (Eds.), *Individual development from 3 to 12: Findings from the Munich longitudinal study* (pp. 61–77). Cambridge, UK: Cambridge University Press.

Sodian, B., Schneider, W., & Perlmutter, M. (1986). Recall, clustering, and metamemory in young children. *Journal of Experimental Child Psychology, 41,* 395–410.

Vygotsky, L. S. (1978). *Mind in society.* Cambridge, MA: Harvard University Press.

Wagner, D. A. (1978). Memories of Morocco: The influence of age, schooling, and environment on memory. *Cognitive Psychology, 10,* 1–28.

Wagner, D. A. (1981). Culture and memory development. In H. Triandis & A. Heron (Eds.), *Handbook of cross-cultural psychology* (Vol. 4, pp. 187–232). Boston: Allyn & Bacon.

Waters, H. S. (2008, July). *Discussion.* In P. A. Ornstein (Chair), *Longitudinal studies on memory development.* Symposium paper presented at the meeting of the International Society for the Study of Behavioural Development, Würzburg, Germany.

Weinert, F. E., & Schneider, W. (Eds.). (1999). *Individual development from 3 to 12.* Cambridge, UK: Cambridge University Press.

Worden, P. E. (1975). Effects of sorting on subsequent recall of unrelated items: A developmental study. *Child Development, 46,* 687–695.

3

Metacognition and Memory Development in Childhood and Adolescence

Wolfgang Schneider

During the last four decades, numerous publications have focused on the development of memory, mostly in children and adolescents (see overviews by Bauer, 2006; Schneider & Bjorklund, 1998; Schneider & Pressley, 1997). Overall, developmental changes in memory capacity, memory strategies, domain-specific knowledge, and metacognitive knowledge were assumed to cause increases in memory performance across childhood and adolescence. Whereas the contribution of developmental changes in memory capacity to improvements in memory performance was generally considered to be rather modest, the relative importance of strategy acquisition, metacognitive knowledge, and domain-specific knowledge for improvements in memory performance were emphasized by most researchers in the field.

CONCEPTUALIZATIONS AND MODELS OF METAMEMORY AND METACOGNITION

In this chapter, the focus is on the development of *metamemory*, that is, metacognitive knowledge about memory and its relationship to memory performance. Research on the development of metamemory was initiated in the early 1970s by Ann Brown, John Flavell, and their colleagues (for reviews, see Brown, Bransford, Ferrara, & Campione, 1983; Flavell, Miller, & Miller, 2002; Schneider & Pressley, 1997). Flavell's (1971) conception of metamemory was global, encompassing knowledge of all possible aspects of information storage and retrieval. Accordingly, metamemory included (but was not limited to) knowledge about memory functioning, difficulties, and strategies. Flavell and Wellman (1977) distinguished between two main metamemory categories, "sensitivity" and "variables." The "sensitivity" category referred to mostly implicit, unconscious behavioral knowledge of when memory is necessary, and thus was very close to subsequent definitions of *procedural metacognitive knowledge*. The "variables" category referred to explicit, conscious, and factual knowledge about the importance of person, task, and strategy variables for memory performance. This is also known as *declarative metacognitive knowledge*. Flavell and Wellman (1977) assumed that these categories and subcategories should be conceived of as overlapping and interactive. For instance, people with well-developed metamemory should know that different individuals do not always solve a problem equally well (i.e., there are person x task interactions), and that the strategy chosen to solve a particular problem depends largely on person and task characteristics (i.e., there are person x strategy x task interactions). One impression that could be gleaned from the early research carried out by Flavell and his colleagues was that a lot of metacognitive development was complete by age 8 or 9 (e.g., Kreutzer, Leonard, & Flavell, 1975). One motivation for Ann Brown's (1978; Brown et al., 1983) reconceptualization of metamemory was to counteract this impression, by focusing on procedural metamemory ("here-and-now-memory monitoring") and children's text processing. Research carried out by Brown and colleagues was able to demonstrate that metacognitive abilities develop quite slowly during the school years, and that there was room for improvement even in adolescents and adults (see Brown et al., 1983).

In a seminal paper, Flavell (1979) argued that metamemory was not isolated from knowledge about other aspects of the mind, and he generalized the metamemory taxonomy developed in Flavell and Wellman (1977) to *metacognition* in general. Although various definitions of the term *metacognition* have been used in the literature on cognitive development, the concept has usually been broadly and rather loosely defined as any knowledge or cognitive activity that takes as its object, or regulates, any aspect of any cognitive enterprise (cf. Flavell et al., 2002). Obviously, this conceptualization refers to people's knowledge of their own information-processing skills, as well as to knowledge about the nature of cognitive tasks, and about strategies for coping with such tasks. Moreover, it also includes executive skills related to monitoring and self-regulation of one's own cognitive activities. Flavell (1979) described three major facets of metacognition, namely, metacognitive knowledge, metacognitive experiences, and metacognitive skills, that is, strategies controlling cognition. According to Flavell et al. (2002), declarative metacognitive knowledge refers to the segment of world knowledge that has to do with the human mind and its doings. Metacognitive experiences refer to a person's awareness and feelings elicited in a problem-solving situation (e.g., feelings of knowing), and metacognitive skills are believed to play a role in many types of cognitive activity such as oral communication of information, reading comprehension, attention, and memory.

The taxonomy of metamemory presented by Flavell and Wellman (1977) was not intended to be exhaustive. Since the late 1970s, a number of additions and changes have been suggested (for comprehensive reviews, see Holland-Joyner & Kurtz-Costes, 1997; Schneider, 1999; Schneider & Pressley, 1997). For instance, Paris and Oka (1986) introduced a component labeled *conditional metacognitive knowledge* that focused on children's ability to justify or explain their decisions concerning memory activities. Whereas the declarative metamemory component first introduced by Flavell and Wellman (1977) focused on "knowing that," conditional metamemory referred to "knowing why." The procedural metamemory component emphasized by Brown and colleagues, that is, children's ability to monitor and self-regulate their memory-related behavior, refers to "knowing how" and plays a major role in complex cognitive tasks such as comprehending and memorizing text materials.

Although subsequent conceptualizations of metacognition expanded the scope of this theoretical construct, they also made use of the basic distinction between declarative and procedural knowledge. For instance, Wellman (1990) linked the declarative metacognitive component to the broader concept of children's *theory of mind*, which focuses on classes of knowledge about the inner mental world and cognitive processes that develop during the preschool years. Pressley, Borkowski, Schneider, and colleagues systematically considered declarative and procedural components of metacognition in developing a theoretical model that emphasized the dynamic interrelations among strategies, monitoring abilities, and motivation (e.g., Pressley, Borkowski, & O'Sullivan, 1985; Pressley, Borkowski, & Schneider, 1987, 1989). In their extension of the theoretical framework of metacognition, Pressley and colleagues proposed an elaborate model, the *good information-processing model*, that linked aspects of procedural and declarative metacognitive knowledge to other features of successful information processing. According to this model, sophisticated metacognition is closely related to the learner's strategy use, domain knowledge, motivational orientation, general knowledge about the world, and automated use of efficient learning procedures. All of these components are assumed to interact. For instance, specific strategy knowledge influences the adequate application of metacognitive strategies, which in turn affects knowledge. As the strategies are carried out, they are monitored and evaluated, which leads to expansion and refinement of specific strategy knowledge.

Overall, the distinction between declarative and procedural metacognitive knowledge is widely accepted in developmental and educational psychology. Although these components are generally conceived of as relatively independent, empirical findings suggest that they can mutually influence each other (see Schneider, Körkel, & Weinert, 1987; Schraw, 1994). For instance, knowing about one's own tendency to commit easy errors may lead to increased self-regulatory activities in test situations.

It should be noted that the conceptualizations of metacognition outlined above and originally elaborated by developmental psychologists actually differ in several aspects from models developed in the fields of general psychology, social psychology, and the psychology of aging. For instance, popular conceptualizations of metacognition in the field of cognitive psychology exclusively elaborate on the procedural component, focusing on the interplay between monitoring and self-control (see Koriat, 2007; Nelson, 1996). On the other hand, when issues of declarative metacognitive knowledge are analyzed in the fields of social psychology and gerontology, the focus is on a person's *beliefs* about cognitive phenomena and not on veridical knowledge. More recent conceptualizations of metacognition developed in the field of educational psychology subsume the procedural and declarative components of metacognition to the superconstruct of *self-regulation* (e.g., Efklides, 2001, 2008; Schunk & Zimmerman, 1998). Recent developments also include cognitive neuroscience models of metacognition (cf. Shimamura, 2000). Overall, the popularity of the metacognition construct is mainly due to the fact that it seems crucial for concepts of everyday reasoning and those assessing scientific thinking as well as social interactions.

Assessment of Metamemory

Measures of Declarative Metamemory

A variety of measures have been used to capture what children know about memory. As noted by Cavanaugh and Perlmutter (1982), measures assessing *declarative metamemory* are taken without concurrent memory assessment (independent measures), whereas measures of *procedural metamemory* are collected simultaneously with the measurement of memory activity (concurrent measures).

Most measurements of *declarative metamemory* in children have used interviews or questionnaires. One of the earliest and best-known interview studies on declarative metamemory was carried out by Kreutzer et al. (1975) who assessed children's knowledge about person, task, and strategy variables relevant to memory performance in different settings. Although no information on reliability was provided for this metamemory battery of 14 items, subsequent replications and extensions carried out in the 1980s showed that reliability was not a major problem (see Belmont & Borkowski, 1988; Cavenaugh & Borkowski, 1980; Kurtz, Reid, Borkowski, & Cavanaugh, 1982; Schneider, Borkowski, Kurtz, & Kerwin, 1986). More recent interview and questionnaire construction procedures seem even better from a psychometric perspective, however. For instance, Schlagmüller, Visé, and Schneider (2001) began with an extensive item pool and then conducted pilot testing, dropping items that were not sufficiently reliable or did not seem to be otherwise valid. The resulting questionnaire tapped metamemory related to everyday memory situations, semantic categorization tasks, and memory for text. Overall, internal consistency was alpha = .77 for the total scale, and the test–retest correlation after 4 months was .71. For similar construction principles, see Hasselhorn (1994). One of the advantages of the questionnaires developed by Belmont and Borkowski (1988) and Schlagmüller et al. (2001) was that they could be used in group settings and also administered to relatively young children between 6 and 12 years of age.

Problems with the assessment of declarative metamemory via interviews and questionnaires were caused by the reliance on verbal self-report, which may be particularly difficult for young children. To avoid such problems, alternative nonverbal assessment procedures such as videotape illustrations of memory strategies were used (for details, see the overviews in Holland-Joyner & Kurtz-Costes, 1997; Schneider & Pressley, 1997). In the procedure developed by Justice (1985, 1986), children were presented with various memory strategies (e.g., looking, naming, rehearsing, and grouping) on a videotape. After watching the videotapes and naming the strategies, children made pairwise comparisons of the strategies.

To ensure that children provide all their available metacognitive knowledge in a test situation, Best and Ornstein (1986) used a peer tutoring assessment procedure where older children (e.g., third or sixth graders) were asked to teach a memory strategy such as sorting items into semantic categories to younger children (e.g., first graders). Tutors' instructions were taped and subjected to content analyses. The measure of metamemory was the extent to which the instructions include appropriate strategy instructions.

Overall, these alternative methods alleviated some of the problems usually related to the use of questionnaire measures. However, these measures still created difficulties when applied to older children and adolescents, particularly when knowledge about text processing was assessed. For instance, when the author of this chapter was first asked to construct such a metacognition measure for the first international Programme for International Student Assessment (PISA) study in 2000, pilot data were disappointing. Although the measure was perfectly reliable, it lacked validity. One of the reasons for this was that not only did good text information processors identify suitable strategies and indicate that they used such strategies most of the time, but even poor text processors intuitively selected the better strategies and pretended that they would use these strategies all of the time. As expected, this was not confirmed by the actual text-processing data, yielding nonsignificant correlations between metamemory, strategy use, and memory performance. In fact, one paradoxical outcome of this research was that low achievers came out with higher metamemory scores than high achievers.

To avoid such problems, more sophisticated measures of metacognition have to be used with older children and adolescents. Schlagmüller and Schneider (2007) came up with a standardized measure of metacognition that was based on a revised test instrument developed for PISA 2000 (see Artelt, Schiefele, & Schneider, 2001). This instrument taps adolescents' knowledge of strategies that are relevant during reading and for the comprehension as well as the recall of text information. For each of six scenarios, students have to evaluate the quality and usefulness of five different strategies available for reaching the intended learning or memory goal. The rank order of strategies obtained for each scenario is then compared with an optimal rank order provided by experts in the field of text processing. The correspondence between the two rankings is expressed in a metacognition score, indicating the degree to which students are aware of the best ways to store and remember text information.

Measures of Procedural Metamemory

Concurrent measures of metamemory are characterized by the presence of simultaneous memory activity. Here, children and adolescents are asked to judge their memory performance either shortly before, during, or after working on a memory task. The most studied type of procedural metamemory is self-monitoring, that is, evaluating how well one is progressing (see Brown et al., 1983; Schneider & Lockl, 2002). The developmental literature has focused on performance prediction or *ease-of-learning (EOL) judgments, judgments of learning (JOL)*, and *feeling-of-knowing (FOK) judgments*, and also has explored some aspects of control and self-regulation such as allocation of study time and termination of study (recall readiness).

EOL judgments occur in advance of the learning process, are largely inferential, and refer to items that have not yet been learned (Nelson & Narens, 1994). The corresponding memory paradigm is performance prediction. A classic EOL task refers to the prediction of one's own memory span. Individuals are presented incrementally longer lists of materials to be learned, such as pictures, words, or figures, and are asked to indicate whether they could still recall a list that long. Children's memory is then tapped using the same lists. Comparisons of the predictor value with actual memory span yields the metamemory indicator. Performance prediction accuracy can be measured for a variety of memory tasks, including list-learning paradigms and text-learning tasks (cf. Schneider, Körkel, & Weinert, 1990).

JOL judgments occur during or soon after the acquisition of memory materials and are predictions about future test performance on recently studied (and probably still recallable) items. Typically, paired-associate learning tasks are used in this context. After completion of a learning trial, participants are shown the stimuli of a given pair and have to indicate how confident they are whether they will remember the correct item response either immediately or 10 minutes later. Some studies also assessed children's *postdictions* (e.g., Pressley, Levin, Ghatala, & Ahmad, 1987). After having memorized a list of items, children were asked how many items they had correctly recalled. Overall, the database concerning children's performance in JOL tasks is still rather small compared to the large body of literature addressing JOLs in adults.

A number of developmental studies have explored children's *FOK* judgments (e.g., Butterfield, Nelson, & Peck, 1988; Lockl & Schneider, 2002). These judgments occur either during or after a learning procedure and are judgments about whether a currently unrecallable item will be remembered at a subsequent retention test. Typically, children are shown a series of items and asked to name them. When children cannot recall the name of an object given its picture, they are asked to indicate whether the name could be recognized if the experimenter provided it. These FOK ratings are then related to subsequent performance on the recognition test that included nonrecalled items.

Whereas self-monitoring involves knowing where you are with regard to your goal of understanding and memorizing task materials, self-regulation includes planning, directing, and evaluating one's mnemonic activities (cf. Flavell et al., 2002). Some developmental studies have addressed aspects of children's *control and self-regulation processes* such as termination of study (recall readiness) and allocation of study time (see the review by Schneider & Pressley, 1997). *Recall readiness* assessments are made after learning materials have been studied at least once. Typically, participants are asked to continue studying until their memory of the materials to be learned is perfect. After children indicate that they have reached this goal, their memory performance is tested.

Another example of self-regulation skills concerns the *allocation of study time*. This research observes how learners deploy their attention and effort when studying lists of items. As already noted by Brown et al. (1983), the ability to attend selectively to relevant aspects of a memory task is a traditional index of a learner's understanding of the task. Developmental studies on the allocation of study time have examined whether schoolchildren and adults were more likely to spend more time on less well-learned material. For instance, after a first free recall trial, participants had to distinguish between recalled and nonrecalled items (monitoring component), and were then asked to select half of the items for additional study (self-regulation component). Other developmental studies using paired-associate learning tasks compared study times for objectively easy and difficult pairs, and related this information to learning outcomes. One problem with the paradigm of the allocation of study time is that it may not only tap metacognitive processes but may also be influenced by motivational variables (see Schneider & Lockl, 2002).

THE DEVELOPMENT OF METAMEMORY IN CHILDREN AND ADOLESCENTS

Precursors of Metamemory: Knowledge of "Mental Verbs" and Acquisition of a "Theory of Mind"

A basic requirement for the acquisition of (declarative) metamemory is an appropriate understanding of mental verbs such as *thinking, forgetting*, or *knowing*. Although Kreutzer et al. (1975) provided evidence that the youngest participants in their study (kindergarten children) could properly apply mental verbs, it has proven more difficult to determine preschoolers' knowledge of mental verbs. Early studies with preschoolers on the issue (e.g., Misciones, Marvin, O'Brien, & Greenburg, 1978; Johnson & Wellman, 1980), as well as more recent ones (e.g., Astington & Olson, 1990; Schwanenflugel, Fabricius, & Alexander, 1994), all demonstrated that young children's competent use of mental verbs was highly constrained. Obviously, acquiring this kind of knowledge is a long-term development, with children's understanding limited compared to adults' understanding.

Since the early 1980s, there has been study of preschoolers' metacognition motivated by Perner's (1991) and Wellman's (1990) conceptualizations of children's *theory of mind* (see also Sodian, 2005), which emphasizes important classes of knowledge about the inner mental world that children acquire by the ages of 3 to 4. From this age on, children develop a rudimentary understanding of mental verbs such as "thinking" or "remembering" and can separate mental processes from external behaviors associated with them. They then gradually learn to recognize that the mental world can be differentiated into processes such as remembering, knowing, and guessing (i.e., they acquire knowledge about distinct mental processes). Although 3- to 4-year-olds are not generally capable of differentiating these processes, older preschoolers already make distinctions that are very similar to those of adults.

The relationship between the development of language, theory of mind development, and metamemory development has only recently been systematically explored in longitudinal studies. For instance, Astington and Jenkins (1999) and de Villiers and Pyers (2002) found that language competence predicted theory-of-mind development, but not the reverse. Whereas these studies did not focus on longitudinal relationships among knowledge of mental verbs, theory of mind, and subsequent metamemory, this issue was carefully analyzed in a recent longitudinal study carried out in our lab (see Lockl & Schneider, 2006, 2007; Schneider, Lockl, & Fernandez, 2005). Here, the assumption was that both early theory-of-mind competence and metacognitive vocabulary (i.e., knowledge of mental verbs) should affect subsequent knowledge of memory. Findings showed that metacognitive vocabulary, theory of mind, and general metamemory improved considerably over the preschool years. In accord with previous results, mean performance on the mental verb and metamemory assessments was far from ceiling, indicating that knowledge of mental verbs and knowledge about memory strategies is not particularly rich before children enter school. Another interesting finding was that test–retest stabilities were moderate for the three constructs under study (about .50). This suggests that individual differences in the development of metacognitive vocabulary, theory of mind, and metamemory already exist at an early age. Last but not least, results of hierarchical regression analyses indicated that there is a predictive relationship between children's acquisition of metacognitive vocabulary, their theory of mind, and their metamemory. Both early theory of mind and metacognitive vocabulary made reliable and substantial contributions to the prediction of metamemory even when individual differences in nonverbal intelligence and general vocabulary were taken into account. Given that prior metamemory also predicted subsequent metacognitive vocabulary, findings seem to indicate a reciprocal association and do not support the assumption of a clear-cut cause–effect relationship.

Development of Declarative Metamemory

In the classic interview study by Kreutzer et al. (1975), children in kindergarten and grades 1, 3, and 5 were asked about person, task, and strategy variables. For example, children were asked if they ever forgot things, if it was easier to recall the gist of a story than to recall it verbatim, and what they could do to find a jacket they had lost while at school. Overall, the results of this study and related assessments (e.g., Myers & Paris, 1978; Schneider et al., 1986; Schneider, Kron, Hünnerkopf, & Krajewski, 2004) indicated substantial improvements on most of the variables as a function of age. Regarding person variables, only the older schoolchildren realized that memory skills vary from person to person and from one situation to the next. On several items, kindergarteners overestimated their own capabilities, assuming that they always remembered well and that they were better at remembering than their friends.

This does not mean that young children do not possess any adequate knowledge about memory. Even the kindergarteners in the Kreutzer et al. (1975) study knew that remembering many items is more difficult than remembering just a few, and the majority of these children also knew that using external devices (e.g., writing telephone numbers down) helps in remembering information (see Beal, 1985; O'Sullivan, 1993; Schneider & Sodian, 1988, for confirmatory findings). However, although young children do have a basic understanding of memory, factual knowledge about the importance of task characteristics and memory strategies develops more rapidly once children enter school. Knowledge about the usefulness of memory strategies was tapped in several studies that focused on organizational strategies (see the reviews by Schneider, 1999; Schneider & Lockl, 2002). Preferences for the most appropriate (sorting and clustering) strategies were not found before the ages of 8 or 10, and reasonable justifications for such preferences were not always provided.

Similar age trends were observed when the interaction of memory variables was considered. In a classic study, Wellman (1978) presented memory problems to 5- and 10-year-olds. Each problem consisted of ranking three picture cards, each of which contained a memorizing scenario. Whereas all of the children solved the simple problems tapping a single task variable such as the impact of number of items on memory performance, substantial developmental differences were found for the complex memory problems varying two aspects (e.g., number of items and type of strategy). Only a very small proportion of the younger age group were able to judge the complex memory problems appropriately. The available data indicate that interactive memory knowledge develops very slowly. This development continues well into adolescence (see Schneider & Pressley, 1997).

Taken together, the empirical evidence illustrates important changes in declarative metamemory over time. Using sensitive methods that minimize demands on the child, it has been possible to demonstrate some rudimentary knowledge about memory functioning in preschoolers. Knowledge of facts about memory develops significantly during the course of elementary school and is already impressive by 11 or 12 years of age (cf. Pressley & McCormick, 1995; Schneider & Lockl, 2002). Nonetheless, declarative metamemory is not complete by the end of childhood. It seems important to note that even though metacognitive knowledge increases substantially between young childhood and young adulthood, there is also evidence that many adolescents (including college students) demonstrate little knowledge of powerful and important memory strategies when the task is to read, comprehend, and memorize complex text materials (cf. Brown et al., 1983; Garner, 1987; Pressley & Afflerbach, 1995).

Development of Procedural Metamemory

Early research focusing on monitoring showed that even young children seem to possess the relevant skills, particularly when the memory tasks were not very difficult (see reviews by Holland-Joyner & Kurtz-Costes, 1997; Schneider & Pressley, 1997). However, the evidence regarding developmental trends was not consistent, with some studies showing better performance in younger than in older children, and others illustrating age-correlated improvement. More recent studies exploring developmental trends in monitoring and self-regulation (as well as the interaction between these two components) were helpful in clarifying the situation and will be summarized next.

According to Nelson and Narens (1990, 1994), self-monitoring and self-regulation correspond to two different levels of metacognitive processing that interact very closely. Self-monitoring refers to keeping track of where you are with your goal of understanding and remembering (a bottom-up process). In comparison, self-regulation or control refers to central executive activities and includes planning, directing, and evaluating your behavior (a top-down process).

Monitoring Skills in Children

The most studied type of procedural metamemory is that of self-monitoring, that is, evaluating how well one is progressing (cf. Borkowski, Milstead, & Hale, 1988; Brown et al., 1983; Schneider, 1998). As noted above, the developmental literature has focused on monitoring components such as EOL judgments, JOL, and FOK judgments. What are the major developmental trends? In short, the findings suggest that even young children possess monitoring skills, and that developmental trends are not entirely clear, varying as a function of the paradigm under study. Whereas young kindergarten children tend to overestimate their performance when EOL judgments are considered, EOL judgments can be already accurate in young elementary school children. Apparently, young children's overestimations of future performance are not due to metacognitive deficiencies, but are at least partially caused by children's wishful thinking and their belief that effort has a powerful effect on performance (see Schneider, 1998). When children's postdictions were assessed in children ranging between 7 and 10 years of age, rather accurate judgments were found even for the younger age groups. However, older children performed significantly better. In most of the relevant studies, subtle improvements over the elementary school years were found (see Pressley & Ghatala, 1990; Schneider & Lockl, 2002, 2008).

Given that only a few developmental studies focused on JOLs occurring during or soon after the acquisition of memory materials, the situation is not yet clear. Overall, findings support the assumption that children's ability to judge their own memory performance after a study of test materials seems to increase over the elementary school years. However, even young children are able to monitor their performance quite accurately when judgments are not given immediately after study but are somewhat delayed.

A number of studies have explored children's FOK judgments and accuracy (e.g., Cultice, Somerville, & Wellman, 1983; DeLoache & Brown, 1984). Overall, most of the available evidence on FOK judgments suggests that FOK accuracy improves continuously across childhood and adolescence (e.g., Wellman, 1977; Zabrucky & Ratner, 1986). Again, however, the pattern of developmental trends is not entirely clear. In a study that avoided a methodological problem apparent in previous research on FOK judgments, Butterfield et al. (1988) showed that 6-year-olds' FOK judgments were actually more accurate than those of 10-year-olds and 18-year-olds. Obviously, this finding did not square well with the results of previous research. A more recent study by Lockl and Schneider (2002) using the same experimental paradigm could not replicate the outcomes reported by Butterfield et al. (1988) but was more in accord with the older findings described above. Taken together, it seems fair to state that more recent studies assessing monitoring abilities in JOL or FOK tasks demonstrate rather small developmental progression in children's monitoring skills (see also Roebers, von der Linden, Howie, & Schneider, 2007).

Research on autobiographical memory, in particular, eyewitness testimony, has repeatedly shown that young children's memory accounts are less accurate than those of older children and adults (for a review, see Bruck & Ceci, 1999). Although different factors such as young children's sometimes poor domain knowledge, their limited encoding skills, and their greater suggestibility account for some of the age differences, monitoring deficits also play a role. For instance, children's ability to recognize the correct sources of information (source monitoring) develops between the ages of 4 and 8 (see Roberts, 2000). Different approaches have been used to improve young children's memory accuracy, either by showing children how to screen out wrong answers (Koriat, Goldsmith, Schneider, & Nakash-Dura, 2001) or to increase their accuracy motivation by rewarding correct answers (Roebers, Moga, & Schneider, 2001).

More recent research on autobiographical memory development indicates that the type or class of memory situation may influence results. For instance, Ghetti, Lyons, Lazzarin, and Cornoldi (2008) assessed children's and adults' ability to monitor retrieval processes by examining confidence judgments associated with accurate memories whose strength was experimentally manipulated (e.g., to-be-remembered actions were either bizarre or common). Ghetti and colleagues found that 7-year-olds successfully monitored differences in strength between memories for both enacted and imagined actions. However, compared with 10-year-olds and adults, 7-year-olds exhibited deficits in monitoring differences in memory strength among imagined actions as well as deficits in monitoring memory absence. Overall, the results of this research suggest that critical changes in monitoring abilities occur after age 7, and that memory monitoring is not a unitary process but may depend on the memory class or type under consideration.

The Relation between Monitoring and Control Processes in Children

An important reason to study metacognitive monitoring processes is because monitoring is supposed to play a central role in directing how people study. Numerous studies including adult participants have shown that individuals use memory monitoring, especially JOLs, to decide which items to study and how long to spend on them (e.g., Metcalfe, 2002; Nelson, Dunlosky, Graf, & Narens, 1994; Nelson & Narens, 1990; Son & Metcalfe, 2000). However, little is known about how children use monitoring to regulate their study time. A classic paradigm suited to further explore this issue refers to the *allocation of study time*. Research on study time allocation observes how learners deploy their attention and effort. As already noted by Brown et al. (1983), the ability to attend selectively to relevant aspects of a problem-solving task is a traditional index of learner's understanding of the task. Developmental studies on the allocation of study time examined whether schoolchildren and adults were more likely to spend more time on less well-learned material (e.g., Masur, McIntyre, & Flavell, 1973; Dufresne & Kobasigawa, 1989; Lockl & Schneider, 2004). All of these studies reported an age-related improvement in the efficient allocation of study time. That is, older children (from age 10 on) spent more time studying hard items than they spent studying easy items, despite the fact that even many young children were able to distinguish between hard and easy pairs. Thus, developmental differences were not so much observed in the metacognitive knowledge itself but in its efficient application to self-regulation strategies.

Although the available developmental research seems to confirm the basic assumption that monitoring influences control processes, recent research with adults has challenged this position, suggesting that self-regulatory processes influence metacognitive monitoring. For instance, Koriat, Ma'ayan, and Nussinson (2006) proposed that study time is actually used by the learner as a cue for encoding fluency under what they called the *memorizing effort heuristic*, meaning that easily studied items are more likely to be remembered than items that require more effort to study. Accordingly, metacognitive judgments are basically data-driven: study time duration is taken retrospectively as a cue for the feeling of mastery. Thus greater effort (longer study time) is associated with lower JOLs, suggesting that the cause-and-effect relation is actually from control to monitoring. The results of Koriat et al. (2006) not only confirmed this assumption but also showed evidence for the "monitoring affects control" hypothesis, indicating that the relationships between monitoring and control can be more complex than originally assumed. First developmental studies on this issue confirm the assumption that this is also true for children, indicating that evidence for the "control affects monitoring" model increases with age (e.g., Koriat, Ackerman, Lockl, & Schneider, 2008).

METAMEMORY–MEMORY RELATIONSHIPS

From a developmental and educational perspective, the metamemory concept seems well suited to explain children's "production deficiencies" on a broad variety of memory tasks. Early empirical research on metamemory was stimulated by the belief that young children do not spontaneously use memory strategies because they are not familiar with memory tasks and are unable to judge the advantages of memory strategies such as rehearsal or categorization. Metamemory researchers assumed that this situation should change after children enter school and are confronted with numerous memory tasks. Experience with such tasks should improve strategy knowledge, which in turn should exert a positive influence on memory behavior (e.g., strategy use). Thus, a major motivation behind studying metamemory and its development was the assumption that although links between metamemory and memory may be weak in early childhood, they should become much stronger with increasing age.

Whereas a first series of investigations of the metamemory–memory link yielded only weak support (see reviews by Brown et al., 1983; Cavanaugh & Perlmutter, 1982), subsequent analyses showed more positive outcomes (Schneider, 1985; Schneider & Pressley, 1997; Wellman, 1983). Overall, the empirical findings indicate a robust relationship between metamemory and memory, even though the associations are not extremely strong. For instance, a statistical meta-analysis of 60 studies (with more than 7,000 participants) produced an average correlation of .41 (Schneider & Pressley, 1997, p. 220). The size of the correlation seems to depend on factors such as type of task, age of children, task difficulty, and timing of metamemory assessment (before or after the memory task). See Table 3.1 for a detailed description of findings reported by Schneider and Pressley (1997).

As can be seen from Table 3.1, children's metamemory makes a reliable and moderately strong contribution to their strategic behavior and performance in a variety of memory tasks. Obviously, the correlations for monitoring observed in laboratory tasks are greater than those for organizational strategies at the younger age levels but not for older schoolchildren. Interestingly, whereas clear developmental trends were found for the correlation between metamemory and strategy use, similar age trends for monitoring in laboratory tasks were not observed.

From the early 1980s on, multivariate experimental designs and also comprehensive field studies have been used to examine the complex relationships among metamemory, domain knowledge, memory behavior

TABLE 3.1. Overall Correlations between Metamemory and Memory, Classified by Kind of Study and School Grade of Subjects

	School grade					
	K	1/2	3/4	5/6	7+	Average
Memory monitoring (laboratory tasks)	.39 (5)	.45 (7)	.35 (10)	.42 (8)	.59 (2)	.39 (16)
Memory monitoring (text processing)	.24 (2)	—	.28 (3)	.49 (10)	.41 (4)	.44 (15)
Memory monitoring (training studies)	—	.52 (4)	.37 (10)	.37 (10)	.28 (1)	.40 (13)
Organizational strategies (clustering)	.12 (1)	.15 (6)	.41 (14)	.47 (5)	—	.33 (43)
Organizational strategies (training studies)	—	.39 (10)	.32 (19)	—	—	.37 (36)

Note. Adapted from Schneider and Pressley (1997). Copyright 1997 by Lawrence Erlbaum Associates, Inc. Adapted by permission.

(strategy use), and memory performance, as well as their relationship with other important variables such as intelligence, memory capacity, and motivation (e.g., see Borkowski, Peck, Reid, & Kurtz, 1983; DeMarie, Miller, Ferron, & Cunningham, 2004; Körkel & Schneider, 1992; Kurtz et al., 1982; Schneider et al., 1987; Schneider, Schlagmüller, & Visé, 1998). For instance, Schneider et al. (1998) assessed the relationships among Verbal IQ, memory capacity, domain knowledge, declarative metamemory, use of a semantic organizational strategy, and recall in a sort-recall task in 155 third and fourth graders. As can be seen from Figure 3.1a, metamemory was affected by both Verbal IQ and memory capacity. Although there was only a modest direct contribution of metamemory to the prediction of recall, the indirect link via strategic behavior was much stronger (about .6). As a consequence, individual differences in declarative metamemory explained a large proportion in the variance of the recall data. Similar findings were also reported by DeMarie et al. (2004), who also illustrated the importance of declarative metamemory for explaining individual differences in strategy use and memory performance in different age groups ranging from kindergarteners to fifth graders.

A somewhat different pattern of findings was reported by Schneider et al. (1998) when the sort-recall task was based on soccer items, and when children's knowledge of soccer was used as an additional predictor variable. Now soccer knowledge turned out to be the most powerful predictor, explaining the lion's share in children's recall variance. However, metamemory still kept its indirect influence via strategy use (sorting), even though the respective path coefficients were considerably lower than those obtained in the first model. See Körkel and Schneider (1992) for similar findings using a memory for text paradigm.

When Flavell and Wellman (1977) introduced their taxonomy of metamemory, they already pointed out that one cannot always expect to find a strong connection between memory knowledge and memory behavior because individual differences in the learners' motivation to carry out the task may be a critical factor. Several multivariate studies on the metamemory–memory link included indicators of learning motivation. For example, Schneider et al. (1987) assessed the additional impact of motivation in a large sample of 300 third and fifth graders, estimating separate but structurally identical causal models for the two age groups. One interesting finding was that the only difference in the two models concerned the impact of motivation. Whereas success motivation did not play a role in predicting third graders' memory performance, it had a robust effect on fifth graders' recall (see Figure 3.1b). Obviously, the impact of motivation increases over the school years (for similar findings in the area of text processing and recall, see Artelt et al., 2001; Van Kraayenoord & Schneider, 1999).

(a)

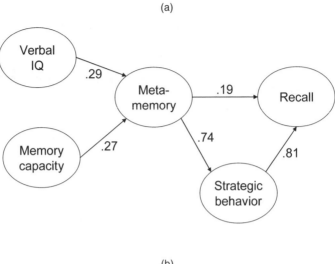

(b)

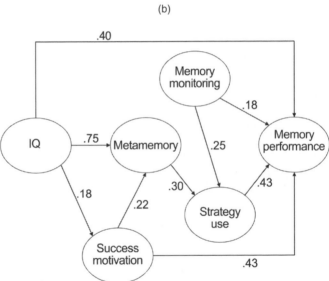

FIGURE 3.1. Examples of causal modeling procedures illustrating metamemory–memory relationships. (a) Causal model depicting metamemory–memory relationships in a sort-recall task. Adapted from Schneider, Schlagmüller, and Visé (1998). Copyright 1998 by Instituto Superior de Psicologia Aplicada. Adapted by permission. (b) Causal model illustrating impacts of IQ, metamemory, and motivation on memory performance in a sort-recall task. Adapted from Schneider, Körkel, and Weinert (1987). Copyright 1987 by the International Society for the Study of Behavioral Development. Adapted by permission.

Overall, the findings of various multivariate analyses confirm that the causal relation between metamemory and memory is complex. Metamemory sometimes has an indirect effect on recall, as when knowledge about categorization strategies leads to semantic grouping during the study period, which in turn produces better recall (see Hasselhorn, 1995; Weinert, Schneider, & Knopf, 1988). Moreover, the influence seems to be bidirectional (see Flavell et al., 2002; Schneider & Pressley, 1997). That is, metamemory can influence memory behavior, which in turn leads to enhanced metamemory. Finally, many other relevant variables such as IQ, domain knowledge, memory capacity, and motivation significantly contribute to the explanation of memory differences. Obviously, these empirical findings are in accord with the core assumptions of the good information-processing model (Pressley, Borkowski, & Schneider, 1989), which provides a detailed theoretical account of the complexity of these interactional processes.

THE IMPORTANCE
OF METACOGNITION FOR EDUCATION

Several studies on the development of memory and metamemory have emphasized the importance of educational contexts for developmental changes, particularly when the acquisition of memory strategies is concerned. Most of memory development is not so much a product of age but of education and practice. For instance, in a recent longitudinal study on memory development from kindergarten age to the end of elementary school, Kron-Sperl, Schneider, and Hasselhorn (2008) repeatedly presented the children of their sample with a sort-recall task without giving any specific strategy cues. When performance of these children was compared with that of random samples of schoolchildren who received this task for the first time, substantial practice effects were found. Children in the longitudinal sample not only outperformed the control children regarding strategy use and memory performance, but also showed better task-specific memory. Obviously, it does not require much effort to improve children's strategy knowledge. There is broad agreement that one way in which parents and teachers can facilitate cognitive development is by the development of children's metacognition (see Carr, Kurtz, Schneider, Turner, & Borkowski, 1989; Coffman, Ornstein, McCall, & Curran, 2008; Ornstein, Coffman, Grammer, San Souci, & McCall, in press). Both classic and recent studies on this issue show that there is still room for improvement in this regard, but that considerable progress can be found.

During the last 20 years or so, several attempts have been made to apply metacognitive theory to educational settings (cf. Paris & Oka, 1986; Moely et al., 1986; Moely, Santulli, & Obach, 1995; Palincsar, 1986; Pressley, 1995; Pressley, Goodchild, Fleet, & Zajchowski, 1989). Observational studies carried out by Moely and colleagues and Ornstein and colleagues showed that teachers vary widely in the extent to which they foster children's metacognitive development. Individual differences in teachers' mnemonic style were found to affect students' acquisition of memory strategies (see Coffman et al., 2008; Ornstein et al., in press). In particular, low-achieving students appear to benefit from a highly mnemonic classroom environment.

One interesting and effective approach to teaching knowledge about strategies was developed by Palinscar and Brown (1984). Here, teachers and students take turns executing reading strategies that are being taught with instruction occurring in true dialogue. Strategic processes are made very overt, with plenty of exposure to modeling of strategies and opportunities to practice these techniques over the course of a number of lessons. The goal is for children to discover the utility of reading strategies, and for teachers to convey strategy-utility information as well as information about when and where to use particular strategies. Teachers using reciprocal instruction assume more responsibility for strategy implementation early in instruction, gradually transferring control over to the student (see Palincsar, 1986, for an extensive description of the implementation of reciprocal instruction; see Rosenshine & Meister, 1994, for a realistic appraisal of its benefits).

During the 1980s and 1990s, numerous studies explored the efficiency of strategy training approaches in school (for a review, see Schneider & Pressley, 1997). The basic assumption was that although children in most cases do not efficiently monitor the effectiveness of strategies they are using, they can be trained to do so. For instance, in a training program carried out by Ghatala and colleagues (e.g., Ghatala, Levin, Pressley, & Goodwin, 1986) elementary school children were presented with paired-associate learning tasks. Before studying these lists, some children received a three-component training. They were taught (1) to assess their performance with different types of strategies, (2) to attribute differences in performance to use of different strategies, and (3) to use information gained from assessment and attribution to guide selection of the best strategy for a task. As a major result, it was shown that even children 7 to 8 years of age can be taught to monitor the relative efficacy of strategies that they are using and to use utility information gained from monitoring in making future strategy selections.

Another more large-scale approach concerns the implementation of comprehensive evaluation programs that aim at assessing the systematic instruction of metacognitive knowledge in schools. As emphasized by Holland-Joyner and Kurtz-Costes (1997), both Moely and Pressley, with their colleagues, have conducted very ambitious programs of evaluating effective instruction in public school systems. For instance, Pressley and colleagues found that effective teachers regularly incorporated strategy instruction and metacognitive information about effective strategy selection and modification as a part of daily instruction. It seems important to note that strategy instruction was not carried out in isolation but integrated in the curriculum and taught as part of language arts, mathematics, science, and social studies. In accord with the assumption of the good information-processing model outlined above (cf. Pressley et al., 1989), effective teachers did not emphasize the use of single strategies but taught the flexible use of a range of procedures that corresponded to subject matter, time constraints, and other task demands. On most occasions, strategy instruction occurred in groups, with the teachers modeling appropriate strategy use. By comparison, the work by Moely and colleagues (e.g., Moely, Santulli, & Obach, 1995) illustrated that the effective teaching process described by Pressley and coworkers does not necessarily constitute the rule, and that effective teachers may represent a minority group in elementary school classrooms. Taken together, the careful documentations of instructional procedures carried out by Pressley, Moely, and their research groups have shown that there is a lot of potential for metacognitively guided instructional processes in children's everyday learning.

Other researchers have focused on the relationship between measures of metacognitive knowledge and children's school performance. For instance, Geary, Klosterman, and Adrales (1990) explored the relationship between declarative metamemory and academic performance in second and fourth graders. The sample not only included "normal" elementary school children but also children with learning disabilities. Not surprisingly, Geary et al. (1990) found that fourth graders performed better than second graders on the metamemory battery, and that metamemory–memory relationships increased with age, even though the link was moderate at best. Contrary to expectations, however, children with learning disabilities did not perform differently from academically normal children.

Other recent research explores the utility of the metacognition concept in research with older children and adolescents, assessing the predictive potential of metacognitive knowledge and skillfulness in reading and mathematics (e.g., Artelt et al., 2001; Mevarech & Kramarski, 1997, 2003; Veenman, Kok, & Blöte, 2005; see also the contributions in Desoete & Veenman, 2006). Overall, these studies confirm the view that metacognitive knowledge and self-regulated insightful use of learning strategies not only are influential in elementary school children but also predict math performance and reading comprehension in secondary school settings, even after differences in intellectual abilities have been taken into account. They also give evidence that metacognitive knowledge relevant for school-related domains can still be effectively trained in late childhood and early adolescence.

Despite the fact that strategy instruction in classrooms is difficult and that empirical studies are still rare, there are plenty of good reasons to believe that the situation will improve in the future. There are now metacognitive training programs available that provide long-term strategy instruction and promise long-lasting success (cf. Schneider & Pressley, 1997). One precondition for increasing the use of such metacognition-related teaching is to increase teachers' understanding of the conceptual foundations of effective learning. As long as teachers do not think in information-processing terms, it will be difficult to establish progress in this field. However, recent changes in teacher education let us believe that teachers will understand information processing much better soon, enabling them to implement strategy training programs in the classroom that pay off for most students.

REFERENCES

Artelt, C., Schiefele, U., & Schneider, W. (2001). Predictors of reading literacy. *European Journal of Psychology of Education, 16,* 363–383.

Astington, J. W., & Jenkins, J. M. (1999). A longitudinal study of the relation between language and theory of mind development. *Developmental Psychology, 35,* 1311–1320.

Astington, J. W., & Olson, D. R. (1990). Metacognitive and metalinguistic language: Learning to talk about thought. *Applied Psychology: An International Review, 39,* 77–87.

Bauer, P. J. (2006). Event memory. In D. Kuhn & R. S. Siegler (Eds.), *Handbook of child psychology: Vol. 2. Cognition, perception, and language* (6th ed., pp. 373–425). New York: Wiley.

Beal, C. R. (1985). Development of knowledge about the use of cues to aid prospective retrieval. *Child Development, 56,* 631–642.

Belmont, J. M., & Borkowski, J. G. (1988). A group-administered test of children's metamemory. *Bulletin of the Psychonomic Society, 26,* 206–208.

Best, D. L., & Ornstein, P. A. (1986). Children's generation and communication of mnemonic organizational strategies. *Developmental Psychology, 22,* 845–853.

Borkowski, J. G., Milstead, M., & Hale, C. (1988). Components of children's metamemory: Implications for strategy generalization. In F. E. Weinert & M. Perlmutter (Eds.), *Memory development: Universal changes and individual differences* (pp. 73–100). Hillsdale, NJ: Erlbaum.

Borkowski, J. G., Peck, V. A., Reid, M. K., & Kurtz, B. E. (1983). Impulsivity and strategy transfer: Metamemory as mediator. *Child Development, 54,* 459–473.

Brown, A. L. (1978). Knowing when, where and how to remember: A problem of metacognition. In R. Glaser (Ed.), *Advances in instructional psychology* (Vol. 1, pp. 77–165). Hillsdale, NJ: Erlbaum.

Brown, A. L., Bransford, J. D., Ferrara, R. A., & Campione, J. C. (1983). Learning, remembering, and understanding. In J. H. Flavell & E. M. Markham (Eds.), *Handbook of child psychology: Vol. 3. Cognitive development* (pp. 77–166). New York: Wiley.

Bruck, M., & Ceci, S. J. (1999). The suggestibility of children's memory. *Annual Review of Psychology, 50,* 419–439.

Butterfield, E. C., Nelson, T. O., & Peck, V. (1988). Developmental aspects of the feeling of knowing. *Developmental Psychology, 24,* 654–663.

Carr, M., Kurtz, B. E., Schneider, W., Turner, L. A., & Borkowski, J. G. (1989). Strategy acquisition and transfer among American and German children: Environmental influences on metacognitive development. *Developmental Psychology, 25,* 765–771.

Cavanaugh, J. C., & Borkowski, J. G. (1980). Searching for metamemory–memory connections: A developmental study. *Developmental Psychology, 16,* 441–453.

Cavanaugh, J. C., & Perlmutter, M. (1982). Metamemory: A critical examination. *Child Development, 53,* 11–28.

Coffman, J. L., Ornstein, P. A., McCall, L. E., & Curran, P. J. (2008). Linking teachers' memory-relevant language and the development of children's memory skills. *Developmental Psychology, 44,* 1640–1654.

Cultice, J. C., Somerville, S. C., & Wellman, H. M. (1983). Preschoolers' memory monitoring: Feeling-of-knowing judgments. *Child Development, 54,* 1480–1486.

DeLoache, J. S., & Brown, A. L. (1984). Where do I go next?: Intelligent searching by very young children. *Developmental Psychology, 20,* 37–44.

DeMarie, D., Miller, P. H., Ferron, J., & Cunningham, W. R. (2004). Path analysis tests of theoretical models of children's memory performance. *Journal of Cognition and Development, 5,* 461–492.

Desoete, A., & Veenman, M. (Eds.). (2006). *Metacognition in mathematics education.* Haupauge, NY: Nova Science.

de Villiers, J., & Pyers, J. (2002). Complements to cognition: A longitudinal study of the relationship between complex syntax and false-belief understanding. *Cognitive Development, 17,* 1037–1060.

Dufresne, A., & Kobasigawa, A. (1989). Children's spontaneous allocation of study time: Differential and sufficient aspects. *Journal of Experimental Child Psychology, 47,* 274–296.

Efklides, A. (2001). Metacognitive experiences in problem solving: Metacognition, motivation, and self-regulation. In A. Efklides, J. Kuhl, & R. M. Sorrentino (Eds.), *Trends and prospects in motivation research* (pp. 297–323). Dordrecht, The Netherlands: Kluwer.

Efklides, A. (2008). Metacognition: Defining its facets and levels of functioning in relation to self- and co-regulation. *European Psychologist, 13*, 277–287.

Flavell, J. H. (1971). First discussant's comments: What is memory development the development of? *Human Development, 14*, 272–278.

Flavell, J. H. (1979). Metacognition and cognitive monitoring. A new area of cognitive-developmental inquiry. *American Psychologist, 34*, 906–911.

Flavell, J. H., Miller, P. H., & Miller, S. A. (2002). *Cognitive development.* Englewood Cliffs, NJ: Prentice-Hall.

Flavell, J. H., & Wellman, H. M. (1977). Metamemory. In R. Kail & W. Hagen (Eds.), *Perspectives on the development of memory and cognition* (pp. 3–31). Hillsdale, NJ: Erlbaum.

Garner, R. (1987). *Metacognition and reading comprehension.* Norwood, NJ: Ablex.

Geary, D. D., Klosterman, I. H., & Adrales, K. (1990). Metamemory and academic achievement: Testing the validity of a group-administered metamemory battery. *Journal of Genetic Psychology, 151*, 439–450.

Ghatala, E. S., Levin, J. R., Pressley, M., & Goodwin, D. (1986). A componential analysis of effects of derived and supplied strategy-utility information on children's strategy selections. *Journal of Experimental Child Psychology, 41*, 76–92.

Ghetti, S., Lyons, K. E., Lazzarin, F., & Cornoldi, C. (2008). The development of metamemory monitoring during retrieval: The case of memory strength and memory absence. *Journal of Experimental Child Psychology, 99*, 157–181.

Hasselhorn, M. (1994). Zur Erfassung von Metagedächtnisaspekten bei Grundschulkindern. *Zeitschrift für Entwicklungspsychologie und Pädagogische Psychologie, 26*, 71–78.

Hasselhorn, M. (1995). Beyond production deficiency and utilization inefficiency: Mechanisms of the emergence of strategic categorization in episodic memory tasks. In F. E. Weinert & W. Schneider (Eds.), *Memory performance and competencies: Issues in growth and development* (pp. 141–160). Mahwah, NJ: Erlbaum.

Holland-Joyner, M. H., & Kurtz-Costes, B. (1997). Metamemory development. In N. Cowan (Ed.), *The development of memory in childhood* (pp. 275–300). Hove, UK: Psychology Press.

Johnson, C. N., & Wellman, H. M. (1980). Children's developing understanding of mental verbs: Remember, know, and guess. *Child Development, 51*, 1095–1102.

Justice, E. M. (1985). Preschoolers' knowledge and use of behaviors varying in strategic effectiveness. *Merrill–Palmer Quarterly, 35*, 363–377.

Justice, E. M. (1986). Developmental changes in judgments of relative strategy effectiveness. *British Journal of Developmental Psychology, 4*, 75–81.

Koriat, A. (2007). Metacognition and consciousness. In P. D. Zelazo, M. Moscovitch, & E. Thompson (Eds.), *Cambridge handbook of consciousness* (pp. 289–325). New York: Cambridge University Press.

Koriat, A., Ackerman, R., Lockl, K., & Schneider, W. (2008). *The memorizing-effort heuristic in judgments of learning: A developmental perspective.* Unpublished manuscript, University of Haifa.

Koriat, A., Goldsmith, M., Schneider, W., & Nakash-Dura, M. (2001). The credibility of children's testimony: Can children control the accuracy of their memory reports. *Journal of Experimental Child Psychology, 79,* 405–437.

Koriat, A., Ma'ayan, H., & Nussinson, R. (2006). The intricate relationships between monitoring and control in metacognition. *Journal of Experimental Psychology: General, 135,* 36–69.

Körkel, J., & Schneider, W. (1992). Domain-specific versus metacognitive knowledge effects on text recall and comprehension. In M. Carretero, M. Pope, R. J. Simons, & J. I. Pozo (Eds.), *Learning and instruction: European research in an international context* (Vol. 3, pp. 311–324). New York: Pergamon Press.

Kreutzer, M. A., Leonard, C., & Flavell, J. H. (1975). An interview study of children's knowledge about memory. *Monographs of the Society for Research in Child Development, 40,* no. 159.

Kron-Sperl, V., Schneider, W., & Hasselhorn, M. (2008). The development and effectiveness of memory strategies in kindergarten and elementary school: Findings from the Würzburg and Göttingen longitudinal memory studies. *Cognitive Development, 23,* 79–104.

Kurtz, B. E., Reid, M. K., Borkowski, J. G., & Cavanaugh, J. C. (1982). On the reliability and validity of children's metamemory. *Bulletin of the Psychonomic Society, 19,* 137–140.

Lockl, K., & Schneider, W. (2002). Developmental trends in children's feeling-of-knowing judgements. *International Journal of Behavioral Development, 26,* 327–333.

Lockl, K., & Schneider, W. (2004). The effects of incentives and instructions on children's allocation of study time. *European Journal of Developmental Psychology, 1,* 153–169.

Lockl, K., & Schneider, W. (2006). Precursors of metamemory in young children: The role of theory of mind and metacognitive vocabulary. *Metacognition and Learning, 1,* 15–31.

Lockl, K., & Schneider, W. (2007). Knowledge about the mind: Links between theory of mind and later metamemory. *Child Development, 78,* 148–167.

Masur, E. F., McIntyre, C. W., & Flavell, J. H. (1973). Developmental changes in apportionment of study time among items in a multitrial free recall task. *Journal of Experimental Child Psychology, 15,* 237–246.

Metcalfe, J. (2002). Is study time allocated selectively to a region of proximal learning? *Journal of Experimental Psychology: General, 131,* 349–363.

Mevarech, Z. R., & Kramarski, B. (1997). IMPROVE: A multidimensional method for teaching mathematics in heterogeneous classrooms. *American Educational Research Journal, 34,* 365–394.

Mevarech, Z. R., & Kramarski, B. (2003). The effects of worked-out examples versus metacognitive training on students' mathematical reasoning. *British Journal of Educational Psychology, 73,* 449–471.

Misciones, J. L., Marvin, R. S., O'Brien, R. G., & Greenburg, M. T. (1978). A developmental study of preschool children's understanding of the words "know" and "guess." *Child Development, 48,* 1107–1113.

Moely, B. E., Hart, S. S., Santulli, K., Leal, L., Johnson, T., Rao, N., et al. (1986).

How do teachers teach memory skills? *Educational Psychologist, 21,* 55–71.

Moely, B. E., Santulli, K. A., & Obach, M. S. (1995). Strategy instruction, metacognition, and motivation in the elementary school classroom. In F. E. Weinert & W. Schneider (Eds.), *Memory performance and competencies: Issues in growth and development* (pp. 301–321). Mahwah, NJ: Erlbaum.

Myers, M., & Paris, S. G. (1978). Children's metacognitive knowledge about reading. *Journal of Educational Psychology, 70,* 680–690.

Nelson, T. O. (1996). Consciousness and metacognition. *American Psychologist, 51,* 102–116.

Nelson, T. O., Dunlosky, J. Graf, A., & Narens, L. (1994). Utilization of metacognitive judgments in the allocation of study during multitrial learning. *Psychological Science, 5,* 207–213.

Nelson, T. O., & Narens, L. (1990). Metamemory: A theoretical framework and new findings. In G. Bower (Ed.), *The psychology of learning and motivation: Advances in research and theory* (Vol. 26, pp. 125–173). New York: Academic Press.

Nelson, T. O., & Narens, L. (1994). Why investigate metacognition? In J. Metcalfe & A. P. Shimamura (Eds.), *Metacognition: Knowing about knowing* (pp. 1–25). Cambridge, MA: MIT Press.

Ornstein, P., Coffman, J., Grammer, J., San Souci, P., & McCall, L. (in press). Linking the classroom context and children's memory skills. In J. Meece & J. Eccles (Eds.), *Handbook of research on schools, schooling, and human development.* New York: Sage.

O'Sullivan, J. T. (1993). Applying cognitive developmental principles in classrooms. In R. Pasnak & M. L. Howe (Eds.), *Emerging themes in cognitive development* (pp. 168–187). New York: Springer.

Palincsar, A. S. (1986). The role of dialogue in providing scaffolded instruction. *Educational Psychologist, 21,* 73–98.

Palincsar, A. S., & Brown, A. L. (1984). Reciprocal teaching of comprehension-fostering and comprehension-monitoring activities. *Cognition and Instruction, 1,* 117–175.

Paris, S. G., & Oka, E. R. (1986). Children's reading strategies, metacognition, and motivation. *Developmental Review, 6,* 25–56.

Perner, J. (1991). *Understanding the representational mind.* Cambridge, MA: MIT Press.

Pressley, M. (1995). What is intellectual development about in the 1990s? In F. E. Weinert & W. Schneider (Eds.), *Memory performance and competencies: Issues in growth and development* (pp. 1–25). Hillsdale, NJ: Erlbaum.

Pressley, M., & Afflerbach, P. (1995). *Verbal protocols of reading: The nature of constructively responsive reading.* Hillsdale, NJ: Erlbaum.

Pressley, M., Borkowski, J. G., & O'Sullivan, J. T. (1985). Children's metamemory and the teaching of memory strategies. In D. L. Forrest-Pressley, G. E. MacKinnon, & T. G. Waller (Eds.), *Metacognition, cognition, and human performance* (Vol. 1, pp. 111–153). Orlando, FL: Academic Press.

Pressley, M., Borkowski, J. G., & Schneider, W. (1987). Cognitive strategies: Good strategy users coordinate metacognition and knowledge. In R. Vasta

& G. Whitehurst (Eds.), *Annals of child development* (Vol. 5, pp. 89–129). New York: JAI Press.

Pressley, M., Borkowski, J. G., & Schneider, W. (1989). Good information processing: What it is and what education can do to promote it. *International Journal of Educational Research, 13,* 857–867.

Pressley, M., & Ghatala, E. S. (1990). Self-regulated learning: Monitoring from text learning. *Educational Psychologist, 25,* 19–33.

Pressley, M., Goodchild, F., Fleet, J., & Zajchowski, R. (1989). The challenges of classroom strategy instruction. *Elementary School Journal, 89,* 301–342.

Pressley, M., Levin, J. R., Ghatala, E. S., & Ahmad, M. (1987). Test monitoring in young children. *Journal of Experimental Child Psychology, 43,* 96–111.

Pressley, M., & McCormick, C. (1995). *Advanced educational psychology for educators, researchers, and policymakers.* New York: HarperCollins.

Roberts, K. P. (2000). An overview of theory and research on children's source monitoring. In K. P. Roberts & M. Blades (Eds.), *Children's source monitoring* (pp. 11–58). Mahwah, NJ: Erlbaum.

Roebers, C., Moga, N., & Schneider, W. (2001). The role of accuracy motivation on children's and adults event recall. *Journal of Experimental Child Psychology, 78,* 313–329.

Roebers, C., von der Linden, N., Howie, P., & Schneider, W. (2007). Children's metamemorial judgments in an event recall task. *Journal of Experimental Child Psychology, 97,* 117–137.

Rosenshine, B., & Meister, C. (1994). Reciprocal teaching: A review of the research. *Review of Educational Research, 64,* 479–530.

Schlagmüller, M., & Schneider, W. (2007). *WLST 7–12. Würzburger Lesestrategie Wissenstest für die Klassen 7 bis 12.* Göttingen: Hogrefe.

Schlagmüller, M., Visé, M., & Schneider, W. (2001). Zur Erfassung des Gedächtniswissens bei Grundschulkindern: Konstruktionsprinzipien und empirische Bewährung der Würzburger Testbatterie zum deklarativen Gedächtnis. *Zeitschrift für Entwicklungspsychologie und Pädagogische Psychologie, 33,* 91–102.

Schneider, W. (1985). Developmental trends in the metamemory–memory behavior relationship: An integrative review. In D. L. Forrest-Pressley, G. E. MacKinnon, & T. G. Wallers (Eds.), *Metacognition, cognition and human performance* (Vol. 1, pp. 57–109). New York: Academic Press.

Schneider, W. (1998). The development of procedural metamemory in childhood and adolescence. In G. Mazzoni & T. O. Nelson (Eds.), *Monitoring and control processes in metacognition and cognitive neuropsychology* (pp. 1–21). Mahwah, NJ: Erlbaum.

Schneider, W. (1999). The development of metamemory in children. In D. Gopher & A. Koriat (Eds.), *Attention and performance XVII: Cognitive regulation of performance: Interaction of theory and application* (pp. 487–513). Cambridge, MA: MIT Press.

Schneider, W., & Bjorklund, D. F. (1998). Memory. In D. Kuhn & R. S. Siegler (Eds.), *Handbook of child psychology: Vol. 2. Cognition, perception and language* (pp. 467–521). New York: Wiley.

Schneider, W., Borkowski, J. G., Kurtz, B. E., & Kerwin, K. (1986). Metamemory and motivation: A comparison of strategy use and performance in German and American children. *Journal of Cross-Cultural Psychology, 17,* 315–336.

Schneider, W., Körkel, J., & Weinert, F. E. (1987). The effects of intelligence, self-concept, and attributional style on metamemory and memory behavior. *International Journal of Behavioral Development, 10,* 281–299.

Schneider, W., Körkel, J., & Weinert, F. E. (1990). Expert knowledge, general abilities, and text processing. In W. Schneider & F. E. Weinert (Eds.), *Interactions among aptitudes, strategies, and knowledge in cognitive performance* (pp. 235–251). New York: Springer.

Schneider, W., Kron, V., Hünnerkopf, M., & Krajewski, K. (2004). Development of young children's memory strategies: First findings from the Würzburg Longitudinal Study. *Journal of Experimental Child Psychology, 88,* 193–209.

Schneider, W., & Lockl, K. (2002). The development of metacognitive knowledge in children and adolescents. In T. J. Perfect & B. L. Schwartz (Eds.), *Applied metacognition* (pp. 224–257). Cambridge, UK: Cambridge University Press.

Schneider, W., & Lockl, K. (2008). Procedural metacognition in children: Evidence for developmental trends. In J. Dunlosky & R. A. Bjork (Eds.), *A handbook of metamemory and memory* (pp. 391–410). New York: Psychology Press.

Schneider, W., Lockl, K., & Fernandez, O. (2005). Interrelationships among theory of mind, executive control, language development, and working memory in young children: A longitudinal analysis. In W. Schneider, B. Sodian, & R. Schumann-Hengsteler (Eds.), *Young children's cognitive development* (pp. 259–284). Mahwah, NJ: Erlbaum.

Schneider, W., & Pressley, M. (1997). *Memory development between 2 and 20.* Hillsdale, NJ: Erlbaum.

Schneider, W., Schlagmüller, M., & Visé, M. (1998). The impact of metamemory and domain-specific knowledge on memory performance. *European Journal of Psychology of Education, 13,* 91–103.

Schneider, W., & Sodian, B. (1988). Metamemory–memory behavior relationships in young children: Evidence from a memory-for-location task. *Journal of Experimental Child Psychology, 45,* 209–233.

Schraw, G. (1994). The effect of metacognitive knowledge on local and global monitoring. *Contemporary Educational Psychology, 19,* 143–154.

Schunk, D. H., & Zimmerman, B. J. (Eds.). (1998). *Self-regulated learning: From teaching to self-reflective practice.* New York: Guilford Press.

Schwanenflugel, P. J., Fabricius, W. V., & Alexander, J. (1994). Developing theories of mind: Understanding concepts and relations between mental activities. *Child Development, 65,* 1546–1563.

Shimamura, A. P. (2000). Toward a cognitive neuroscience of metacognition. *Consciousness and Cognition, 9,* 313–323.

Sodian, B. (2005). Theory of mind: The case for conceptual development. In W. Schneider, R. Schumann-Hengsteler, & B. Sodian (Eds.), *Interrelationships among working memory, theory of mind, and executive functions* (pp. 95–130). Mahwah, NJ: Erlbaum.

Son, L. K., & Metcalfe, J. (2000). Metacognitive and control strategies in study-time allocation. *Journal of Experimental Psychology: Learning, Memory, and Cognition, 26*(1), 204–221.

Van Kraayenoord, C. E., & Schneider, W. (1999). Reading achievement, meta-cognition, reading self-concept and interest: A study of German students in grades 3 and 4. *European Journal of the Psychology of Education, 14,* 305–324.

Veenman, M., Kok, R., & Blöte, A. (2005). The relation between intellectual and metacognitive skills in early adolescence. *Instructional Science, 33,* 193–211.

Weinert, F. E., Schneider, W., & Knopf, M. (1988). Individual differences in memory development across the life-span. In P. B. Baltes, D. L. Featherman, & R. M. Lerner (Eds.), *Life-span development and behavior* (Vol. 9, pp. 39–85). Hillsdale, NJ: Erlbaum.

Wellman, H. M. (1977). Preschoolers' understanding of memory-relevant variables. *Child Development, 48,* 1720–1723.

Wellman, H. M. (1978). Knowledge of the interaction of memory variables: A developmental study of metamemory. *Developmental Psychology, 14,* 24–29.

Wellman, H. M. (1983). Metamemory revisited. In M. T. H. Chi (Ed.), *Trends in memory development research* (pp. 31–51). Basel: Karger.

Wellman, H. M. (1990). *The child's theory of mind.* Cambridge, MA: MIT Press.

Zabrucky, K., & Ratner, H. H. (1986). Children's comprehension monitoring and recall of inconsistent stories. *Child Development, 57,* 1401–1418.

Part II

MATH AND SCIENCE

4

Self-Explanations Promote Children's Learning

Robert S. Siegler
Xiaodong Lin

Increasing children's learning of mathematical and scientific material is a major national priority. Numerous high-level national commissions and panels have called on researchers to address these vital needs (e.g., National Mathematics Advisory Panel, 2008; National Science Board, 2008). One particularly promising technique for improving learning in these areas is encouraging learners to explain for themselves phenomena they observe, statements by teachers and textbooks, and answers to problems. In this chapter, we examine research illustrating the beneficial effects of encouraging learners to generate such explanations, as well as describing the theoretical and methodological background that led us to conduct the studies.

In the first main section, we describe our theoretical and methodological approach to studying children's learning. In the second, we describe several recent studies that apply this theoretical and methodological approach to understanding when and how self-explanations increase learning. In the third section, we consider the cognitive mechanisms that underlie self-explanation effects.

OVERLAPPING WAVES THEORY AND MICROGENETIC METHODS

Children's thinking is much more variable than is recognized within most theories of cognitive development. Different children use different strategies; individual children use different strategies on different problems within a single session; individual children often use different strategies to solve the same problem on two occasions close in time; and children sometimes use multiple strategies on a single problem. This variability has important consequences for cognitive development. Children who know and use varied strategies can fit them more precisely to the demands of different problems and to their own strengths and weaknesses than can children who have fewer strategies at their disposal. Moreover, in a wide range of circumstances, the number of initial strategies that children use is positively related to their learning (Siegler, 1994). Theories that simplify cognitive development into a sequence of stages, theories, or principles, in which each new cognitive structure replaces the previous one, divert attention away from these important phenomena.

To capture these findings regarding cognitive variability, as well as findings regarding the ways in which children choose among the varied approaches and the ways in which cognitive change occurs, Siegler (1996) proposed overlapping waves theory. The basic assumption of this theory is that development is a process of variability, choice, and change. As illustrated in Figure 4.1, the theory posits that children typically know and use varied strategies for solving a given problem at any one time. With age and experience, the relative frequency of each strategy changes, with some strategies becoming less frequent (Strategy 1), some becoming more frequent (Strategy 5), some becoming more frequent and then less frequent (Strategies 2 and 4), and some never becoming very frequent (Strategy 3). In addition to changes in relative use of existing strategies, new strategies are discovered (Strategies 3, 4, and 5), and some older strategies abandoned (Strategy 1).

In many cases, several of these patterns are evident within a single study. Consider a study of number conservation (Siegler, 1995) in which 5-year-olds were given a pretest and four learning sessions. During the learning sessions, children needed to explain the logic underlying the experimenter's answer on each trial. Over the course of the experiment, reliance on the relative lengths of the two rows of objects decreased, reliance on the type of transformation that had been performed increased, reliance on counting stayed at a constant low level, and answering "I don't know" first increased and then decreased. Interestingly, roughly half of the 5-year-olds first used the most advanced type of reasoning, reliance on the type of transformation, on a pretest trial. For these children, learning involved increased reliance on transformational reasoning; for the others, it involved discovery of the new approach as well as increasing reliance on it.

As this example illustrates, an important feature of overlapping waves theory is that it provides a means of integrating qualitative and

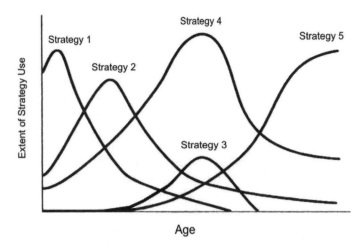

FIGURE 4.1. The overlapping waves model of cognitive change.

quantitative aspects of learning within a single framework. The approach recognizes that children discover qualitatively novel strategies and concepts; it also recognizes that much development is due to quantitative shifts in the frequency and efficiency of execution of strategies and in the adaptiveness of choices among them. Learning clearly involves both qualitative and quantitative changes; there is no reason for developmental theories to focus on one to the exclusion of the other.

Microgenetic methods have proven particularly useful for investigating the questions about learning processes that are raised by overlapping waves theory. Such methods have three main properties:

1. Observations span the period of rapidly changing competence.
2. Within this period, the density of observations is high, relative to the rate of change.
3. Observations are analyzed intensively, with the goal of inferring the representations and processes that gave rise to them.

The second property is especially important. Densely sampling changing competence during the period of rapid change provides the temporal resolution needed to understand the learning process. If children's learning usually proceeded in a beeline toward advanced competence, such dense sampling of ongoing changes would be unnecessary. We could examine thinking before and after changes occurred, identify the shortest path between the two states, and infer that children moved directly from the less advanced one to the more advanced one. Detailed observations of ongoing changes, however, indicate that such beelines are the exception rather than the rule (Siegler, 2006). Cognitive changes involve regressions as well as progressions, odd transitional states that are present only briefly but that are crucial for the changes to occur, generalization along some dimensions from the beginning of learning but lack of generalization along other dimensions for years thereafter, and many other surprising features. Simply put, the only way to find out how children learn is to track their progress carefully while they are learning.

The logic of densely sampling changes as they occur is not unique to the microgenetic approach; the same logic underlies a number of other methods. One example is neural imaging methods such as functional magnetic resonance imaging (fMRI). The dense temporal sampling of brain activity allowed by increasingly powerful magnets and software has led to many insights into the neural substrate of performance, and increasingly of cognitive development as well (e.g., Casey, 2001; Diamond & Amso, 2008). Other neural techniques such as single-cell recording are based on the same logic, as are behavioral techniques such as eye movement analysis (Just & Carpenter, 1987). In all cases, the dense sampling of performance over time allows insights into cognitive processes. One area in which such dense sampling of changing performance has proven useful is examining when and how self-explanations contribute to learning.

SELF-EXPLANATIONS

Self-explanations are inferences that learners generate regarding causal connections among objects and events. The inferences can concern how procedures cause their effects, how structural aspects of a system influence its functioning, how people's reasoning leads to their conclusions, how characters' motivations within a story results in their behavior, and so on. In short, self-explanations are inferences concerning "how" and "why" events happen.

The ability to infer causal connections is present from very early in life. Infants in their first year sometimes infer connections between physical causes and their effects (Cohen & Cashon, 2006). Infants and toddlers also remember events that reflect a coherent causal sequence better than ones in which the causality is unclear (Bauer, 2006). Thus, the ability to explain the causes of events seems to be a basic property of human beings, one that influences many aspects of cognition, including memory, problem solving, and conceptual understanding.

Although infants and toddlers can generate causal connections, older children and adults often fail to do so. This poses a particular problem in mathematics and science instruction. Mathematics and science teachers frequently lament the fact that their students know how to execute procedures but have no idea why the procedures work. Such patterns reflect failures of self-explanation (as well as of instruction). The problem can be illustrated in the context of buggy subtraction (VanLehn, 1983). On problems requiring borrowing across a zero, such as 704–337, second through fifth graders generate a variety of incorrect answers. These answers usually reflect misunderstandings of how the procedure works rather than carelessness. For example, children often borrow across a zero without decrementing the number from which the borrowing was done. On 704–337, this would produce the answer 477. Such procedures reflect children (almost) knowing the long subtraction procedure but not understanding why subprocedures within it are legitimate and why other subprocedures would not be.

Another type of evidence for the importance of self-explanations comes from studies of individual differences in learning. One difference between better and worse learners is the degree to which they try to explain what they are learning. In a wide range of areas, including physics, biology, algebra, and computer programming, frequency of explaining the logic underlying statements in textbooks is positively related to learning the material covered in the textbook (Chi, Bassok, Lewis, Reimann, & Glaser, 1989; Chi, De Leeuw, Chiu, & LaVancher, 1994; Nathan, Mertz, & Ryan, 1994; Pirolli & Recker, 1994; Renkl, Stark, Gruber, & Mandl, 1998). The kinds of explanations that seem most effective involve constructing causal connections between procedures and their effects, as well as between structural, functional, and behavioral aspects of systems and subsystems (Roy & Chi, 2005).

The positive relation between learning and generation of self-explanations does not seem attributable to people of higher ability generating a greater number of explanations than those of lower ability. Both high and low scorers on standardized achievement tests who generate a greater number of such explanations learn more than those who do not (Chi et al., 1994). Nor is it attributable to those who generate a greater number of explanations spending more time on the task. Generating explanations does take time, but equating the time spent on the task by having a control group read the textbook material twice did not result in as much learning as generating the explanations on a single reading (Chi et al., 1994).

Another type of evidence for the positive effects of self-explanations on learning comes from studies of mathematics teaching practices in Japan (Stigler & Hiebert, 1999). Levels of mathematics learning in Japan are at consistently high levels. For example, in one comparison of fifth graders, mean level of math achievement in all 10 Minneapolis schools that were examined was below the mean level of any of the schools examined in a comparable community in Japan (Stevenson & Lee, 1990). One contributing factor to these differences seems to be a differing degree of emphasis on generating explanations for why mathematical algorithms work. In Japanese classrooms, both teachers and students spend considerable time trying to explain why solution procedures that differ superficially nonetheless generate the same answer. They also spend considerable time analyzing why seemingly plausible approaches yield incorrect answers. Encouraging children to explain why procedures work appears to promote deeper understanding of them than simply describing the procedures, providing examples, and encouraging students to practice them—the typical approach to mathematics instruction in the United States (Stigler & Hiebert, 1999).

Thus, when we began the present series of investigations, we knew that amount of self-explanation and amount of learning were correlated. We did not know, however, whether there was a causal relation between the two. It might be the case, for example, that more intelligent and more highly motivated children might learn more and generate more explanations, but the self-explanatory activity might not cause the greater learning. Only by randomly assigning children to conditions under which they were or were not encouraged to engage in explanatory activity could causal linkages between the two be drawn.

The particular form of self-explanation instruction that we have examined involves asking children to explain the outcome of an event or the reasoning of another person. In particular, children are presented a problem, they advance an answer, they receive feedback concerning the correct answer, and then the experimenter asks them, "Why do you think that happened" or "How do you think I knew that"? This instructional procedure was of particular interest because it can be used on virtually any task, is easy to execute, and can be used with a wide range of age groups.

The detailed data about learning that is yielded by microgenetic methods provided a means for finding out not only whether such encouragement to advance self-explanations enhanced learning but also why it did or did not work for individual children. The investigations presented in this chapter have been aimed at answering seven main questions:

1. Is self-explanation causally related to learning, as well as being correlated with it?
2. Do young children, as well as older individuals, benefit from encouragement to provide explanations?
3. Is explaining other people's reasoning more useful than explaining your own reasoning?

4. What individual difference variables influence ability to benefit from self-explanations?
5. Is explaining both correct and incorrect reasoning more useful than just explaining correct reasoning?
6. Does explaining general rules of the problem solving or specific implementation of the rules lead to greater learning?
7. How does encouragement to explain generate its effects?

Explaining Number Conservation

The first context in which we examined the causal influence of self-explanations involved 5-year-olds performing number conservation problems (Siegler, 1995). The task closely resembled the classic Piagetian procedure. Children were shown two parallel rows, each with the same number of objects (7, 8, or 9, depending on the item), arranged in 1:1 correspondence. At the beginning of each trial, after children agreed that the two rows had the same number of objects, one of the rows was transformed spatially (by lengthening the row, shortening it, or leaving the length unchanged) and quantitatively (by adding an object, subtracting an object, or doing neither). The experimenter called attention to both spatial and numerical transformations, by saying, for example, "Now I'm spreading this row out and I'm taking an object away from it." Children in all groups were then asked whether they thought the transformed row had more objects, fewer objects, or the same number of objects as the untransformed row.

Children whose pretest performance indicated that they did not yet know how to solve number conservation problems spent four sessions participating in one of three training procedures. One group of children received feedback alone; they advanced their answer and were immediately told whether it was correct or not (*feedback-only condition*). A second group of children stated their answers, were asked, "Why do you think that?," and then were given feedback on their answer, as in the feedback-only condition (*explain-own-reasoning condition*). Examining this condition allowed us to determine whether describing one's own conservation reasoning was causally related to learning, as has been found in some contexts (e.g., Kastens & Liben, 2007).

A third group of children advanced their answers, received feedback, and then were asked by the experimenter, "How do you think I knew that?" (*explain-correct-reasoning condition*). This last condition, in which the child needed to explain the way in which the experimenter reached the conclusion that she did, was of greatest interest. Having children explain another person's correct reasoning combines the advantages of discovery and didactic approaches to instruction. It is like discovery-oriented approaches in that it requires the child to generate a relatively deep analysis of a phenomenon without being told how to do so. It is like didactic approaches in that it focuses the child's attention on correct reasoning. Thus, it combines some of the efficiency of didactic instruction with some of the motivating properties of discovery.

The results were clear: As hypothesized, encouraging 5-year-olds to explain the reasoning underlying the experimenter's answer resulted in their learning more than feedback alone or feedback in combination with requests to explain their own reasoning. Children who were asked to explain the experimenter's reasoning increased their percent correct from 17% on the pretest to 72% in the final training session. The corresponding percentages for the children in the other two conditions were an improvement from 13% to 31% in the group asked to explain their own reasoning and from 9% to 41% in the group that was not asked to provide any explanation. The differential gains were largest on the most difficult problems, those on which relying on the length cue led to the wrong answer.

These findings, though interesting, could have been obtained in a conventional training study. Other results from the study, however, could not have been obtained without the trial-by-trial analysis of change made possible by microgenetic methods. The advantages of the microgenetic data were especially evident in analyzing the performance and learning of children in the explain-correct-reasoning group, the group that showed the greatest learning.

One such finding was that even in a logical domain such as number conservation, a variety of ways of thinking coexisted both before and during the instruction was presented. Children explained the experimenter's reasoning in five qualitatively distinct ways: the type of numerical transformation, the relative lengths of the rows, counting the objects in each row, saying the objects were just moved back and forth, and saying that they didn't know why the experimenter had answered as she had. Variability of reasoning was evident in all phases of the experiment. On the pretest, only 7% of children relied on a single strategy on all trials. Of the other children, 20% used two approaches, 47% used three approaches, and 27% used four approaches. Thus, the large majority of children used three or more strategies on the pretest. This diversity of strategy use continued during the four training sessions.

The microgenetic design also made possible detailed analysis of the way in which the request to explain the experimenter's reasoning produced its effects. On the pretest, children explained most of their answers by saying that the row they chose was longer (or by saying that the two rows had the same number of objects because the rows were equally long). When initially asked to explain the experimenter's reasoning in the first training session, most children could not generate a good explanation; their most frequent response was that they didn't know why the experimenter had answered as she had. This explanation was used more than twice as often as explanations in which they cited the type of transformation. However, by the second training session, children were citing the type of transformation just as often as saying that they did not know, and in the third and fourth training sessions, their most frequent explanation was that the experimenter had based her judgment on the type of transformation. Thus, the predominant change was children deemphasizing length and emphasizing the type of transformation that was performed.

How did the children who benefited from the requests to explain the experimenter's reasoning differ from those who did not benefit? To answer this question, a regression analysis was conducted in which several characteristics of children and their pretest performance were used to predict amount of learning (defined as percent correct answers over the four training sessions). Three predictors accounted for 65% of the variance in learning: number of different explanations that the child used on the pretest (right or wrong), whether the child ever advanced two explanations on a single pretest trial, and the child's age. The first two predictors—number of different explanations and use of multiple explanations on a single trial—both indicated that the children who learned the most were the children whose pretest performance was the most variable.

This finding of a positive relation between initial variability and learning is consistent with results from studies in which rats, pigeons, and adult humans have been presented with experimental procedures that increased their behavioral variability (Baer, 1994; Neuringer, 1993; Stokes, Lai, Holtz, Rigsbee, & Cherrick, 2007). It also is consistent with results from microgenetic studies in which children's understanding is assessed on each trial via both gesture and speech. A child whose gestures and speech on a pretest reflect divergent reasoning is more likely to learn than one whose gestures and speech reflect the same reasoning (Goldin-Meadow, 2001; Goldin-Meadow & Alibali, 2002). Verbal inarticulateness, as reflected in false starts and long pauses, also is positively related to learning (Perry & Lewis, 1999).

The positive relation between initial variability and later learning makes a great deal of sense. Use of more varied approaches increases opportunities to explore the task environment and to discover heretofore unexpected aspects of it. Relatively great initial variability also may be indicative of openness to new approaches. In addition, part of the effectiveness of many forms of instruction may lie in their leading children to try more varied approaches. In the Siegler (1995) study, for example, children who were asked to explain the experimenter's reasoning advanced more different types of explanations than did peers who were asked to explain their own reasoning. Thus, part of the reason for the effectiveness of requests to explain the experimenter's reasoning may have been that it encouraged generation of varied possibilities, some of which were more effective than the approaches that children usually used.

The findings from the Siegler (1995) study of number conservation suggested answers to four of the six questions about self-explanation posed earlier in this chapter. With regard to the first question, encouraging children to explain other people's reasoning is causally related to learning. Children who were randomly assigned to explain the experimenter's reasoning learned more than children who explained their own reasoning. Studies conducted in other laboratories have shown that the people whose reasoning is being explained need not be present for the positive effects to emerge, though having another person present can facilitate transfer (Rittle-Johnson, Saylor, & Swygert, 2008).

The results also indicated positive answers to the second and third questions. Young children (5-year-olds) benefited from being asked to explain other people's reasoning, and explaining other people's correct reasoning was more beneficial than explaining children's own reasoning. Since then, even younger children (4-year-olds) have been found to learn from requests to explain another person's relational reasoning (Honomichl & Chen, 2006). With regard to the fourth question, individual differences in learning were positively related to variability of initial reasoning. Additional experiments were necessary, however, to address the fifth and sixth questions.

Explaining Mathematical Equality

Within overlapping waves theory, and within recent computer simulation models that embody that theory, such as the Associative Strategy Choice Model (ASCM) and the Strategy Choice and Discovery Simulation (SCADS) (Shrager & Siegler, 1998; Siegler & Araya, 2005; Siegler & Shipley, 1995), adoption of new approaches depends not only on the degree to which experiences encourage generation of that approach but also on the degree to which experiences discourage use of other approaches. Within these models, the two learning processes—generation of new approaches and reduction of use of older ones—are distinct both conceptually and empirically. Experiences that elicit generation of new approaches, even approaches that are clearly superior to previous ones, often lead to only small reductions in use of previous approaches, at least initially (Kuhn & Franklin, 2006; Miller & Coyle, 1999; Miller

& Seier, 1994). Considerable use of the new, superior strategy often is needed before it predominates. Conversely, when an existing approach leads to negative feedback, children often reduce their use of the existing approach without having discovered superior alternatives; they guess or oscillate among alternatives (Kuhn, Garcia-Mila, Zohar, & Andersen, 1995; Perry & Lewis, 1999; Siegler & Chen, 1998; Siegler & Svetina, 2002). Thus, the likelihood of using a new strategy can be increased in two ways: by increasing its own strength or by decreasing the strength of alternative strategies.

This issue arises frequently in instructional contexts in which less advanced previous approaches continue to be used after more advanced new approaches are learned. Overlapping waves theory suggests that the best way to increase the use of the new, more advanced approaches should be to increase their strength and also to decrease the strength of less advanced approaches. In the context of self-explanation, having children explain both why correct approaches are correct and why incorrect approaches are incorrect should be more effective than only explaining why correct approaches are correct. Explaining how correct answers were generated and why they are correct should increase the strength of correct procedures, and explaining how incorrect answers were generated and why they are wrong should decrease the strength of incorrect procedures.

Siegler (2002) tested this prediction on the mathematical equality task developed by Perry, Church, and Goldin-Meadow (1988). This task involves problems of the form $A + B + C =$ ____ $+ C$. Third and fourth graders find such problems surprisingly difficult. For example, they usually answer $3 + 4 + 5 =$ ____ $+ 5$ by writing "12." This answer reflects an add-to-equal-sign strategy, in which the children add all numbers to the left of the equal sign. The next most common answer to the problem is 17, which reflects an add-all-numbers strategy (Goldin-Meadow & Alibali, 2002). Both approaches reflect limited understanding of what the equal sign means. The third and fourth graders seem to interpret it as a signal to add the relevant numbers rather than as an indication that the values on the two sides of the equal sign need to be equivalent.

Siegler (2002) presented third and fourth graders with a pretest, training, and a posttest on mathematical equality problems. The pretest and posttest included three types of problems: $A + B + C =$ ____ $+ C$ (C problems), $A + B + C =$ ____ $+ B$ (B problems), and $A + B + C =$ ____ $+ D$ (D problems). These problems differed in the relation of the number after the equal sign to the numbers before it. On "C problems," the number after the equal sign was identical to the rightmost number before it (e.g., $3 + 4 + 5 =$ ____ $+ 5$). On "B problems," the number after the equal sign was identical to the middle number before it (e.g., $3 + 4 + 5 =$ ____ $+ 4$).

On "D problems," the number after the equal sign did not match any of the numbers before it (e.g., $3 + 4 + 5 = \underline{\quad} + 6$).

The reason for including these three kinds of problems was that they were solvable by different types of strategies and showed varying distances of transfer. One strategy—just add the first two numbers—worked only on C problems. A second strategy—ignore the number that is present on both sides of the equal sign, and add the other two numbers—worked on both B and C problems but not on D problems. Two other strategies worked on B, C, and D problems. One of these optimal strategies was to create equal values on the two sides of the equal sign (e.g., on $3 + 4 + 5 = \underline{\quad} + 5$, add the numbers on the left, and solve $12 = \underline{\quad} + 5$). The other optimal strategy was to subtract from both sides, the number on the right side of the equation (e.g., on $3 + 4 + 5 = \underline{\quad} + 5$, subtract 5 from both sides and solve $3 + 4 = \underline{\quad}$). Thus, presenting the B, C, and D problems allowed assessment of children's strategy use before and after training.

The training procedure included 10 problems. The ones of greatest interest were the six C items, such as $3 + 4 + 5 = \underline{\quad} + 5$. The other four items were standard three-term addition problems with no numbers on the right side of the equal sign, such as $5 + 6 + 7 = \underline{\quad}$. These four foils were included to prevent children from developing a set to blindly add the first two numbers on all problems. Performance on these foils was virtually perfect in all conditions and will not be described further.

Children received the 10 problems under one of three training conditions. Children in the *explain-own-reasoning condition* were asked to answer a problem and to explain their reasoning, and then were given feedback about the answer (either "You're right, the answer is N" or "Actually, the correct answer is N"). Children in the *explain-correct-reasoning condition* were also asked to answer a problem and given feedback. They then were told that a child at another school had answered N, which was the correct answer, and asked how they thought the child had generated that answer and why they thought it was correct. Finally, children in the *explain-correct-and-incorrect-reasoning condition* were presented the same procedure, except that they were asked to explain not only the reasoning of a hypothetical child who had generated the right answer but also the reasoning of a hypothetical child who had generated a wrong answer. The wrong answer that children in this condition needed to explain matched the answer that would have been generated by the procedure that that child had used most often on the pretest.

Pretest performance of this sample closely resembled that described in previous studies in which this task was used. Children usually employed the add-to-equal-sign strategy (they answered "12" on $3 + 4 + 5 = \underline{\quad} + 5$). A minority of children used the add-all-numbers approach (they answered "17" on this problem). Percent correct was 0% for children in all three conditions, and average solution time was around 10 seconds in all conditions. (This summary of pretest performance excludes the performance of the nine children who answered most pretest items correctly and therefore did not participate further in the study.)

The children in all three conditions learned a considerable amount during training. However, those children who were asked to explain both why correct reasoning was correct and why incorrect reasoning was incorrect learned more than those in the other two groups. These differences were maintained on the posttest. Children who were asked to explain both correct and incorrect reasoning improved from 0% correct on the pretest to about 70% correct during training and on the posttest. Children in the other two groups progressed from 0% correct answers on the pretest to about 50% correct during training and on the posttest.

The superior posttest performance of children who explained both correct and incorrect answers during training was due largely to their being better able to solve the problems that required relatively deep understanding (B and D problems). Analysis of changes in explanations during the training phase made clear the source of this effect. Children in all groups greatly decreased their use of the add-to-equal-sign strategy that had predominated on the pretest. The decrease occurred more quickly in the group in which children needed to explain why that strategy was wrong, but over the six trials it occurred in all three groups to large extents. However, the groups differed considerably in the new strategies that children adopted. Children who only received feedback and explained their own reasoning largely adopted the simplest strategy, that of adding A + B. In contrast, children who explained both why correct answers were correct and why incorrect ones were incorrect were more likely to use the more conceptually advanced strategies of equalizing the two sides or eliminating the constant on the right side of the equal sign by subtracting its value from both sides.

The strategies that children adopted to explain correct answers during the training period proved to be very predictive of their own posttest performance. Frequency of adopting one of the two advanced strategies correlated $r = .77$ with percent correct on the B problems on the posttest and $r = .86$ with percent correct on the D problems on the posttest. In contrast, percent use of the more superficial A + B explanations during training correlated $r = -.70$ with percent correct on the B problems on the posttest and $r = -.76$ with percent correct on the D problems. Thus, asking children to explain why correct answers were correct and why incorrect answers were incorrect led to deeper understanding of the problems, as indicated by adoption of strategies that would solve a broader range of problems rather than just the problems in the initial training set.

Changes in solution times over the six trials of the training period shed additional light on the change process for children in the three groups. On Trial 1, times for children in all three groups were around 12 seconds. The lack of difference made sense, because children in all groups had been treated identically up to this point. However, for those children who were asked to explain either correct reasoning or correct and incorrect reasoning at the end of Trial 1, solution times approximately doubled on Trial 2. On Trial 3, solution times of children who were asked to explain both correct and incorrect reasoning started to decline and the times continued to decline thereafter. In contrast, mean solution times of children who were asked to explain only correct answers increased to 26 seconds on Trial 3, before decreasing substantially over the remaining trials.

Why did the solution times of children asked to explain another child's reasoning show these changes? Consideration of data on each child's trial of last error during the training phase suggested a simple explanation. Most children who were asked to explain both correct and incorrect reasoning made their last error on Trial 2. The next most common outcome was for their last error to occur on Trial 3. Thus, their solution times for explaining the correct reasoning increased from Trial 1 to 2, when they became confused about how the correct answer was generated, and the times decreased thereafter as the children increasingly understood how to generate the correct answer. In contrast, most children who were asked only to explain the correct answer did not make their last error until Trial 3, and a number of them made their last error on Trial 4. This suggested that one or more incorrect procedures continued to compete with the correct procedure for a longer time, resulting in their solution time on Trial 3 being much greater than that of children who explained both correct and incorrect answers.

Thus, requests to explain correct answers, or correct and incorrect answers, led to an initial period of cognitive ferment, characterized by incorrect answers and very long solution times. Then children induced one or more strategies for solving the problems, and thus for explaining correct answers. This led to their consistently answering correctly and to their solution times becoming much shorter. Children who were asked to explain both correct and incorrect answers tended to cease relying on their previous incorrect approach more quickly than did children who only were asked to explain correct answers, and they tended to settle on more widely applicable new strategies.

These findings are reminiscent of previous ones indicating that just prior to discoveries, children show increasingly variable answers (Siegler & Svetina, 2002), increased solution times (Siegler & Jenkins, 1989), increased verbal disfluency (Perry & Lewis, 1999), increased gesture–

speech mismatches (Alibali & Goldin-Meadow, 1993), and increased cognitive conflict (Piaget, 1952). They also are reminiscent of the previously described number conservation findings from Siegler (1995), in which pretest variability was positively related to subsequent learning. In all cases, learning seems to involve children moving from incorrect approaches to a state of high uncertainty and variability, and then to a period in which the uncertainty and variability gradually decrease as children increasingly rely on more advanced approaches. The process occurs much faster in situations such as number conservation and mathematical equality, in which the less advanced approaches generate wrong answers, than in situations such as addition and time telling, in which the less advanced approaches generate correct answers but do so relatively inefficiently. Thus, in addition to supporting the previous conclusions that self-explanations are causally related to learning and that explaining correct answers promotes learning more effectively than explaining one's own answers, results of this study also suggest an answer to Question 5: Children do learn more from being asked to explain both why correct answers are correct and why incorrect answers are incorrect than from being asked only why correct answers are correct.

Explaining Water Displacement

To examine the generality of the beneficial effects of explaining incorrect as well as correct answers, and to examine age differences in these effects, Siegler and Chen (2008) asked children to explain outcomes on a scientific reasoning task, Inhelder and Piaget's (1958) water displacement problem. On each trial, first through fourth graders were presented two identical beakers containing equal amounts of water. Then, the children were shown two objects, told, for example, that one object was heavier but the other was larger, informed that both would float or that both would sink, and asked to predict which object would cause the water to rise higher.

Children were randomly assigned to one of three experimental conditions, which differed in the type of explanations that the experimenter requested. Children in the *explain-correct-and-incorrect-answers* condition were asked to explain both why the observed outcome occurred and why the other outcome did not. To elicit explanations of correct answers, they were told, "Look carefully and see if you can figure out why the water level in this container is higher than in that one." To elicit explanations regarding incorrect answers, they were told: "A child from another school thought that the water level in this container would be higher than in that one after we put these two blocks into the containers. Why do you think she thought this container would have a higher water level? Do you know why she was wrong?" Children in the *explain-correct-answers* condition were asked to explain why the observed water displacement occurred but not why the alternative did not. Children in the *explain-own-answers* condition were asked before the blocks were placed in the water to explain the basis of their own prediction.

The complexity of the water displacement problem stems from the fact that one variable (weight) determines water displacement when objects float, whereas a different variable (volume) determines displacement when they sink. To state the principle more formally: Sunken objects displace a quantity of water equal to their volume; floating objects displace a quantity of water equal to their weight.

Children's likelihood of using the correct rule on the posttest was substantially influenced by the type of explanation they were asked to provide and by the rule they had used on the pretest. On the pretest, 0% of children in all three groups met the criteria for use of the correct rule, which was 80% correct answers on the 18 problems. On the posttest, the correct rule was used by 49% of children who were asked to explain both why the observed outcome occurred and why the opposite outcome did not occur, by 28% of children who were asked to explain only why the observed outcome occurred, and by 6% of children who were only asked to explain their own reasoning. The correct rule was used on the posttest by significantly more children who explained both the correct and incorrect answers than by children who only explained the correct answer, and by significantly more children in both groups than in the group that explained their own answer.

The probability of children learning was also influenced by their pretest rule. Among children who used the most advanced incorrect approach on the pretest, 57% used the correct rule on the posttest. In contrast, 41% of those who used the second most advanced incorrect approach on the pretest, 18% of those who used the third most advanced approach on the pretest, and 0% of those who used the least advanced approach on the pretest progressed to the most advanced rule on the posttest.

Effects of the type of explanatory activity also varied with children's age. Among the third and fourth graders, those who were asked to explain both correct and incorrect answers were more likely to use the correct rule on the posttest than were children who were asked to explain correct answers (67% vs. 37%), and children who were asked to explain correct answers adopted the correct rule more often than children asked to explain their own answers (37% vs. 5%). In contrast, among the first and second graders, frequency of correct rule use on the posttest showed a similar trend, but one that was less dramatic and not statistically significant (33% vs. 20% vs. 6%.) These age effects, however, were entirely accounted for by differences in children's pretest rules. Older and younger children who used the same rule on the pretest showed comparable progress on the posttest.

Depth of search appeared to be particularly important in explaining the greater learning of children who were asked to explain why incorrect answers were wrong as well as why correct answers were correct. The importance of searching one's knowledge base deeply rather than shallowly can be seen particularly clearly in how children rejected the single most common incorrect pretest approach: the more-is-more rule. On problems on which the blocks were equivalent on one dimension but unequal on the other (e.g., equal volume, unequal weight), children using the more-is-more rule would rely on the dimension on which the blocks were unequal (in this example, they would choose the block that was heavier). On problems on which the blocks were unequal on both dimensions (one block heavier and the other block larger), children using the more-is-more rule would guess.

Consider the likely reaction of children using the more-is-more approach after being given negative feedback on problems where one block was heavier and the other larger. If only asked to explain the correct answer (the observed outcome), children using "more-is-more" logic could generate a plausible answer with a superficial search of their knowledge base. They could simply cite the variable associated with the correct outcome. Thus, if one object was larger, and the water into which it was placed rose more, the child could easily explain the outcome by saying that the water rose more because the object placed in it was bigger (as most children did). This would allow children to believe they had explained the outcome without forcing them to confront the inadequacies in their way of thinking about the problem. Such shallow processing may explain the seeming anomaly of only 18% of children who used the more-is-more rule on the pretest progressing to the correct rule on the posttest, despite their citing both weight and volume on the pretest. Such children may simply have responded to negative feedback by searching for a dimension whose values were unequal and that matched the dimensions cited in the question.

In contrast, being asked to explain why the incorrect answer was incorrect raised questions that were less easily dismissed. In the example in the previous paragraph, more-is-more logic does not explain why, for example, the larger object did not raise the water level more; indeed, more-is-more logic predicts that the larger object should have produced this effect. This puzzle seems likely to have increased the depth of search for an explanation for the puzzling outcome. In particular, it may have led them to encode other dimensions that were part of the problem description to see if they might explain the observation. Thus, requests to explain incorrect answers may have led children to wonder whether the fact that the objects sometimes floated and sometimes sank had anything to do with the outcome. Such requests may also have led children to reason that a sunken object would displace the same amount of water no matter what its weight, but that a floating object would displace more water if it rode lower in the water, and that perhaps the amount of weight would influence how high the floating object rode in the water. Thus, requests to explain why plausible effects do not occur can increase depth of processing and lead to encoding of previously ignored dimensions that might explain the puzzling outcomes.

Explaining Control of Variables

Children are not the only ones who benefit from generating self-explanations; adult learners also benefit from generating them, as indicated by Lin and Lehman's (1999) study of preservice science teachers who were asked to explain either a general control of variables rule for problem solving or a specific implementation of the rule. The control of variables scheme requires holding extraneous variables constant while systematically varying one or more factors of interest. It has long been viewed as a central competence within science education. Yet people of all ages have difficulties understanding and applying the general procedure to test scientific hypotheses (Ross, 1988; Sneider, Kurlich, Pulos, & Friedman, 1984).

A meta-analysis of 65 studies that examined effects of instruction on solving control of variable problems demonstrated the benefits of having students explain concepts and procedures associated with the control of variables approach (Ross, 1988). However, the meta-analysis did not specify what types of self-explanation were most helpful for learning.

Lin and Lehman (1999) predicted that asking preservice science teachers to explain why, how, and when they used the control of variables scheme to solve specific problems would help them understand the approach more deeply, as well as helping them understand how their experimental activities affected the quality of problem-solving outcomes. The effects of explaining how the approach was used to solve specific problems were expected to be greater than those of explaining the general control-of-variables approach or explaining learners' evaluation of the quality of their experimental activities. The logic was that having learners explain their efforts to implement the general approach in specific contexts was more likely to force them to confront incompleteness, ambiguity, or contradictions in their understanding. This, in turn, was expected to lead to more precise understanding of where experimental activities went wrong, more frequent revision of experiments, and greater planning and monitoring of experimental activities to avoid similar future problems.

To test this hypothesis, Lin and Lehman (1999) randomly assigned 88 preservice teachers to one of three experimental conditions. The conditions differed in the types of explanations that a computer program requested them to generate before, during, and after they conducted computer-simulated biology experiments. Participants in the *general-rule-explanation* condition were asked to explain general rules for conducting experiments involving multiple variables; they also were asked to describe the variables they were testing and the experimental results. Participants in the *rule-implementation* condition were asked to explain their plan for conducting specific variable control experiments, why they set up the experiments in the way they did, how they decided what to test next, and how they decided that they had run enough experiments to draw conclusions. Participants in the *confidence-explanation* condition were asked to explain how confident they felt about their reasoning and experimental activities.

We chose to examine these three types of explanations because they represent major components of metacognition (Brown, 1987; Flavell, 1987). According to Brown and Flavell, metacognition involves understanding of the task, cognitive processes involved in performing the task, and emotional states during learning. We predicted that explaining one's own problem-solving processes (when, how, and why certain actions were taken) was most likely to engage people in the core of metacognitive self-assessment: planning, monitoring, evaluating, and revising. Therefore, these explanatory activities were expected to lead to the largest learning gains, including far transfer.

A pretest-training-posttest design was used to assess students' ability to apply the knowledge gained from the computer-simulated control of variable experiments to near and far transfer problems. The near transfer problem required students to solve problems with levels of difficulty and problem contexts closely similar to those in the training problems. The far transfer problem required students to solve much more complex control of variables problems in a completely different context than the problems encountered during training. Lin and Lehman also collected online data to analyze changes in the preservice teachers' experimental designs and self-explanations during training.

On the pretest, and also on the near transfer problem on the posttest, preservice teachers in all three groups performed comparably. The three groups also spent comparable amounts of time on the learning tasks during all three phases of the study. In contrast, on the far transfer problem, participants in the rule implementation condition significantly outperformed those in the other two groups: rule-implementation condition = 18.09, general-rule-explanation condition = 16.69, and confidence-explanation condition = 16.59. To understand why, Lin and Lehman examined the experimental designs, and the types of explanations learners offered for them, in the three conditions. Participants who were asked to explain how they implemented the rules in their variable control designs (i.e., participants in the rule-implementation condition) reported monitoring their activities, revising their designs, and engaging in other metacognitive activities far more often than participants in the other two conditions—on 79% of experiments for those asked to explain their rule implementations versus 16% of experiments for those asked to explain the general control of variables rule and 6% of experiments for those asked to explain their confidence in their designs.

The explanations generated by participants in the rule-implementation condition indicated greater depth of processing than those produced by peers in the other conditions. To illustrate, after being asked to conduct experiments to decide if isopod insects were affected more by the moisture or by the light, a prospective teacher in the rule-implementation condition provided the following representative explanation:

> "I plan to set up the isopods in the trough with a light source, a light bulb, at one end and the dark paper for the other end, and then I would switch the sides between the two because this procedure will allow me to make sure that the variable, position of the light, would not affect the behaviors of the isopods, ... rather it is the degree of light that affected their behaviors. I want to learn how my designs would affect the control of other factors in the experiments. It is not a matter of simply controlling the moisture variable, while experimenting with light. It is much more complex than that, I think...."

In contrast, explanations such as this one were common in the other groups:

> "Now I am very confused and I don't know how I got these results. I probably should replicate what I have got so far to see if I will get the same results.... "

Lin and Lehman also examined changes in the participants' problem-solving strategies over the course of training. Roughly 90% of the first three experiments of participants in all three conditions were unsystematic or confounded. On these trials, the preservice teachers often tested the moisture and light variables at the same time, or they tested the effects of the presence of a variable but not the effects of its absence. In general, they tended to jump around testing different variables. However, after the initial three trials, 75% of participants in the rule-implementation condition adopted a systematic approach to testing the effects of the two variables. These participants thoroughly tested the effects of one variable before testing the effects of a different variable or setting up more complex tests. In contrast, only 40% of participants in the general-rule condition and 34% of those in the confidence-explanation condition adopted systematic experimental approaches. Such systematic testing allowed participants to improve their understanding of the effects of each variable.

The fine-grained analysis of change over trials in the preservice teachers' online explanations and problem-solving strategies indicated three main reasons why explaining implementations of the control of variables strategy yielded greater learning than the other types of explanations. One reason was that asking students to explain their rule implementations stimulated them to plan and monitor subsequent design activities. Consider this comment by a participant in the rule-implementation condition:

> "When I was responding to the computer prompts that asked me how would I plan my experiments, I stopped and thought for almost 5 minutes about what I should do. I thought about what were the goals for the experiments.... You know, when you are using computers, you always feel pressed to rush through to get the right solutions. Now I had to think about my plans and look at what I have done ... where I was heading.... Going through these thoughts actually helped me become more efficient later on."

Second, explaining specific rule implementation helped participants assess their own problem-solving activities. In particular, it helped them specify where they had gone wrong, what they did not understand, and what they still needed to find out. Most participants in the other two groups were aware in a general way of what they did not know; they often made statements such as "I am confused" or "I don't know." However, the students in the rule-implementation group tended to be more specific about what they did not know. For example, one of them said:

> "I was able to do controlling variables by holding the light variable constant while testing moisture. However, I was unable to notice other potentially confounding variables ... like the amount of water I poured into each trough and the amount of sand that I put under the trough.... But how could I tell which variables may potentially confound moisture testing? I really needed instructions on how to decide which variables were potentially confounding variables.... I could not find any instructions within the computer program."

Finally, this level of monitoring and evaluation helped students identify specific conditions that limited their understanding. The more in-depth monitoring and evaluation then set the stage for students to explore alternative experimental designs.

Connecting scientific principles with specific actions is crucial to fully understanding the principles (Brown et al., 1993; Lin, Schwartz, & Hatano, 2005). The principles help learners to organize their thinking, to perceive analogies, and to develop abstract knowledge representations (Chi & VanLehn, 1991; Gick & Holyoak, 1983). In addition, by understanding the big ideas behind general procedures, and how these big ideas relate to specific implementations of them, students may transcend contextual differences to flexibly solve novel problems (Brown & Campione, 1994; Lin, 2001; Salomon & Perkins, 1989).

EXPLAINING THE EFFECTS OF EXPLAINING

Self-explanation seems likely to generate its effects through several distinct mechanisms. Data from the present studies of number conservation, mathematical equality, water displacement, and control of variables provide evidence for at least four of them.

One way in which encouragement to explain exercises its effects is to increase the probability of the learner seeking an explanation at all. When people are told that an answer is wrong, they often simply accept the fact without thinking about why it is wrong or how they might generate correct answers in the future. The number conservation data provide evidence regarding this source of effectiveness. Children who were told that their answer was wrong and which answer was right, but who were not asked to explain why the correct answer was correct, did not increase the accuracy of their answers over the course of the four sessions. In contrast, children who received the same feedback, but who also were asked to explain how the experimenter had generated the correct answer, did increase their accuracy. Further, those children who showed the largest increases in successfully explaining the experimenter's reasoning also showed the largest increases in generating correct answers on their own. Thus, encouragement to generate self-explanation seems to work partially through encouraging children to try to explain observed outcomes.

A second way in which encouragement to explain exercises its effects is through increasing the depth of explanatory efforts. The study of the mathematical equality task provides relevant evidence. Children in all three groups succeeded in finding ways to solve the problems by the second half of the training period. However, children who were asked to explain correct and incorrect answers appeared to search considerably more deeply. They more often generated conceptually more sophisticated solutions, such as balancing the values on the two sides of the equal sign. In contrast, children who were only given feedback usually generated solutions to the training problems that happened to work on those problems but were not generally applicable (the A + B strategy). Thus, encouraging generation of explanations also seems to promote a deeper search than might be undertaken otherwise.

Similarly, on the water displacement task, the effects of explaining both correct and incorrect answers were especially great among children who had used the more-is-more rule on the pretest. The more-is-more approach involves predicting that when the blocks are equal on one dimension and unequal on the other (e.g., equal on weight and unequal on volume), then the block that is greater on the unequal dimension will produce greater displacement. The more-is-more approach also involves predicting that when one block is greater on one dimension and the other block on the other dimension, the child will guess. This approach allows correct answers to be explained in quite superficial ways; the child simply cites the dimension on which the block that produced the greater displacement was greater. However, explaining why the incorrect answer was incorrect cannot be done through such a superficial matching process. For example, why shouldn't the block of the greater size have displaced more water? This dilemma seems likely to have led children to encode dimensions that they previously ignored, for example, whether the blocks sunk or floated, and to try to relate those variables to which block raised the water more. Calin-Jageman and Ratner (2005) also suggested that the positive effects of requesting explanation can arise through children widening the range of variables that they encode.

The findings on the control of variables scheme provide converging evidence. The preservice teachers who needed to explain their specific implementations of the control of variables scheme engaged in greater depth of processing than peers who explained the general scheme or their confidence in their own experimental activities. The effect appears to have been driven by teachers who explained the specific implementations of the control of variables approach engaging in deeper processing. This deeper processing included greater planning of experiments, monitoring of one's problem-solving activities, specificity of criticisms of those activities, and revision of experimental designs.

It should be noted that both of these mechanisms also have the effect of increasing the variability of the procedures that children attempt. For example, in the number conservation study, children who were asked to explain the experimenter's answer generated a greater number of strategies than did children who were only given feedback concerning their own answers. This difference was present despite feedback per se often increasing variability of responses (Neuringer, 1993). Thus, increasing the likelihood of searching for an explanation and the depth of the search if one is undertaken seem to operate in part by increasing the range of strategies that children attempt.

A third likely mechanism involves changing the accessibility of effective and ineffective ways of thinking. The most directly relevant evidence here comes from the mathematical equality study. Children who were asked to explain why incorrect answers were incorrect as well as why correct answers were correct showed more rapid decreases in use of their previous A + B + C strategy than did children who were only asked to explain why correct answers were correct. The self-criticisms of preservice teachers suggest that asking them to explain how they implemented the control of variables scheme produced a similar effect. This was what models such as ASCM and SCADS would predict. Instructional approaches that not only strengthen effective approaches but that also weaken ineffective ones should increase the likelihood of retrieving the effective approaches and decrease the likelihood of retrieving ineffective ones.

A fourth set of mechanisms involves more general processes related to engagement with the task. One concerns motivational effects. Learning is more enjoyable when what you are learning makes sense. By encouraging children to make sense of their observations, encouragement to generate explanations achieves this motivating effect. Another general benefit involves increased time spent actively engaged in thinking about the problem. The more time that children spend trying to understand why correct answers are correct and why incorrect answers are incorrect, the more they are likely to learn.

Thus, these microgenetic studies yielded answers to the questions posed at the beginning of the chapter. They demonstrated that:

1. Encouragement to explain other people's reasoning or physical outcomes is causally related to learning.
2. Preschoolers, as well as older children and adults, can benefit from encouragement to explain.
3. Explaining other people's answers is more useful than explaining your own, at least when the other people's answers are consistently correct and your own answers include incorrect ones.
4. Variability of initial reasoning is positively related to learning.
5. Explaining why correct answers are correct and why incorrect answers are incorrect yields greater learning than only explaining why correct answers are correct.
6. The mechanisms through which explaining other people's reason-

ing exercises its effects include increasing the probability of trying to explain observed phenomena; searching in greater depth
for explanations when explanatory efforts are made; increasing
the accessibility of effective strategies relative to ineffective ones;
and increasing the degree of engagement with the task.

Specifying in greater depth and breadth how self-explanations exer-
cise their effects may move us toward the twin goals of describing high-
quality problem solving and helping child and adult learners approach
that ideal in their math and science learning.

REFERENCES

Alibali, M. W., & Goldin-Meadow, S. (1993). Gesture–speech mismatch and
mechanisms of learning: What the hands reveal about a child's state of
mind. *Cognitive Psychology, 25*, 468–523.

Baer, J. (1994). Divergent thinking is not a general trait: A multidomain training
experiment. *Creativity Research Journal, 17*, 35–46.

Bauer, P. J. (2006). Event memory. In W. Damon & R. M. Lerner (Series Eds.) &
D. Kuhn & R. S. Siegler (Vol. Eds.), *Handbook of child psychology: Vol.
2. Cognition, perception, and language* (6th ed., pp. 373–425). Hoboken,
NJ: Wiley.

Brown, A. L. (1987). Metacognition, executive control, self-regulation and other
more mysterious mechanisms. In F. E. Weinert, & R. H. Kluwe (Eds.), *Metacognition, motivation, and understanding* (pp. 65–116). Hillsdale, NJ: Erlbaum.

Brown, A. L., Ash, D., Rutherford, M., Nakagawa, K., Gordon, A., & Campione, J. C. (1993). Distributed expertise in the classroom. In G. Salomon
(Ed.), *Distributed cognition* (pp. 188–228). New York: Cambridge University Press.

Brown, A. L., & Campione, J. C. (1994). Guided discovery in a community of
learners. In K. McGilly (Ed.), *Classroom lessons: Integrating cognitive theory and classroom practice* (pp. 229–270). Cambridge, MA: MIT Press/
Bradford Books.

Calin-Jageman, R. J., & Ratner, H. H. (2005). The role of encoding in the self-
explanation effect. *Cognition and Instruction, 23*, 523–543.

Casey, B. J. (2001). Disruption of inhibitory control in developmental disorders:
A mechanistic model of implicated frontostriatal circuitry. In J. L. McClelland & R. S. Siegler (Eds.), *Mechanisms of cognitive development: Behavioral and neural perspectives* (pp. 327–349). Mahwah, NJ: Erlbaum.

Chi, M. T. H., Bassok, M., Lewis, M., Reimann, P., & Glaser, R. (1989). Self-
explanations: How students study and use examples in learning to solve
problems. *Cognitive Science, 13*, 145–182.

Chi, M. T. H., De Leeuw, N., Chiu, M.-H., & LaVancher, C. (1994). Eliciting
self-explanations improves understanding. *Cognitive Science, 18*, 439–477.

Chi, M. T. H., & VanLehn, K. A. (1991). The content of physics self-explanations. *The Journal of the Learning Sciences, 1*, 69–105.

Cohen, L. B., & Cashon, C. H. (2006). Infant cognition. In W. Damon & R. M. Lerner (Series Eds.) & D. Kuhn & R. S. Siegler (Vol. Eds.), *Handbook of child psychology: Vol. 2. Cognition, perception, and language* (6th ed., pp. 214–251). Hoboken, NJ: Wiley.

Diamond, A., & Amso, D. (2008). Contributions of neuroscience to our understanding of cognitive development. *Current Directions in Psychological Science, 17*, 136–141.

Flavell, J. H. (1987). Speculations about the nature and development of metacognition. In F. E. Weinert & R. H. Kluwe (Eds.), *Metacognition, motivation, and understanding*. Hillsdale, NJ: Erlbaum.

Gick, M. L., & Holyoak, K. J. (1983). Schema induction and analogical transfer. *Cognitive Psychology, 12*, 1–38.

Goldin-Meadow, S. (2001). Giving the mind a hand: The role of gesture in cognitive change. In J. L. McClelland & R. S. Siegler (Eds.), *Mechanisms of cognitive development: Behavioral and neural perspectives* (pp. 5–31). Mahwah, NJ: Erlbaum.

Goldin-Meadow, S., & Alibali, M. W. (2002). Looking at the hands through time: A microgenetic perspective on learning and instruction. In N. Granott & J. Parziale (Eds.), *Microdevelopment: Transition processes in development and learning* (pp. 80–105). Cambridge, UK: Cambridge University Press.

Honomichl, R. D., & Chen, Z. (2006). Learning to align relations: The effects of feedback and self-explanation. *Journal of Cognition and Development, 7*, 527–550.

Inhelder, B., & Piaget, J. (1958). *The growth of logical thinking from childhood to adolescence.* New York: Basic Books.

Just, M. A., & Carpenter, P. A. (1987). *The psychology of reading and language comprehension.* Needham Heights, MA: Allyn & Bacon.

Kastens, K. A., & Liben, L. S. (2007). Eliciting self-explanations improves children's performance on a field-based map skills test. *Cognition and Instruction, 25*, 45–74.

Kuhn, D., & Franklin, S. (2006). The second decade: What develops (and how). In W. Damon & R. M. Lerner (Series Eds.) & D. Kuhn & R. S. Siegler (Vol. Eds.), *Handbook of child psychology: Vol. 2. Cognition, perception, and language* (6th ed., pp. 953–993). Hoboken, NJ: Wiley.

Kuhn, D., Garcia-Mila, M., Zohar, A., & Andersen, C. (1995). Strategies of knowledge acquisition. *Monographs of the Society for Research in Child Development, 60*(4, Serial No. 245).

Lin, X. D. (2001). Designing metacognitive activities. *Educational Technology Research and Development, 49*, 23–40.

Lin, X. D., & Lehman, J. (1999). Supporting learning of variable control in a computer-based biology environment: Effects of prompting college students to reflect on their own thinking. *Journal of Research in Science Teaching, 36*, 837–858.

Lin, X. D., Schwartz, D., & Hatano, G. (2005). Toward teachers' adaptive metacognition. *Educational Psychologist, 40*, 245–255.

Miller, P. H., & Coyle, T. R. (1999). Developmental change: Lessons from micro-genesis. In E. K. Scholnick, K. Nelson, S. A. Gelman, & P. H. Miller (Eds.), *Conceptual development: Piaget's legacy* (pp. 209–239). Mahwah, NJ: Erl-baum.

Miller, P. H., & Seier, W. L. (1994). Strategy utilization deficiencies in children: When, where, and why. In H. W. Reese (Ed.), *Advances in child development and behavior* (Vol. 25, pp. 108–156). New York: Academic Press.

Nathan, M. J., Mertz, K., & Ryan, B. (1994). *Learning through self-explanation of mathematical examples: Effects of cognitive load.* Paper presented at the 1994 annual meeting of the American Educational Research Association.

National Mathematics Advisory Panel. (2008). *Reports of the task groups and subcommittees.* Washington, DC: Author.

National Science Board. (2008). *Science and engineering indicators 2008. Two volumes.* Arlington, VA: National Science Foundation. (Vol. 1, MSB 08-01; Vol. 2, NSB 08-01A)

Neuringer, A. (1993). Reinforced variation and selection. *Animal Learning and Behavior, 21,* 83–91.

Perry, M., Church, R. B., & Goldin-Meadow, S. (1988). Transitional knowledge in the acquisition of concepts. *Cognitive Development, 3,* 359–400.

Perry, M., & Lewis, J. L. (1999). Verbal imprecision as an index of knowledge in transition. *Developmental Psychology, 35,* 749–759.

Piaget, J. (1952). *The child's concept of number.* New York: Norton.

Pirolli, P., & Recker, M. (1994). Learning strategies and transfer in the domain of programming. *Cognition and Instruction, 12,* 235–275.

Renkl, A., Stark, R., Gruber, H., & Mandl, H. (1998). Learning from worked-out examples: The effects of example variability and elicited self-explanations. *Contemporary Educational Psychology, 23,* 90–108.

Rittle-Johnson, B., Saylor, M., & Swygert, K. (2008). Learning from explaining: Does it matter if mom is listening? *Journal of Experimental Child Psychology, 100,* 215–224.

Ross, J. A. (1988). Controlling variables: A meta-analysis of training studies. *Review of Educational Research, 58,* 405–437.

Roy, M., & Chi, M. T. H. (2005). The self-explanation principle in multimedia learning. In R. E. Mayer (Ed.), *The Cambridge handbook of multimedia learning* (pp. 271–286). New York: Cambridge University Press.

Salomon, G., & Perkins, D. N. (1989). Rocky roads to transfer: Rethinking mechanisms of a neglected phenomenon. *Educational Psychologist, 24,* 113–142.

Shrager, J., & Siegler, R. S. (1998). SCADS: A model of children's strategy choices and strategy discoveries. *Psychological Science, 9,* 405–410.

Siegler, R. S. (1994). Cognitive variability: A key to understanding cognitive development. *Current Directions in Psychological Science, 3,* 1–5.

Siegler, R. S. (1995). How does change occur: A microgenetic study of number conservation. *Cognitive Psychology, 28,* 225–273.

Siegler, R. S. (1996). *Emerging minds: The process of change in children's thinking.* New York: Oxford University Press.

Siegler, R. S. (2002). Microgenetic studies of self-explanations. In N. Granott &

J. Parziale (Eds.), *Microdevelopment: Transition processes in development and learning* (pp. 31–58). New York: Cambridge University Press.

Siegler, R. S. (2006). Microgenetic analyses of learning. In W. Damon & R. M. Lerner (Series Eds.) & D. Kuhn & R. S. Siegler (Vol. Eds.), *Handbook of child psychology: Vol. 2. Cognition, perception, and language* (6th ed., pp. 464–510). Hoboken, NJ: Wiley.

Siegler, R. S., & Araya, R. (2005). A computational model of conscious and unconscious strategy discovery. In R. V. Kail (Ed.), *Advances in child development and behavior* (Vol. 33, pp. 1–42). Oxford, UK: Elsevier.

Siegler, R. S., & Chen, Z. (1998). Developmental differences in rule learning: A microgenetic analysis. *Cognitive Psychology, 36*, 273–310.

Siegler, R. S., & Chen, Z. (2008). Differentiation and integration: Guiding principles for analyzing cognitive change. *Developmental Science, 11*, 433–448.

Siegler, R. S., & Jenkins, E. A. (1989). *How children discover new strategies.* Hillsdale, NJ: Erlbaum.

Siegler, R. S., & Shipley, C. (1995). Variation, selection, and cognitive change. In T. Simon & G. Halford (Eds.), *Developing cognitive competence: New approaches to process modeling* (pp. 31–76). Hillsdale, NJ: Erlbaum.

Siegler, R. S., & Svetina, M. (2002). A microgenetic/cross-sectional study of matrix completion: Comparing short-term and long-term change. *Child Development, 73*, 793–809.

Sneider, C., Kurlich, K., Pulos, S., & Friedman, A. (1984). Learning to control variables with model rockets: A neo-Piagetian study of learning in field settings. *Science Education, 68*, 463–484.

Stevenson, H. W., & Lee, S.-Y. (1990). Contexts of achievement. *Monographs of the Society for Research in Child Development, 55*(1–2, Serial No. 221).

Stigler, J. W., & Hiebert, J. (1999). *The teaching gap: Best ideas from the world's teachers for improving education in the classroom.* New York: Free Press.

Stokes, P. D., Lai, B., Holtz, D., Rigsbee, E., & Cherrick, D. (2007). Effects of practice on variability, effects of variability on transfer. *Journal of Experimental Psychology: Human Perception and Performance, 34*, 640–659.

VanLehn, K. (1983). On the representation of procedures in repair theory. In H. P. Ginsburg (Ed.), *The development of mathematical thinking* (pp. 201–253). New York: Academic Press.

5

Bird Experts

A Study of Child and Adult Knowledge Utilization

Harriet Salatas Waters
Theodore E. A. Waters

Two decades ago, developmental psychologists began in earnest to study the role of knowledge in cognitive development (e.g., Carey, 1985, Keil, 1981). Research findings demonstrated far more heterogeneity in development than Piaget's stage theory had anticipated (Flavell, 1982). One of the more dramatic areas of investigation focused on child experts and their abilities to perform in sophisticated and "adult-like" ways provided they possessed the prerequisite knowledge. Child chess experts outperformed adult novices in a variety of tasks challenging their abilities to process and remember chess positions from legitimate chess boards (Chi, 1978). Child dinosaur experts' classification and inference-making skills were tied to their knowledge base about dinosaurs, not to their general developmental level (Chi & Koeske, 1983; Chi, Hutchinson, & Robin, 1989).

A decade later researchers acknowledged the importance of studying the interplay between domain-general and domain-specific skills (e.g., Ceci, 1989; Sternberg, 1989). Recognizing the strengths and weaknesses of both perspectives, researchers moved on to study the details of knowledge acquisition with at least an "eye" to the domain-general components of the process. Sternberg (1989) in particular argued that the question of domain-general versus domain-specific was not an either/or proposition; that development has elements of both and researchers should explore their interaction. In more recent years, the interplay between general strategy use and domain-specific knowledge has been highlighted in studies of scientific thinking (Kuhn, Garcia-Mila, Zohar, & Anderson, 1995; Kuhn & Pearsall, 2000; Schauble, 1996).

Although there has been significant progress in understanding some aspects of the interplay between domain-general and domain-specific knowledge, the discussion has often been focused on important ramifications of how knowledge is represented by those (experts) who have acquired significant knowledge in a particular domain. The end result has been a burgeoning literature on expertise often focused on skilled adult experts (Ericsson, 1996; Sternberg & Grigorenko, 2003; Ericsson, Charness, Feltovich, & Hoffman, 2006). As a consequence, researchers who are interested in the beginnings of expertise in children have been left behind. Comparisons between adult experts and novices simply do not provide insight into how children move toward greater in-depth knowledge and sophisticated strategy use within a particular domain.

DOMAIN-SPECIFIC VERSUS DOMAIN-GENERAL KNOWLEDGE

Early studies of expertise quickly demonstrated that general transfer of skills from one domain to another was limited (Chi, Glaser, & Farr, 1988; Ericsson & Lehmann, 1996), challenging the domain-general perspectives of Piaget and others. To make that case, these studies often placed an expert in a quite different domain from that of his or her expertise, for example, a chemist being asked to address problems from political science. And every time, the experts faltered in addressing problems from the unfamiliar domain. The domain-specific demonstrations from the expertise literature were numerous and dramatic, and developmental psychologists pursued greater understanding of the domain-specific constraints on knowledge acquisition.

Consequently, detailed explorations of how domain-general and domain-specific skills interact across development were not pursued, although the early critiques of the question had left the door open for further investigation. In fact, contributors from a recent edited volume (Roberts, 2007) revisit the issue across several developmental domains, including logical reasoning, theory of mind, and number learning. They argue that domain-general processes are essential, and that domain-specific processes cannot function without them. A similar perspective can be found in Siegler and Alibali's (2005) textbook on children's thinking: "Problem-solving relies on knowledge and processes of many levels of generality. The key issue is how children integrate such diverse information into efficient problem-solving procedures, rather than whether specific or general knowledge is more important" (p. 347). We would add one point of clarification to that description. The best arena for studying that interplay would be within a particular domain, but in a context in which individuals are challenged to use a broad range of general strategic knowledge.

Thus, we have chosen to cast the question in terms of how domain-specific and domain-general knowledge work together within an individual to produce adaptive and flexible problem-solving performance across tasks. Furthermore, we argue that how domain-specific and domain-general knowledge interact changes with both development and experience with differing task demands. In other words, general strategy knowledge not only increases with age but also reflects the types of cognitive demands that individuals have encountered along the way. Different individuals may vary not only in domain knowledge but also in how they use their knowledge, producing diversity in knowledge utilization as well as overall knowledge.

As noted by Chi (2006), there are multiple methodologies for studying expertise. In some studies, the focus is on individuals with extraordinary ability (e.g., a chess expert performing at the highest levels). In others, the comparison is among individuals who vary in their degree of knowledge. Here the difference is often a matter of years of experience, with the understanding that the less knowledgeable individuals can acquire greater expertise with time and effort. In the present case we take the more relativistic approach. We contrast both child and adult bird experts who bring different degrees of domain-specific and general strategic knowledge as they tackle a range of tasks with differing cognitive demands. This methodology is better suited for our developmental pursuits, offering an opportunity to track changes in problem-solving performance as cognitive demands tax an individual's knowledge utilization skills.

A STUDY OF KNOWLEDGE UTILIZATION

The goal of the present investigation was to pursue the interplay between domain-specific knowledge and general strategy knowledge in varying problem-solving contexts with both child and adult experts. Although some studies have used both child and adult participants to track their movement toward greater expertise (e.g., Johnson & Eilers, 1998), in the current study we chose to recruit several already expert individuals. These experts, however, were selected to vary on two key dimensions, developmental level (age) and education (between adults). First, an elementary school child bird expert and an adult bird expert with similar birding experience were recruited. The purpose of recruiting these two individuals was to contrast their facility in using general strategy knowledge to successfully negotiate different task demands given comparable birding knowledge. The adult expert arguably had a more practiced and generalized strategy repertoire than that of the child expert.

A second adult expert with more extensive birding experience than the child or adult expert already recruited was also included in the study. Although this adult possessed more bird knowledge, she had less educational experience than that of the first adult expert. The addition of this adult expert provided an opportunity to contrast the advantages of domain knowledge versus general strategy knowledge. One adult expert had more domain-specific knowledge, the other more general strategy knowledge (a judgment based on his additional years of education). We anticipated that both age and education would provide strategy knowledge above that which was provided by bird knowledge, demonstrating a complex interplay between these factors in the coordination of domain-specific and general strategy knowledge.

To highlight this interplay, all of our bird experts were given two different problem-solving tasks, one more structured in which strategy use was closely related to the characteristics of the materials (*picture sorting*), and one more open-ended where there was little support for appropriate strategy use (*twenty questions*). Although the details of each task are described below, it is clear that any picture-sorting task provides concrete visual information that can guide an individual's performance. A twenty questions task for bird experts (What bird am I thinking of?), however, requires that the individual construct and implement a question-asking strategy without any hints from the interviewer or any observable materials to guide him or her.

Finally, in addition to the contrasts between the child and adult bird experts, we included several groups of control participants that completed all tasks. These were college students, all of whom could be viewed as reasonably knowledgeable about a wide range of general purpose strategies, but with little birding experience (none of the controls reported any significant birding experience). We anticipated that they would tap into general strategies for both problem-solving tasks, but would implement them without the benefit of domain-specific knowledge, providing an interesting contrast to our bird experts.

Child and Adult Experts

All three bird experts recruited for this study were members of a community bird club. They differed, however, in age, education, and experience in birding. The child bird expert was 9 years old and had been a bird watcher since he was 5. One of our adult experts was a 37-year-old university psychology professor who had an equivalent number of years bird watching as the child. He was our well-educated, but less knowledgeable adult expert. The other adult bird expert was a 45-year-old housewife with 2 years of college, 20 years of birding experience, who was a past officer of the New York State Audubon Society. She was our more knowledgeable, less well-educated adult expert. These selections set the stage for two key comparisons. First, how does a child and an adult expert with comparable birding experience apply their knowledge given the differing general strategy knowledge between the two of them. Second, how do two adult experts who vary in education and birding experience manage problem-solving tasks that vary in how structured or open-ended they are.

Factual Information Task

Although we selected the bird experts based on their reported birding experience and their involvement in various bird-related activities, they were also asked to complete a *Factual Information Task* to assess overall level of bird knowledge. The purpose of this task was to match our child and our adult bird expert with comparable years of birding on the basis of factual knowledge as well. In addition, the Factual Information Task was used to establish that our more experienced adult expert had indeed accumulated a broader range of bird knowledge along with her additional years of birding. The task involved a set of 250 questions about birds randomly selected from a bird Trivial Pursuit card set (3,000 questions in total). The questions covered information about field identification, bird behavior, anatomy, history, geography, and so on. Sample questions included:

131. Are rusty blackbirds often found with other blackbird species?
132. Where in southern New Jersey do fantastic numbers of fall migrants collect, waiting for the wind to change before they fly across the open ocean?
133. Which group of seaducks lines its nest with down that is later harvested by Icelanders for down clothing and pillows?
134. In what type of woodlands are western tanagers found?

135. What cuckoos have the nickname the "tickbirds"?
136. What is A. O. U.?
137. What colors are the brown-headed cowbird male?
138. What is the only cormorant that lives in the entire tropical American region of the western hemisphere?

Picture-Sorting Task

The first problem-solving task our bird experts were asked to complete was a bird picture-sorting task. As noted by other researchers who have used picture sorting, this type of task provides more structure and support for completing the task than other more open-ended tasks (Chi et al., 1989; Johnson & Eilers, 1998). A wealth of visual information can prompt relevant bird knowledge in the expert and facilitate grouping patterns based on bird knowledge rather than on superficial perceptual characteristics. Both the child and adult experts had the requisite knowledge that would enable them to group appropriate pictures together, once they identified birds of the same grouping (e.g., birds of prey). Grouping strategies based on common category membership is a well-established strategy for sorting items, one that is learned quite early. Familiar semantic groups like animals, toys, furniture, transportation, and so on, are introduced into young children's picture books and sorting experiences are common in the preschool and early elementary school years.

The three bird experts and the 20 college student controls were asked to sort pictures of birds into piles of birds they thought belonged together. They were told that they were free to decide how many piles were most appropriate. After they completed their sorts, they were asked to explain their groupings. The picture set contained 47 pictures selected from the Audible Audubon set, drawn by various bird artists. Examples of the types of bird drawings used are presented in Figure 5.1. The groups of birds that made up the picture set were selected from different bird orders. They included nine groups of birds: herons, birds of prey, waterfowl, chicken-like birds, shore birds, woodpeckers, and three families of perching birds (crows and jays, thrushes, blackbirds and related birds). Table 5.1 presents the complete listing within each grouping. Performance was judged in terms of overlap with the formal groupings.

Twenty Questions Task

In contrast to the picture-sorting task, the twenty questions task does not provide any concrete support and in fact requires some general-purpose strategic knowledge that children do not acquire early. The best approach to this task is to start with general (superordinate) questions that help

FIGURE 5.1. Sample bird drawings depicting the types of drawings that were sorted by participants.

TABLE 5.1. Bird Groupings Used in the Picture-Sorting Task

1. Herons and Flamingos (order: Ciconiiformes)	4. Chicken-like birds (order: Galliformes)	7. Orioles, grackles, and blackbirds (order: Passeriformes) (family: Emberizidae)
Great egret	California quail	Yellow-headed blackbird
Great blue heron	Bobwhite	Northern oriole
Little blue heron	Ruffed grouse	Eastern meadowlark
Snowy egret	Ring-necked pheasant	Red-winged blackbird
Black-crowned heron		Brown-headed cowbird
Green heron	5. Waders, gulls, and auks (order: Charedriiformes)	Common grackle
2. Hawks and Falcons (order: Falconiformes)	Spotted sandpiper	8. Thrushes (order: Passeriformes) (family: Muscicapidae)
	Marbled godwit	
Bald eagle	Common snipe	Wood thrush
Red-shouldered hawk	Herring gull	Hermit thrush
Northern harrier	Laughing gull	Robin
American kestrel	Common tern	Eastern bluebird
Sharp-shinned hawk		Swainson's thrush
Red-tailed hawk	6. Woodpeckers (order: Piciformes)	Veery
3. Waterfowl (order: Anseriformes)	Yellow-shafted flicker	9. Crows and jays (order: Passeriformes) (family: Coruidae)
	Red-bellied woodpecker	
Canada goose	Red-headed woodpecker	Scrub jay
Mallard	Downy woodpecker	Steller's jay
Pintail	Yellow-bellied sapsucker	Blue jay
Black duck		Common crow

divide the domain of possible birds, and then progress toward more specific questions as the pool of possibilities decreases. As Mosher and Hornsby (1966) and Siegler (1977) noted in their developmental studies on asking questions, it is not until approximately 11–14 years of age that children fully grasp the importance of successively narrowing the range of questions in order to zero in on the answer. Our 9-year old expert had not yet entered that age range, whereas the adult experts should be familiar with the twenty questions' optimal strategy.

In this task, our bird experts and a new group of 20 college student controls were asked to guess what bird the experimenter was thinking about. For the bird experts, the game was played 20 times with an assortment of different birds. Birds that were selected were all commonplace birds (e.g., Canada goose, starling, osprey, bluebird). For the adult controls, each participant was tested only five times, and the questions asked were limited to 15 because of the difficulty in generating questions with so little bird knowledge. All participants were given as much time as needed to generate questions and the experimenter only responded with a "yes" or a "no." Overall performance was assessed in terms of number of birds successfully identified. Use of a superordinate–subordinate "narrowing" strategy was evaluated from the list of questions participants asked for each bird presented.

Key Findings

Factual Information Task

All of our experts had each question read to them and then responded with their answer. Their answers were scored as correct or not, with partial credit given for questions that contained more than one component, for example, "What are the two colors of the male cowbird." The child bird expert and the adult bird expert with similar birding experience correctly answered 51% and 46% of the questions, respectively. An examination of the questions that they answered correctly indicated that the child and adult expert agreed (both correct or both in error) on 71% of the questions, indicating significant overlap between their two knowledge bases. Not surprisingly, the adult expert with greater birding experience answered 71% correct. That proportion was significantly higher than that of the less experienced, better educated expert, $z = 5.85$, $p < .001$, and the child expert, $z = 4.72$, $p < .001$. Twenty college student controls did significantly worse, drawing a blank or answering most of the questions incorrectly. Their mean percent correct was 15%, with a range from 13% to 20%. All three experts did significantly better than the controls, z-tests, $p < .001$.

Picture Sorting

Two different approaches were used to assess how well the different experts sorted the pictures from the nine bird groupings that had been used to select the 47 pictures. One approach focused on whether the nine groupings remained intact in the individual's sort even if they might be grouped with an additional bird or partial set of birds from another grouping. The second approach focused on the homogeneity of the piles instead of the bird groupings per se. These two types of measures were needed because the instructions were open-ended and allowed individuals to construct as many or as few piles of bird pictures as they wanted.

All of the experts did very well in this task, although performance fell short of perfect for the child expert and the adult expert with comparable knowledge. Examining first the intactness of the bird groupings, the child expert maintained the completeness of six of the nine groupings (67%) in his sort (herons, woodpeckers, birds of prey, ducks and geese, waders, gulls, and auks, oriole group). The remaining three groups (thrushes, jays and crows, and chicken-like birds) were dispersed across more than 1 pile. With regard to the homogeneity of the groupings, our child expert produced 6 piles, 3 of which (50%) were both homogeneous ("pure") and complete. Examining next the well-educated adult expert's sort, we once again have six complete bird groupings (67%), with the three remaining groupings dispersed across different piles (thrushes, jays and crows, waders, gulls, and auks). With regard to the homogeneity of the groupings, the adult expert had 4 piles that were both homogeneous and complete out of his 10 piles (40%).

In contrast, the more knowledgeable adult expert produced a close to perfect sort with eight of the nine bird groupings in complete and homogenous piles (89%). The one group that was divided into two piles, the "waders, gulls, auks" group, was divided into two coherent groupings of shore birds and gulls and terns, producing arguably a perfect sort. The more knowledgeable expert also made no mistakes among the three families from the order of *Passeriformes*, whereas both the child expert and the less knowledgeable adult expert had difficulties with these families. Although all three experts did well, the more knowledgeable adult expert did the best among the three. Bird knowledge appears to be the key factor in this task, more significant than age or educational level.

Finally, the adult controls (N = 20) provide an interesting counterpoint to the exceptional performance of our experts. With little bird knowledge to guide them, they relied on apparent differences in physical features (e.g., length of beak, legs) or environment-type considerations (e.g., whether the birds were on a beach or in the trees in the picture). The number of piles ranged from 3 to 27 with a mean of 8.3 piles, standard deviation (SD) = 5.47. In terms of maintaining the intactness of the nine bird groupings, the controls averaged 30% of the bird groups intact. A closer examination, however, indicates that two-thirds of the controls (14 of 20) had three or less of the nine bird groups intact (0%–30%), far less than the 67%–87% of the bird experts. The difference between experts and naïve participants is even more striking when we look for piles that are both complete and homogeneous among the control sorts. The controls averaged 4% with a range of zero to 20%. Thirteen of the 20 controls did not even have a single pile of bird pictures that represented an intact bird grouping.

Twenty Questions

All participants, including the bird experts and controls, asked yes–no questions until they guessed the bird correctly or ran out of questions. Performance was measured both in terms of how many birds (out of 20) were identified correctly and how many questions were required before correct identification. All verbalizations during the task were recorded and transcribed. The order and types of questions (e.g., general or specific) were then examined for evidence of a "narrowing" strategy.

The child bird expert correctly identified 11 of the 20 birds (55%) and averaged 14.6 questions, SD = 6.15, with a range from 4 to 20 questions. In contrast, the adult expert with comparable knowledge identified all 20 birds (100%), averaging 9.7 questions, SD = 4.5, with a range from 4 to 20 questions as well. A t-test comparison of the number of questions used by the child and the adult expert during the twenty questions game produced a significant result, $t(38)$ = 2.88, $p < .01$, two-tailed test, reflecting the different success rates between the two. The more knowledgeable, less educated adult bird expert correctly identified only 15 of the 20 birds (75%) compared to the 100% correct performance of the less knowledgeable, but better educated adult expert. Across the 20 times she played the game, she averaged 12.9 questions, SD = 5.6, with a range from 5 to 20 questions. A t-test comparison of the number of questions used by both adult experts during the twenty questions game produced a significant result, $t(38)$ = 1.98, $p < .05$, two-tailed test. The better educated expert appeared better equipped for the cognitive demands of this task even if he had less bird knowledge and birding experience.

Tables 5.2, 5.3, and 5.4 present several examples from both the child and the adult experts' questioning for bird information. All of the experts' protocols were examined for relative use of general versus specific questions and for the strategic value of the questions. We begin with the less knowledgeable, better educated adult expert's protocols because of his 100% success rate and the greater likelihood that he used more sys-

TABLE 5.2. Adult Expert (Better Educated, Less Bird Knowledge) Twenty Questions—Sample Protocols (100% Correct)

Bird—Canada Goose		Bird—Mourning Dove	
1. Is it a perching bird?	N	1. Is it a perching bird?	N
2. Is it a shore bird or a water bird?	Y	2. Is it bigger than a mockingbird?	Y
3. Is it a duck?	N	3. Is it all one color?	Y
4. Is it a goose?	Y	4. Is it an eastern bird?	Y
5. Is it a North American bird?	Y	5. Does it eat insects?	N
6. Is it a Brant?	N	6. Does it feed on the ground?	Y
7. A Canada?	YES!	7. Is it a dove?	Y
		8. Is it a mourning dove?	YES!

tematic questioning. A number of things are immediately apparent in his performance (see Table 5.2). The questioning format he adopted across the 20 times he played the game was very similar, beginning with exactly the same question for all 20 times, "Is the bird a perching bird?" (Order: *Passeriformes*). Because this order is so large and represents essentially half of living birds, it is the most efficient way to start the questioning. If the answer to this question was "no," this expert then proceeded to ask whether the bird was a shore bird, or a water bird, continuing with questions about whether it was a predatory bird, or perhaps a chicken-like bird, or a woodpecker, and so on. Once our less knowledgeable, better educated adult expert had zeroed in on a particular bird group, he would further narrow down his options with both additional category-type questions and attribute-type questions (color, size, eating habits). Toward the end this adult expert would ask specific questions, "Is it an *X*?" where *X* is a specific bird. In sum, his questioning format appeared to follow a "narrowing" strategy, similar to that first described by Mosher and Hornsby (1966) in their developmental study of questioning strategies with the twenty questions game. In order to confirm this impression, two independent raters evaluated each of 19 question protocols (one taped protocol was unclear and couldn't be evaluated) for significant evidence of the narrowing strategy. Eighteen of the 19 were rated as essentially perfect or close to perfect narrowing formats.

Moving on to the child expert's questioning pattern, we found that he was not generally systematic in producing general, superordinate questions followed by more specific questions. Although he succeeded in identifying 11 of the 20 birds, only five of his questioning protocols were judged as using an essentially perfect or close to perfect narrowing strategy. Table 5.3 includes examples of both a success (Canada

TABLE 5.3. Child Expert Twenty Questions—Sample Protocols (55% Correct Out of 20 Birds)

Bird—Canada Goose		Bird—Mourning Dove			
1. Is it a bird of prey?	N	1. Is it a bird of prey?	N	8. Do I see it every day?	Y
2. Is it small?	N	2. Is it a songbird?	N	9. Is it a starling?	N
3. Is it a blue jay?	N	3. Is it a meat eater? like worms or carrion?	N	10. Grackle?	N
4. Is it big?	Y	4. Is it a seed eater?	Y	11. Little black bird?	N
5. Is it a goose?	Y	5. Is it a goldfinch?	N	12. Cardinal?	N
6. Is it a Canada goose?	YES!	6. Is it in the jay family?	N	13. Is it any color other than white?	Y
		7. Is it a crow?	N	14. Is it a water bird? etc.	N
				Never guesses bird!	

goose) and a failure (mourning dove) in which the child expert did not use a narrowing strategy. The child expert often began with some fairly general questions (Is it a bird of prey? Is it a water bird? Is it a songbird?) that could give him a good start toward a narrowing strategy, but the child was not systematic in building upon those initial questions unless he received a "yes" on his queries about whether the bird was a member of these groups. The difference in the number of protocols that followed a narrowing strategy between the better educated adult and the child expert was in fact significant (18/19 vs. 5/20, $z = 4.43$, $p < .001$).

More intriguing was the approach of our more knowledgeable, but less educated adult expert. Table 5.4 presents examples that reflect the pattern of questions that dominated her protocols. She used almost all attribute-type questions, interspersed with questions about specific birds, and rarely used the type of narrowing strategy that dominated the other adult expert's protocols. She also tended to use questions that if answered "yes" would likely lead to a correct guess (e.g., "Does it have a crest?" or "Does it have an eye ring?"), but would provide very little useful information if the answer was "no." When two independent raters evaluated this expert's twenty question protocols for significant evidence of a narrowing strategy, only 7 of the 20 protocols were judged to reflect a systematic and strategic use of general and specific questions. When compared with the 18 out of 19 rate of the less experienced, better educated adult expert, the use of a narrowing strategy significantly differed between the two adult experts, $z = 3.88$, $p < .001$.

Finally, we examined the protocols from the 20 college controls that

TABLE 5.4. Adult Expert (Greater Bird Knowledge, Less Educated) Twenty Questions—Sample Protocols (75% Correct Out of 20 Birds)

Bird—Canada Goose		Bird—Mourning Dove			
1. Is it larger than a crow?	Y	1. Is it bigger than a crow?	N	9. Does it nest in the East Coast?	Y
2. Would you see it on the coast?	Y	2. Is it bigger than a robin?	Y	10. Does it build a distinctive nest?	Y
3. Is it a raptor?	N	3. Is it a perching bird?	N	11. Does it nest on the ground?	N
4. Is it confined to the water?	N	4. Would it be a shore bird?	N	12. Does it build a large nest?	N
5. Does it have a musical song?	N	5. Is it a duck?	N	13. Is it a very colorful bird?	N
6. Is it a turkey?	N	6. Is it a quail?	N	14. Does it have a large bill?	N
7. Is it a goose.	Y	7. Is it mostly black?	N	etc.	
8. Is it a Canada goose?	YES!	8. Is it a bird that I'd find on the grass?	Y	Never guesses bird!	

attempted this task. The students only successfully guessed 9% of the birds that were presented. Because they had little bird knowledge they could not use bird groupings to help themselves. Instead, they tried to use color, size, location, and even what letter the bird name started with to help themselves. Not surprisingly, they showed little superordinate ordering of questions and often forgot information obtained in earlier questions. Here are some questions from one of the control protocols (Canada goose): Does the bird fly? Is it red? Is it located in North America? Do they fly south? Is it a small bird? Is it a large bird? Is it gray? Is it an eagle? Is it a sparrow? Do people keep them as pets?, and the like. Even when a college student zeroed in on the appropriate bird grouping, he or she was unable to continue, for example, after learning that the bird in question was a hawk, one control guessed "Is it an eagle?" and then commented "That's not a hawk, I don't think I can name any hawks."

Self-Monitoring Skills

The two different cognitive tasks given to our experts varied in the degree of support they provided for implementing an appropriate strategy for successful completion. Consequently, we examined their comments during the tasks to see whether the more challenging cognitive task prompted more self-awareness of strategy use among our experts. Starting with the picture-sorting task, all of the experts had an opportunity to describe their picture sort after they completed the task, explaining why they placed different birds in different piles. Even though the child expert performed quite well, he had very little to say beyond the recognition of the different bird groupings. As he pointed to one, and then to another pile of bird pictures, he simply labeled them as "herons, egrets," "woodpeckers," "hawks, birds of prey," and so on. In contrast, both adult experts provided detailed explanations of their thinking behind their picture sorts. The well-educated, less knowledgeable expert seemed very much aware of the decision-making necessary to decide whether some pictures should be grouped together or not—for example, "The next one is ducks and geese. There's only one goose so I didn't make a pile of it. So, ducks and geese are similar enough that they can stay together," or "The next one is herons. Six kinds of herons. I didn't sort them into white ones and colored ones, which apparently someone might have." The more knowledgeable adult expert also showed similar levels of self-monitoring. For example, she noted the subgroupings within the "birds of prey" group before deciding to keep them together as birds of prey: "If you want to call these all birds of prey, you could, but I separate it into eagle, buteos, accipiters, falcon." Another time, for her "shore bird" pile, she stated "These are shore birds but you could separate it into godwits, sandpipers, and wood godwits."

These differences in explanation suggest that the adult experts were engaging in significantly more self-monitoring of their decision making. Although the child expert might have provided more explanation if prompted further, the information was not offered, and certainly not with the detail that the adult experts spontaneously provided. Furthermore, these differences in spontaneous explanations suggest that self-monitoring in the picture-sorting task was not tied to the amount of knowledge per se. Instead, age seemed to be the key factor. That conclusion is also supported by the high level of self-monitoring that is seen in the mostly "clueless" explanations offered by the adult controls. For example, one control stated, "Generally, I took them and I separated them as land-dwelling, water, ones that are around the water, ones that are primarily flying around in the air, like a predator would. Then I took the most common birds that I knew and I went to this pile here, which was ducks, primarily geese," and so on. Another stated, "These first three, they look mean, and they look like they hang around in groups. These also hang out in groups, according to the pictures, but they are more beautiful. These also hang out in groups, but they all seem alike. They have long claws, short beaks," and so on. We could continue with the control commentaries, but what is striking in these examples is that the controls are very much aware of their categorization efforts and can articulate their criteria although the features selected often seemed ridiculous from a bird knowledge point of view.

Moving on to the twenty questions task, we identified three types of self-monitoring statements: (1) spontaneous clarifications of questions before the experimenter could respond with a "yes" or "no" to the question, (2) repetition of already acquired information before generating a new question, and (3) statements that reflect an awareness of difficulties with the task. Table 5.5 presents examples of these statements from all three experts. The well-educated adult bird expert had the least difficulty with the task, showing confidence in his narrowing strategy for identifying the birds. At no point did he suggest he was having serious difficulties. Perhaps not surprisingly, he produced the least number of self-monitoring statements in this task.

Of greater interest is whether the child expert and the less educated, more knowledgeable adult expert showed higher rates of self-monitor-

TABLE 5.5. Examples of Self-Monitoring during Twenty Questions (Child and Adult Experts)

Spontaneous clarifications

Child expert ($N = 9$):
  "Is it black? Mainly black."
  "Does it make a bucket nest, like an oriole nest?"

Well-educated expert ($N = 5$):
  "Is it more than one color, don't get technical, if you saw it from 10 feet?"

More knowledgeable, less educated expert ($N = 12$):
  "Does it have long legs, say longer than a crow's legs?"
  "Is it yellow? Partially? I mean does it have some yellow?"

Systematic repetition of acquired information

Child expert ($N = 7$):
  "I've got one guess, its got a little bit of red, black, lives in the eastern United States, doesn't live in marshes, bigger than a starling, smaller than a crow."

Well-educated expert ($N = 4$):
  "not a song bird, not a rapter, not a chicken-like bird"

More knowledgeable, less educated expert ($N = 12$):
  "It's not brightly colored, it's larger than a robin, doesn't have a crest."

Awareness of task difficulty

Child expert ($N = 4$):
  "There is nothing else. I'm never going to get this."
  "What other kinds of birds are there?"

Well-educated expert:
  None

More knowledgeable, less educated expert ($N = 37$):
  "Um, I'm not thinking very well today."
  "My trouble is that I forget the questions I've asked."
  "I forgot, we said it was bigger than a robin, or smaller?"

ing as they encountered difficulty with this task. The child expert produced approximately twice the number of clarifications and repetitions of acquired information than the well-educated adult expert. He also made spontaneous comments reflecting his uneven progress—for example, "There is nothing else. I'm never going to get this." Although the child expert showed little self-monitoring during the picture-sorting task, some self-monitoring did seem to kick in when the problem-solving task became cognitively demanding.

So where does our less well-educated, more knowledgeable adult expert stand with respect to self-monitoring in the twenty questions task? She did make spontaneous clarifications to the experimenter, and she repeated acquired information, as did the other experts, but at a slightly higher rate. However, the most dramatic difference concerned the third type of self-monitoring, spontaneous evaluations of progress and a recognition of her own difficulties with the task. Once again, the better educated, less experienced adult expert produced no such verbalizations whereas the child expert produced four such statements. Our more knowledgeable, less well educated expert in fact produced 37 comments that could be grouped into this category. They are particularly instructive because they demonstrate that our more knowledgeable adult expert is aware of her level of expertise (among the best birders in the local Aubodon Society group) and recognizes that she is having difficulty with this task in spite of her expertise.

Much of her difficulties arise from failing to consistently adopt a narrowing strategy across the 20 opportunities to play twenty questions. Instead, she seems to adopt a strategy that is closely tied to the way she uses her knowledge in the real world, that is, how to identify a bird in the field. Questions of size and distinctive features, colors, bird song or call, and the like are very important in effective field identification. As noted earlier, her preference for questions about distinct characteristics worked well if she received a "yes" response from the experimenter, but provided little information if the response was "no." It appears that our more knowledgeable, more experienced bird expert approached the twenty questions task by generating a possible bird after obtaining some information and then tried to "nail down" her guess. Comments such as "I have a bird in mind" and "I didn't think you'd say yes" support that interpretation. Overall, the more knowledgeable, less well-educated expert had a high level of self-awareness of her progress and her approach to the task. But high levels of metacognitive awareness along with extensive bird knowledge did not lead to systematic use of the best (narrowing) strategy for the task in this case. Without experience with this type of task, our more knowledgeable bird expert could not come up with an appropriate strategy for twenty questions.

EFFECTIVE KNOWLEDGE UTILIZATION
AND EDUCATIONAL IMPLICATIONS

Since the early days of studies on expertise, developmental psychologists have come to realize that the interplay between knowledge and strategy use is more complex than that of a simple, direct link (Sternberg, 1989; Crowley, Shrager, & Siegler, 1997, Kuhn, 1996). In the current study of knowledge utilization, we explored the interplay between task demands, age, education, and degree of expertise. Knowledge per se does facilitate problem-solving performance. The comparison between our bird experts and the adult controls makes that clear. But we would argue that effective knowledge utilization is constrained by developmental level, education, and broad experience with different task demands.

With regard to developmental level, a child expert is more likely to have a smaller repertoire of available general purpose strategies than an older expert with comparable knowledge. In part this is due to less experience with a broad range of task demands and less effective self-monitoring during problem solving (i.e., less reflection on what works and what doesn't work). For example, the child bird expert in the current study was less adept in dealing with the more cognitively demanding task of twenty questions when compared to the adult expert with comparable knowledge. Knowledge did increase the likelihood that the child expert would succeed in guessing the bird in question (compared to a nonexpert). In addition, he could use a narrowing strategy if his early success in questioning guided him toward that strategy. But the child expert lacked the systematic and deliberate use of a narrowing strategy that took full advantage of the bird knowledge that he in fact had available.

Perhaps more striking is the constraint that education and experience with varying knowledge use can place on performance. The less well educated adult expert was significantly more knowledgeable than the better educated adult expert (75% vs. 48% correct on the bird Trivial Pursuit questions) and had many more birding years "under her belt." But when it came to the more demanding task, the twenty questions task, the key strategy eluded her. Although she used the narrowing strategy on some of the trials, as did the child expert, she did not recognize the strategy. Based on her own evaluation, there had to be a strategy for generating questions efficiently, but she repeatedly commented that she didn't know what it was. And she was genuinely surprised at her difficulties because, according to her own naïve theory, her extensive bird knowledge should produce a simple and direct link to successful performance.

A closer examination of the interplay between knowledge, age, education, and task demands gives us some indications about how effective strategy use can be prompted in individuals with prerequisite knowledge.

Figure 5.2 presents our view of the key factors that contribute to effective knowledge utilization and recommendations of how we might promote effective knowledge use in the classroom.

Multiple Organizations

Not too long ago, Mannes and Kintsch (1987) explored the advantages of a richly structured knowledge base for science text processing, for both subsequent memory and problem-solving assessments. Their experiments produced an interesting contrast. Providing an outline that matched the organization of the science text to be read enhanced memory performance, but providing an alternative framework for organizing the content in the science text before reading enhanced problem solving. Multiple organizations were an advantage for "learning from text" rather than remembering content per se. Mannes and Kintsch (1987) argued that by "forcing" students to structure information in multiple ways you can prompt deeper, more variable processing and produce a larger number of interknowledge connections. This in turn enhances effective problem solving. More recent studies make a similar point by demonstrating that less coherent texts prompt more active processing and inference making that produce multiple ties to prior knowledge and easy access to knowledge when needed (McNamera, Kintsch, Songer, & Kintsch, 1996; McNamera, 2001).

If that's the rule, then our more knowledgeable expert may have been hampered by her extensive but repetitive use of bird knowledge in the field. Her lack of a more broad-based understanding of how to use knowledge to meet a range of task demands seemed to be her primary problem. Without varied experience in knowledge use, there may have been limited opportunities to construct a richer, more interconnected knowledge base that could be used for flexible and effective problem solving. In contrast, our other adult expert was very well educated, and may have acquired along the way an appreciation of multiple ways of organizing knowledge for adaptive problem solving in the real world. An intriguing question is whether we could encourage more flexible use of knowledge by varying the ways in which information is presented in textbooks and classroom activities. Positive results would have important implications for how we teach in the classroom, particularly in the science classroom.

Self-Monitoring

Researchers have already noted that metacognitive awareness can set the stage for strategy discovery, although it may not be the only factor

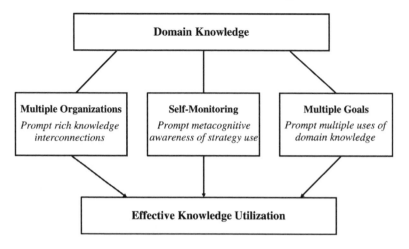

FIGURE 5.2. Building blocks of effective knowledge utilization.

(Crowley et al., 1997; Pressley, 1995). The child expert in the current study showed a particularly interesting pattern of self-monitoring across the different tasks. He seemed less aware of his decision making in the picture-sorting task compared with the two adult experts. But then he really didn't need to engage in high-level self-monitoring in that task. The pictures of the different birds prompted recognition of the familiar bird groupings since he already had the prerequisite knowledge. The twenty questions task was a different situation. The cognitive demands of that task required self-monitoring from all of the participants in order to generate questions. Consequently, we could argue that the child expert might be on the verge of an "Aha! experience" in that situation. After all, he did use the key narrowing strategy on a number of the twenty questions trials.

Perhaps the experimenter could have prompted a link between strategy use and performance in the mind of the child expert. That didn't take place in this study, but the literature on strategy discovery has examples of exactly that process. For example, Siegler and Jenkins (1989) prompted the consistent use of the "min" strategy for addition problems in young children by presenting them challenge problems (20 + 2) after they had shown some use of the "min" strategy (counting up from the larger number, minimizing the number of steps to the answer). The more demanding "challenge" addition problems had the desired effect by prompting recognition of the more efficient "min" strategy. In the area of reading comprehension, Pressley (1998) and others have been strong advocates of comprehension-monitoring training in which strategy use is explicitly modeled by the teacher and then consciously implemented by younger readers. Numerous studies have demonstrated the success of this approach which emphasizes metacognitive awareness of strategy use. Students not only recognize the use of the strategy in the experimental sessions but show broad-based application of comprehension-monitoring strategies in ordinary academic settings (Palincsar & Brown, 1984; Brown, Pressley, Van Meter, & Schuder, 1996). Greater efforts to prompt recognition of links between strategy use and successful problem solving should enhance more effective knowledge utilization in our students.

Multiple Goals

The results of the current study have demonstrated that knowledge plus metacognitive awareness is not the complete story. Our more knowledgeable, but less well educated adult expert had both extensive birding knowledge and engaged in extensive self-monitoring in the twenty questions task. She monitored her question selections, noticing that they were not necessarily helping her, as well as repeatedly commenting on the apparent difficulty of the task. This was combined with her expressed unhappiness in her overall level of performance, missing birds that are commonplace and for which she had a great deal of familiarity. In fact, her performance was quite good, with 15 of the 20 birds in the task being correctly identified. But she struggled every step of the way, and had a very strong sense that there was a way to do this task, but she didn't know what it was. "Why not?"

At this point we can only suggest an answer. But if we examine the questioning patterns of our more experienced, less well educated adult expert, we can identify a questioning strategy closely tied to the way in which she uses her bird knowledge in her everyday birding activities. When you are out in the field and see a bird, you first note some basic physical characteristics: How big it is, does it have distinctive physical features, does it have a distinctive call or song? That information plus context information can help you zero in on identifying the bird in question. Bird watchers can use this strategy effectively to succeed in bird identification in the field. But one must use bird knowledge in a different way in order to narrow down the possible birds that the experimenter is thinking about in the twenty questions task. Our more knowledgeable expert couldn't "break set" and continued to use a strategy that works well out in field but is not well suited for twenty questions.

Thus, greater birding experience constrained our more knowledgeable expert from using her knowledge flexibly and adaptively. In part, this may have been due to the fact that she used her bird knowledge in a redundant way, over and over again, out in the field. Perhaps if she had more versatile use of her knowledge, she would have shown more flexibility in response to the task demands of the twenty questions task. It may be that one of the outcomes of greater education is an understanding of how to adapt knowledge to task demands, or at least it can be. Future research in how multiple goals impact knowledge utilization is imperative.

REFERENCES

Brown, R., Pressley, M., Van Meter, P., & Schuder, T. (1996). A quasi-experimental validation of transactional strategies instruction with low-achieving second-grade readers. *Journal of Educational Psychology, 88*, 18–37.

Carey, S. (1985). *Conceptual change in childhood*. Cambridge, MA: MIT Press.

Ceci, S. J. (1989). On domain specificity … more or less general and specific constraints on cognitive development. *Merrill–Palmer Quarterly, 35*, 131–142.

Chi, M. T. H. (1978). Knowledge structures and memory development. In R. S. Siegler (Ed.), *Children's thinking: What develops?* (pp. 73–96). Hillsdale, NJ: Erlbaum.

Chi, M. T. H. (2006). Two approaches to the study of experts' characteristics. In K. A. Ericsson, N. Charness, P. J. Feltovich, & R. R. Hoffman (Eds.), *The Cambridge handbook of expertise and expert performance* (pp. 21–30). New York: Cambridge University Press.

Chi, M. T. H., Glaser, R., & Farr, M. J. (Eds.). (1988). *The nature of expertise.* Hillsdale, NJ: Erlbaum.

Chi, M. T. H., Hutchinson, J. E., & Robin, A. F. (1989). How inferences about novel domain-related concepts can be constrained by structured knowledge. *Merrill–Palmer Quarterly, 35*, 27–62.

Chi, M. T. H., & Koeske, R. D. (1983). Network representations of a child's dinosaur knowledge. *Developmental Psychology, 19*, 29–39.

Crowley, K., Shrager, J., & Siegler, R. S. (1997). Strategy discovery as a competitive negotiation between metacognitive and associative mechanisms. *Developmental Review, 17*, 462–489.

Ericsson, K. A. (Ed.). (1996). *The road to excellence: The acquisition of expert performance in the arts and sciences, sports, and games.* Mahwah, NJ: Erlbaum.

Ericsson, K. A., Charness, N., Feltovich, P. J., & Hoffman, R. R. (Eds.). (2006). *The Cambridge handbook of expertise and expert performance.* Cambridge, UK: Cambridge University Press.

Ericsson, K. A., & Lehmann, A. C. (1996). Expert and exceptional performance: Evidence on maximal adaptations on task constraints. *Annual Review of Psychology, 47*, 273–305.

Flavell, J. H. (1982). On cognitive development. *Child Development, 53*, 1–10.

Johnson, K. E., & Eilers, A. T. (1998). Effects of knowledge and development on superordinate level categorization. *Cognitive Development, 13*, 515–546.

Keil, F. C. (1981). Constraints on knowledge and cognitive development. *Psychological Review, 88*, 197–227.

Kuhn, D. (1996). Is good thinking scientific thinking? In D. Olson & N. Tor-rance (Eds.), *Modes of thought: Explorations in culture and cognition* (pp. 261–281). Cambridge, UK: Cambridge University Press.

Kuhn, D. (2000). Does memory development belong on an endangered topic list? *Child Development, 71,* 21–25.

Kuhn, D., Garcia-Mila, M., Zohar, A., & Andersen, C. (1995). Strategies of knowledge acquisition. *Monographs of the Society for Research in Child Development, 60*(4, Serial No. 245).

Kuhn, D., & Pearsall, S. (2000). Developmental origins of scientific thinking. *Journal of Cognition and Development, 1,* 113–129.

Mannes, S., & Kintsch, W. (1987). Knowledge organization and text organiza-tion. *Cognition and Instruction, 4,* 91–115.

McNamara, D. S. (2001). Reading both high-coherence and low-coherence texts: Effects of text sequence and prior knowledge. *Canadian Journal of Experi-mental Psychology, 55,* 51–62.

McNamara, D. S., Kintsch, E., Songer, N. B., & Kintsch, W. (1996). Are good texts always better? Interactions of text coherence, background knowledge, and levels of understanding in learning from text. *Cognition and Instruction, 14,* 1–43.

Mosher, F. A., & Hornsby, J. R. (1966). On asking questions. In J. S. Bruner, R. R. Olver, & R. M. Greenfield (Eds.), *Studies in cognitive growth* (pp. 86–103). New York: Wiley.

Palincsar, A. S., & Brown, A. L. (1984). Reciprocal teaching of comprehension-fostering and monitoring activities. *Cognition and Instruction, 1,* 117–175.

Pressley, M. (1995). What is intellectual development about in the 1990's?: Good information processing. In F. Weinert & W. Schneider (Eds.), *Memory per-formance and competencies: Issues in growth and development* (pp. 375–404). Hillsdale, NJ: Erlbaum.

Pressley, M. (1998). Comprehension strategies instruction. In J. Osborn & F. Lehr (Eds.), *Literacy for all: Issues in teaching and learning* (pp. 113–133). New York: Guilford Press.

Roberts, M. J. (Ed.). (2007). *Integrating the mind: Domain general versus domain specific processes in higher cognition.* New York: Psychology Press.

Schauble, L. (1996). The development of scientific reasoning in knowledge-rich contexts. *Developmental Psychology, 32,* 102–119.

Siegler, R. S. (1977). The twenty questions game as a form of problem solving. *Child Development, 42,* 395–403.

Siegler, R. S., & Alibali, M. W. (2005). *Children's thinking* (4th ed.). Upper Sad-dle River, NJ: Prentice-Hall.

Siegler, R. S., & Jenkins, E. (1989). *How children discover new strategies.* Hills-dale, NJ: Erlbaum.

Sternberg, R. J. (1989). Domain-generality versus domain-specificity: The life and impending death of a false dichotomy. *Merrill–Palmer Quarterly, 35,* 115–130.

Sternberg, R. J., & Grigorenko, E. L. (Eds.). (2003). *Perspectives on the psychol-ogy of abilities, competencies, and expertise.* Cambridge, UK: Cambridge University Press.

6

The Dual Components of Developing Strategy Use

Production and Inhibition

Deanna Kuhn
Maria Pease

Contemporary researchers who study the development of cognitive strategies address a distinctly different set of issues than did those who approached the topic in its infancy in the 1970s. The evolution in study of this topic can be traced from early assumptions that the capacity to behave strategically did not develop until later in childhood to the contemporary recognition that even infants can be strategic. Moreover, the study of strategy development has become much more complex. Rarely do we see over time a simple transition from the application of one kind of strategy to a problem to the application of a new, different strategy. Instead, it is now clear, individuals have a repertory of strategies they bring to a new situation, some more adequate or advanced than others. The task of microgenetic analysis over time, in a context of repeated encounters with the problem, is thus to examine the nature of strategy *selection*, which itself evolves over time (Kuhn & Phelps, 1982; Kuhn, 1995, 2001; Siegler, 2006). The now well-replicated finding is that more advanced modes become more frequent and less advanced ones less frequent, although in an uneven and not entirely predictable way. The period of time in which a mixture of more and less advanced strategies are applied variably may be prolonged.

The implication is that strategy development involves much more than learning to execute a strategy. For the evolution just described to take place, two distinct challenges must be met: The less advanced (and likely more habitual) mode of response must be repeatedly inhibited and the more advanced (and initially weaker) mode of response must be consolidated and strengthened. The question we examine here is this: During the often extended periods of transition observed in microgenetic studies, how are these two challenges related to one another?

Two possibilities seem viable. One is that the two are inversely related, that is, occurrence of the advanced response mode in a given instance makes occurrence of the less advanced mode less likely (the context being one in which exhibiting one does not preclude also exhibiting the other). The other possibility is that the two challenges are met independently— in other words, advanced responses must be executed and less advanced ones must be inhibited, but the one occurrence has no influence on the other one. Whichever of these possibilities is correct, there are two distinct tasks to be accomplished, each with its own set of challenges, if change is to occur. One is increased selection and execution of the better strategy. The other is stronger inhibitory control of the inferior strategy.

These are the two components of strategy development, and their connection to one another, that we examine in the research described in this chapter. Doing so requires us to address all of the themes of this volume. Metacognition, we claim, is central to strategy selection. And the instructional implications of our topic are significant. How are the multiple challenges of strategy development met in instructional contexts? And how are these developmental challenges best supported?

THE PROBLEM CONTEXT: UTILIZING STRATEGIES OF INVESTIGATION AND INFERENCE IN INQUIRY

The problem context in which we examine these questions is the complex, multifaceted one of scientific inquiry, although we focus on the inference phase of the inquiry process, thus also situating the task in the research literature on inductive multivariable causal inference (Kuhn & Dean, 2004). In self-directed scientific inquiry (see Lehrer & Schauble, 2006, or Zimmerman, 2007, for review of studies), the individual has access to a database and is asked to plan and execute an investigation and to draw and justify inferences regarding the relations among variables depicted in the database. Typically, multiple potential independent variables may influence a dependent variable, and the task is to examine the database and make inferences regarding which of the variables bear a causal relation to the outcome and which do not.

Here we focus on the conclusions individuals draw on the basis of their investigation, as these constitute the culmination of the inquiry process. We divide them into the two broad categories of valid judgments and invalid judgments (Schauble, 1990; Kuhn, Schauble, & Garcia-Mila, 1992; Kuhn, Garcia-Mila, Zohar, & Andersen, 1995). *Valid judgments* are judgments the individual draws on available evidence to justify, in a manner adequate to support the judgment. (Specific examples are presented later.) *Invalid judgments* are those lacking justification adequate to support them. Valid judgments (that a variable is causal or noncausal) are therefore always correct, whereas invalid judgments may be incorrect or correct (regarding the variable's true causal status). In the multivariable causal context described, a valid judgment requires the individual to have accessed from the database and compared at least two instances that differ with respect to only a single variable (what has come to be known as a *control-of-variables* strategy), allowing an inference to be made regarding how variation in that variable affects outcome. The strategy application that leads to a valid judgment therefore requires intention and planning, to identify appropriate instances to compare to one another, to secure them from the database while withholding any inferential judgment, and then to analyze the pattern of outcomes as the basis for making a judgment of causality (that the focal variable makes a difference) or noncausality (that it does not).

An invalid causal (or noncausal) judgment, in contrast, can be made quickly and intuitively, by observing no more than a single instance and outcome. When justification for such a judgment is solicited, the most common one is co-occurrence (or association): Because a particular level of a variable was present when the outcome occurred, that variable is implicated as having played a role in the outcome. Occasionally, an invalid judgment may make reference to a previous instance in which both variable and outcome were absent, but no comparative analysis is undertaken across instances (especially one that would identify uncontrolled variables). The most common type of invalid judgment, however, is one that ignores the evidence entirely and is based on retrieval of the respondent's previous knowledge or beliefs regarding the content at hand. (Examples of each of these types are presented shortly). The reasoning required to produce invalid judgments of any of these types is therefore minimal. Each of the types has been found to occur among both children and adults but to diminish with age and with experience with problems that entail investigatory and inference skills (Kuhn et al., 1995). Microgenetic analyses of performance over time reveal the typical pattern of prolonged periods of mixed usage of both valid and invalid inference strategies, with a gradual increase over time in the proportion of use of valid strategies (Kuhn et al., 1992, 1995; Schauble, 1990, 1996).

In the context of interpreting a single outcome from the database, an individual can thus make both valid and invalid judgments, in so doing presumably drawing on multiple kinds of inference strategies. Of five variables that are identified, with levels of each occurring in conjunction with an outcome across a succession of instances, for example, an individual might make the valid judgment that a particular variable is causal on the basis of a comparison of the outcome in the current instance to a previous one in which the level of only this variable differed and the outcome varied (i.e., a controlled comparison). At the same time, as has been documented to happen frequently, in responding to this instance the individual might also identify a second variable as causal, but on the basis only that a level of this variable also was present in conjunction with the outcome being examined and therefore must have contributed to it. Other than declaring a variable causal or noncausal, a third option with respect to each of the variables is to suspend judgment and claim that the causal status of that variable is not yet certain.

Hence, in evaluating a given instance (an outcome in conjunction with different levels of the five identified variables), while only one judgment is made about any one variable, multiple judgments (of causality, of noncausality, or of uncertainty)—valid or invalid—may be made regarding the variables identified in the instance. In subsequently evaluating another instance, these judgments (regarding a variable's causal status) may change. Judgments have been observed to fluctuate as individuals evaluate successive instances (Kuhn et al., 1995; Schauble, 1990).

A MICROGENETIC INVESTIGATION

In the context of the scientific inquiry problem we have described, change can be examined not only in the knowledge an individual acquires about the causal system but also in the strategies of investigation and inference by means of which this knowledge is acquired (Kuhn, 1995; Kuhn et al., 1995). Researchers who have used the microgenetic method report a similar pattern of change. At all points multiple strategies are available and applied, but change occurs in the form of a shifting frequency distribution (Kuhn, 2001; Kuhn & Phelps, 1982; Kuhn et al., 1995) or overlapping waves (Siegler, 1996, 2006). That is, with continued engagement less effective strategies come to be used less frequently and more effective strategies begin to be used more frequently.

The data we bring to bear on this question here are microgenetic (Kuhn, 1995; Siegler, 2006) data—that is, they entail repeated observations of the same individuals engaged in the same or similar problems over time, allowing examination of patterns of change across time. The data are drawn from a larger 3-year longitudinal study in which we follow the development of inquiry skills among students beginning in their fourth-grade year as they encounter a sequence of problems of increasing complexity (Kuhn & Pease, 2008). The specific analyses presented here, addressed to the specific question we have identified, were not included in the report of that study as they were not central to the longitudinal developmental questions that were the focus of that work.

Our purpose in examining microgenetic data in the present work, then, is not the typical one of examining patterns of change over time. Instead, we turn to such data to address the particular question identified above: whether occurrence of more and less advanced response modes operate independently or are (inversely) related to one another. This is a different question from that of how they change over time. One type of judgment may become more frequent and another type less frequent over time, but this does not tell us whether one of these trends in some way governs or influences the other or whether the two trends take place independently of one another. Repeated-observation data involving individuals working on the same or similar problems over time are necessary to address our question as the question is one about variation in responses to the same kind of problem on different occasions.

One other feature of our research design that warrants noting at the outset is that participants' problem-solving activity is situated in a social context. During most sessions, students work on the task in pairs. We regard this feature as advantageous in any case, since cognition very frequently occurs in a social context. But it also stands to provide a second, less direct kind of evidence regarding the independence of the two components of strategy change. Other people can serve as external influences on individual cognition. In particular, the thinking they display is likely to have an influence on an individual's propensity to rely on one or the other mode of response. Moreover, it is possible that this external influence functions differently in the respective cases of the two different modes.

As our participants worked most of the times with a series of changing partners (except for initial and subsequent individual assessments), we sought to examine how the social context of working with a same-level, higher level, or lower level peer influenced a participant's propensity to make judgments of the two types. Conceivably, this influence of social context on performance may be different for the two kinds of judgments. One, for example, as we in fact speculated might be the case, may be more susceptible to social influence than those regarded as of a more advanced type. If any such differences (in the effect of social context) across the two kinds of judgments do in fact emerge, they stand to serve as additional evidence of a second, less direct type, regarding the independence of the two modes.

The 34 fifth-grade students reported on here began participation in our larger, longitudinal study of the development of inquiry skills when the students were fourth graders and continued through their sixth-grade year (Kuhn & Pease, 2008). Students were from an urban independent school serving a socioeconomically and ethnically diverse population. As would be expected among this age group, all 34 met a criterion of being in the process of developing scientific inquiry skills. Specifically, they showed variable usage (across occasions) of effective and ineffective strategies, as detailed below. One participant was eliminated because he showed no variation (i.e., exclusive use of ineffective strategies) at all sessions.

Students worked with inquiry software for one or sometimes two 45-minute periods per week, except when occasional special school activities or field trips intervened. Students worked in pairs, with pair composition varying across sessions, except for the initial one or two sessions allocated to initial assessment of individual skill levels, and a later final assessment carried out individually for the same purpose. The sessions on which the present analyses are based began in late October of the fifth-grade school year and continued into early May. Due to school absences and other reasons students had to be away from class, the number of sessions a student participated in varied across students, from a low of 8 to a high of 15 (mean = 10.53).

A sample of one version of the software, *Earthquake Forecaster*, is presented in Figures 6.1–6.4. *Earthquake Forecaster*, and several other parallel programs are multimedia inquiry software programs created with Adobe Director multimedia authoring software as Flash files (Kuhn & Dean, 2005; Kuhn, Katz, & Dean, 2004). The program requires students to assess the causal status of five dichotomous variables in contributing to the level of earthquake risk. The introduction to the program explains the importance of developing means to predict earthquakes in order to protect others and maintain safety. To accomplish this, students must learn which features do and do not make a difference. Of the five features that students investigate in *Earthquake Forecaster*, two have no effect and three have simple (noninteractive) causal effects.

After the initial introduction, students are asked to choose what they will find out about in their first selection of an instance (or case) to examine (see Figure 6.1). Students identify whether they are or are not finding out about a feature by clicking the feature picture(s) corresponding to their choice(s). Then, students construct an instance of their own choosing, by selecting the level of each feature (see Figure 6.2). These choices yield an outcome displayed in the form of a gauge representing the earthquake risk level. Students are then asked to make and justify any causal or noncausal inferences they believe to be justified regarding the

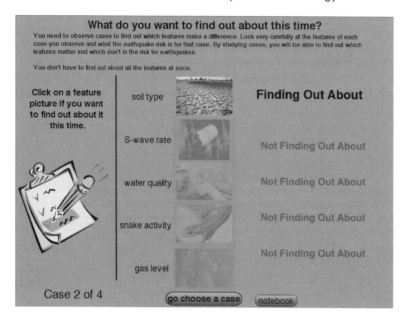

FIGURE 6.1. Find out screen.

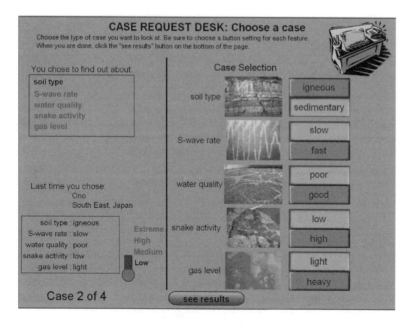

FIGURE 6.2. Case request screen.

status of any of the features (Figure 6.3). Or, for each feature, they have the option of suspending judgment (Figure 6.3). The final screen prompts the student to enter any notes they wish to (Figure 6.4).

Each of the screens shown in Figures 6.1–6.4 is depicted as it would appear during the course of the second instance the student chooses for investigation. For second and subsequent instances, the screen includes not only the outcome for the current instance the student is investigating but also shows the outcome for the instance chosen immediately preceding this one. After the student answers questions regarding the outcome of the fourth instance and is prompted to make any additional notes that may be desired, the program thanks the student for participating and shuts down.

After the initial one to two sessions assessing individual skill levels, students began working in pairs on different versions of the software that were structurally equivalent to *Earthquake Forecaster*. The pair made a single joint response at each prompted point in the program, and this response was taken as the response for each of the individuals that made up the pair. The work was done in a 45-minute class that met twice a week for most of the school year. The class was described to students explicitly as a class in inquiry, which was defined for the class as ways of asking

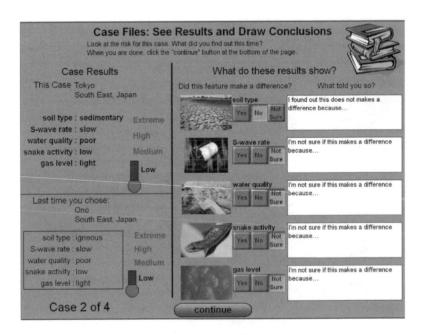

FIGURE 6.3. Results and conclusions screen.

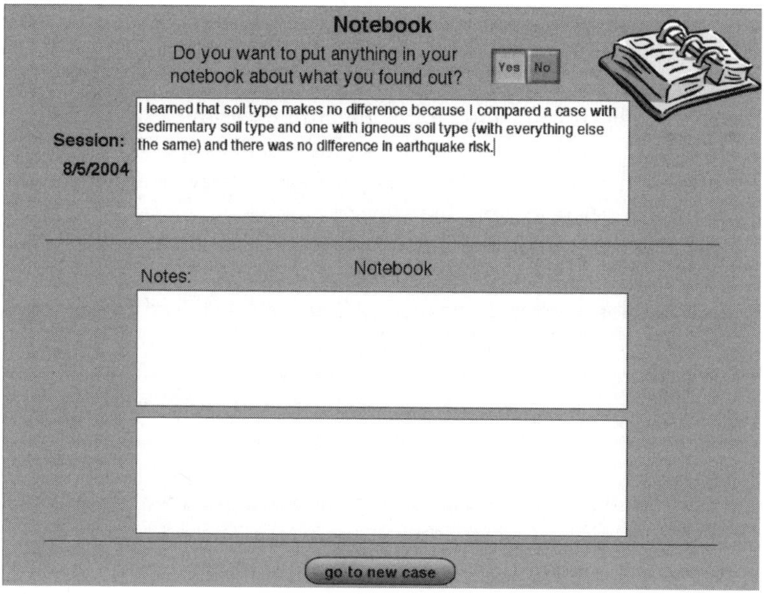

Notebook

Do you want to put anything in your notebook about what you found out? [Yes] [No]

Session: 8/5/2004

I learned that soil type makes no difference because I compared a case with sedimentary soil type and one with igneous soil type (with everything else the same) and there was no difference in earthquake risk.

Notes: Notebook

go to new case

FIGURE 6.4 Notebook screen.

questions and seeking answers. In working with a partner, students were instructed not to divide the task (i.e., for one student to make responses to one segment of the program and the other student to another) and sufficient adult "coaches" circulated among students to ensure this did not happen. Students were instructed instead to discuss each question or choice with their partner and not to respond until agreement had been reached between them.

The first program student pairs worked on was *Avalanche Hunter*. Wind type, snow-type cloud cover, soil, and slope were the five binary variables potentially having causal effects on avalanche risk. Each content version of the software also contained a prediction module that students worked on, to apply one's learning (by predicting outcomes from different variable constellations), but here we focus on just the inquiry strategies themselves and in particular the inference phase of the inquiry process. Work with *Avalanche Hunter* continued from late October to mid-December, by which time the majority of students had achieved a high degree of mastery, although, as detailed below, they still showed less than 100% consistent optimal strategy usage.

Other more advanced forms of the software were elaborations of the structure of the basic program. These enhanced the challenge of students' inquiry by introducing more complex forms of evidence. Beyond the scaffolding provided by the software itself, the two adult "coaches" supervising the sessions provided one further scaffold in the form of encouragement to find out about one variable at a time (as necessary, among students who did not formulate this intention without assistance). This scaffold was introduced as earlier work (Kuhn & Dean, 2005) had shown it to be highly effective in structuring students' activity and enhancing progress in investigatory and inference strategies.

Following winter vacation, when inquiry sessions resumed in mid-January, a new form of *Avalanche Hunter* was introduced, one in which one variable (cloud cover) had twice as large an effect as the other causal variables, and students were asked to indicate whether any of the variables were more important than any others. By mid-February two-thirds of the students had mastered this problem and were ready to move on (they had correctly identified all causal and noncausal effects using appropriate methods and justifications for inferences), while the remaining one-third did not meet this criterion and were provided more practice with the basic software. The latter group thus switched to new content to maintain their interest: the *Ocean Voyage* program (in which ancient ships varying on five dimensions vary in the success of their voyages), which did not contain any further structural advance. During this same period, the more advanced group also worked with *Ocean Voyage*, but in their case a more advanced probabilistic version of *Ocean Voyage* was introduced, one in which the outcome for a particular constellation of variable levels was not constant but rather took the form of a distribution with one outcome (voyage distance) most frequent but adjacent outcomes of lesser and greater distance also occurring but with lower frequency.[1] Students thus had to compare results over multiple trials with the same constellation (of variable levels) in order to make informative comparisons between two constellations.

In late March there occurred for all students a phase of individual assessment, returning to the basic structure of *Earthquake Forecaster*. The purpose was to assess how much progress each student had made individually, in the absence of the influence of working with a peer. Students individually required between one and two sessions to complete the *Earthquake Forecaster* program (both investigation and prediction modules) at least once.

Following completion of the individual assessment, and a brief vacation, at the end of April and through mid-May, all students encountered a final new data structure, presented within the *Earthquake Forecaster* content, in which two of the three causal variables interacted with one another.[2] Students returned to working in pairs and worked with the interaction database from one to four times depending on the time available.

Identification of Strategies and Classification of Judgments

In one cycle of the program, the participant (or pair of participants) had the opportunity to examine four instances. A valid judgment is not possible until a second instance is examined for comparison with the first. Hence, valid judgments become possible following examination of the second instance. A second valid judgment becomes possible following examination of the third instance (since the third can be compared to the first or second), and a third valid judgment becomes possible following examination of the fourth instance. If the individual or pair continue on the same occasion to engage in a second iteration of the program, the fifth instance they examine allows for the possibility of another valid judgment, and so on. The number of possible valid judgments at a single session therefore ranged from a low of one (since participants occasionally failed to complete a cycle at a given session) to a high of 11, with a median of three.

Each instance, beginning with the first, in contrast, allowed for the possibility of 5 invalid judgments, since an invalid judgment of causality or noncausality could be made about each of the five variables for each of the four instances in the cycle. The range of possible invalid judgments per session thus ranged from a low of 5 to a high of 60, with a median of 20 (4 judgments × five variables). Additional evidence regarding a judgment came from the justification the individual (or pair) offered for it. The four principal types of justifications for determinate inferences appear in Table 6.1. For ease of comparison, the examples in Table 6.1 all refer to the same variable and to a judgment of causality. Justifications of noncausal judgments are parallel except that no difference (in outcome) is present and the respondent accordingly concludes that the variable does not make a difference to the outcome.

In order to generate the fourth justification type, note, the student would have had to construct the two instances in order to compare them and draw the appropriate inference. In the case of the first three types, no such intentional construction of instances is necessary. For Type 1, no instances of evidence are invoked to support the judgment. For Type 2, any single instance will suffice, and in Type 3 just about any two instances, with no fixed relation to one another, will suffice.

It is on this basis, then, that we regarded the fourth type as signaling a more reflective, analytic type of processing. Generation of a controlled comparison is unlikely to happen by chance (and, indeed, rarely occurred in the absence of the appropriate justification). Even once the evidence has been generated, the student must recognize its relevance, make the relevant comparison, and draw the appropriate conclusion. Although the

TABLE 6.1. Types of Justifications for Determinate Judgments (of Causality or Noncausality)

Justification type	Example
1. Absence of evidence-based justification	"The heavy gas level means high risk, because the gas has bad chemicals in it."
2. Single-instance justification	"The heavy gas level increases the risk, because here you have heavy gas and the risk is high."
3. Cross-instance uncontrolled comparison	"The heavy gas level increases the risk, because here you have heavy gas and the risk is high. Before, when the level of everything was good, the risk was low."
4. Cross-instance controlled comparison	"In this instance only the gas level changed, compared to the last instance, and the risk increased. So the gas level makes a difference."

first three types in Table 6.1 arguably involve some level of reasoning, it is neither complex nor effortful and can be accomplished by the sort of covariation assessment that even infants are capable of (Alloy & Tabachnik, 1984).

Note we do not include indeterminacy judgments ("not sure") in the analysis since the kind of processing underlying them is likely to vary. An indeterminacy judgment might arise from a close analysis of the available evidence and recognition that the evidence is insufficient to permit an inference regarding causality. Or it might arise from a nonreflective subjective sense of uncertainty. Typical justifications for indeterminacy judgments, for example, "I'm not sure yet," are often difficult to distinguish in this respect. Accordingly, only determinate judgments (the variable makes a difference or doesn't make a difference) were coded. Two indices were calculated for each individual (or pair) at each session, as the basis for further analysis. One was the proportion of valid determinate judgments (the proportion being the number of valid judgments divided by the number of possible valid judgments). The other was the proportion of invalid determinate judgments (the number of invalid judgments divided by the number of possible invalid judgments).

Patterns of Change over Time

The general pattern of change evident in earlier studies (Kuhn et al., 1995; Schauble, 1990) appeared in the present work as well, when children worked most of the time with partners. Examining change first of all in terms of qualitative patterns, at the initial individual assessment six of 34 students made all possible valid judgments (the exact number possible varying slightly across individuals depending on how many instances they constructed) and showed no invalid judgments, thus performing at ceiling on both of these dimensions.[3] (None of these six maintained this record, however, when they went on to work with partners.) At the individual posttest, the number of students performing at ceiling on both dimensions increased to nine of 34. Nineteen of the 34 showed at least one of these achievements (maximum possible valid judgments or no invalid judgments), compared to 11 at the pretest. Of the remaining 15, who did not achieve ceiling performance on either dimension, nine showed progress on both dimensions (increasing valid inferences and decreasing invalid ones) and an additional three showed progress on one or the other. Among those students who showed progress only on one of the two dimensions, most progressed on the dimension of reduction of invalid judgments.

Quantitative analysis of the change data confirmed that the group as a whole made significant progress on both dimensions, with repeated-measures analysis of variance yielding a significant effect of time (initial vs. final assessment) with respect to proportion of valid judgments (which increased over time) and proportion of invalid judgments (which decreased over time). Proportion of valid judgments increased from a mean of .392 to a mean of .794 across the two assessments, $F(1,29) = 20.73, p < .05$ (partial eta squared = .417). Also significant was the effect of time with respect to the proportion of actual invalid judgments to possible invalid judgments (the latter number depending on the number of instances examined). This proportion decreased from a mean of .381 to a mean of .113 across the two assessments, $F(1, 29) = 23.67, p < .05$ (partial eta squared = .449).

An illustration of one student's change over time appears in Figure 6.5. A second student's record appears in Figure 6.6. In each the solid line represents valid inferences and the dotted line invalid inferences. Individual sessions occurred on occasions, 1, 11, and 12 for Anna and on occasions 1, 10, and 11 for Sasha. On all other occasions, participants worked with a partner. As reflected in Figures 6.5 and 6.6, performance is highly variable over time. This variability can be attributed to a combination of the student's own intraindividual variability (as documented in earlier research in which participants worked alone) and variability attributable to the influence of the partner. In both the cases shown, variability diminishes over time, but does not disappear, as valid judgments increase in frequency and invalid judgments decrease.

Connections between Applications of Superior Strategies and Inhibition of Inferior Strategies

We turn now to the central question posed in the present study—the relation between appearance of valid judgments and appearance of invalid

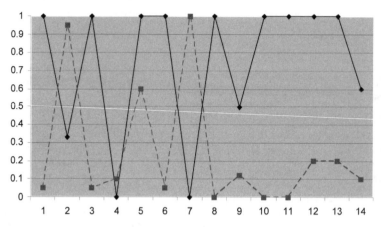

FIGURE 6.5. Anna's performance over time. Varying effect sizes were introduced at Session 6 and probabilistic effects at Session 8. Interaction effects were introduced at Session 12. Solid line depicts proportion of valid judgments that were made (relative to the total number of valid judgments possible, which varied based on the number of instances the student constructed). Dotted line depicts proportion of invalid judgments (again, relative to the total number of invalid judgments possible).

judgments. We first looked for any evidence that patterns of performance over time differed for the two kinds of judgments. Such differences would be suggestive of independence in their functioning. Examining the charts of performance over time (like those shown in Figures 6.5 and 6.6) for each of the participants, a participant's variability over time appeared to be somewhat greater in making valid judgments than in making invalid judgments. To verify this difference, we computed for each participant the standard deviation (in proportion of valid judgments) across all of that participant's sessions, first for valid judgments and then for invalid judgments. This analysis supported our observation. For 28 of the 34 participants, standard deviation was higher for valid judgments than invalid judgments. Median standard deviations across participants (based on percentage scores from 0 to 1.00 for each participant) were .41 for valid judgments and .28 for invalid judgments, a significant difference, $F(1, 33)$ = 39.28, $p < .001$ (partial eta squared = .543).

The next question we asked is whether such a relation emerges in the individual data, when participants are working alone. For this purpose we examined first the pretest data and then the posttest data to ascertain whether a relation appeared. For each we examined the relationship between students' pretest (or posttest) scores for valid judgments and pretest (or posttest) scores for invalid judgments. We included only those

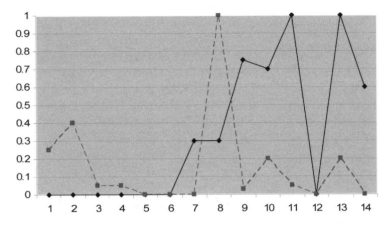

FIGURE 6.6. Sasha's performance over time.

participants who showed variability on both dimensions (across the multiple instances the participant evaluated in this assessment). Omitted were those (identified above) who had reached asymptote of perfect performance on both dimensions. The data take the form of the same percentages illustrated in Figures 6.5 and 6.6.

Using these percentages, comparisons can be made across individuals and across judgment types within individuals. Within individuals, a negative association would be predicted if the two judgment types are related, that is, high likelihood of making valid judgments, presumably driven by an analytic system, would be associated with low likelihood of making invalid judgments, presumably driven by a heuristic system. Because these percentages can be assumed to have no more than ordinal properties, the nonparametric gamma index of association was calculated for each participant. The gamma statistic G, first discussed by Goodman and Kruskal, is appropriate for measuring the relation between two ordinally scaled variables (Siegel & Castellan, 1988).

For the pretest individual data, the association between proportion of valid judgments and proportion of invalid judgments was negative, as expected, but did not reach an .05 level of significance.[4] For the posttest individual data, this association similarly was negative but did not reach an .05 level of significance. A scatter plot for the posttest data is shown in Figure 6.7. The scatter plot for the pretest appears very similar and is not shown. As seen there, deviations from an inverse association are frequent—some individuals make a high proportion of valid judgments but also make a high proportion of invalid judgments, while others make a low proportion of both kinds of judgments.[5]

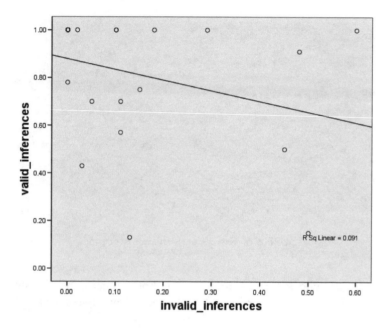

FIGURE 6.7. Relations between valid and invalid judgments in individual post-test data.

We turned next to the intervening sessions when participants worked with a partner. It is possible that a relation between the two kinds of judgments emerges only here, when the influence of a partner increases the variability in a participant's judgments. We thus examined performance over time while students worked with partners and investigated whether any relation appears between a given participant's level of functioning in making valid judgments and level of functioning in making invalid judgments. For this analysis, each participant's record of performance over time was examined individually. Because we had information about each participant's level of functioning when working alone, we were less interested in an absolute level of performance and rather whether this level in the dyadic context was higher, lower, or equivalent to the participant's own level when working alone.

Accordingly, for each dyadic session the proportion of a participant's valid judgments was compared to the same proportion when the participant worked alone,[6] and categorized as either higher, lower, or equal to the solitary level. A parallel categorization was made for invalid judgments. The majority of participants showed varied records in this respect, on occasions performing at a level equivalent to their individual level, on others below it, and on others above it. This variability was influenced by how often an individual's pairing was with a more able, less able, or equally able partner, as we go on to examine.

For each participant, the ordinal gamma statistic was again employed to examine the relation between an individual's level of functioning relative to partner in making valid judgments and level of functioning making invalid judgments. The gamma statistic showed a significant (inverse) relation at the .05 level for only six of the 34 participants. When the .01 level of significance is used, only three of the 34 are significant. We can thus draw the same essential conclusion we did in examining records of individual performance. The relative frequency of valid judgments and relative frequency of invalid judgments do not appear to be related.

Does Social Influence on Production versus Inhibition Differ?

These findings led us to ask the question of what might be related to the variability over time in a participant's level of functioning in making the two kinds of judgments. In particular we were curious about the likely influence of the partner. Does a partner affect the two kinds of judgments in the same way? To examine partners' influence, on every occasion in which a participant worked with a partner, we identified the partner's level of functioning as higher than, equal to, or lower than the participant's, separately for valid judgments and invalid judgments. Partner's level of functioning was identified in the same way as was the participant's level of functioning but the comparison determining the designation of high, low, or equal in this case was between the participant's and the partner's individual level of functioning.[6] Since the relation of the participant's and the partner's level was a matter of chance (partners were not assigned to represent particular degrees of mismatch), most participants' records contained a mixture of the three types (partner higher than, equal to, or lower than participant), although in a few cases not all three types appeared. For the sample as a whole, the median percentage of occasions at which the partner was more able was 43.5%, was equally able was 20%, and was less able was 25%.[7] These percentages are similar when broken down by type of judgment (valid or invalid).

Using the same gamma statistic and analytic procedure described above, for valid judgments we found statistically significant positive relations for 68% of the individual participant's records[8] between the level of the participant's functioning (assessed as his or her individual level) and the level of the partner relative to the participant. For invalid judgments, the gamma coefficient was less often significant but still well above a chance level—35% of participants showed a significant positive relation between the level of the participant's functioning and the level of the partner's functioning relative to the participant. Significant gamma coefficients (which have a potential range of −1.00 to +1.00) ranged from .78 to 1.00 across the sample. These high positive associations signify that a higher functioning partner tended to improve a participant's performance (relative to his or her individual level), while a lower functioning partner tended to weaken the participant's performance.

These results, confirming that partners did have an influence on one another, led us to examine finally the interesting question of the relative degree of social influence and hence performance variability for the two types of judgments, valid versus invalid, as well as for the two types of influence: a higher functioning partner (with the potential to improve one's performance) and a lower functioning partner (with the potential to weaken one's performance). To conduct this analysis, we computed for each participant the percentage of dyadic sessions in which their performance improved (relative to individual level) when working with a higher level partner and the percentage in which it declined when working with a lower level partner, separately for valid judgments and for invalid judgments.

These data were subjected to a two-way repeated-measures analysis of variance with judgment type (valid vs. invalid) one factor and partner level (higher or lower than participant) as the other. (Cases in the "equivalent" category were not examined.) The dependent variable was the proportion of instances in which the participant's performance shifted (relative to solitary level) in the direction of the partner (i.e., was higher in the case of a superior-performing partner or was lower in the case of an inferior-performing partner). The means for the four resulting cells appear in Table 6.2. As reflected there, both partner level and judgment type were shown to have an effect. The effect of judgment type was significant, $F(1, 33) = 9.63$, $p < .004$ (partial eta squared = .226), as was the effect of partner type, $F(1.33) = 4.31$, $p < .046$ (partial eta squared = .116). The interaction between the two was nonsignificant, $F(1,33) = .162$, $p = .69$. The numbers in parentheses in Table 6.2 are the respective medians. While very similar to the means, they establish that the patterns reflected in Table 6.2 are not the product of only a few extreme-scoring participants.

In sum, these analyses suggest that the social context of working with a partner does influence an individual's performance. A partner is more often influential in raising a participant's functioning than in lowering it. A partner's influence (either positive or negative), moreover, is more pronounced in the case of invalid judgments (which need to be inhibited to improve performance) than it is in the case of valid judgments (which need to be constructed to improve performance).[9]

TABLE 6.2. Proportion of Occasions in Which a Partner Influenced
Participant's Level, by Judgment Type and Direction of Partner Mismatch

	Participant improved with superior partner	Participant declined with inferior partner
Valid judgments	38.88 (30)	27.88 (24)
Invalid judgments	49.76 (50)	35.06 (30)

Note. Improvement is defined as a higher level of functioning than that shown by the participant when performing alone. Decline is defined as a lower level than that shown by the participant when performing alone. Numbers in parentheses are the respective medians.

CONCLUSIONS: TOWARD A DUAL-PROCESS MODEL

The various analyses we report here all support the independence model, both those that directly examine the relation between judgments associated with two response modes and those that show differential effects of other variables, notably social influence, on judgments associated with the respective modes. These findings warrant replication with different populations of different age levels and with different kinds of tasks. The task we employed, however, is a generic one (that can employ any content) and represents the kind of multivariable causal induction that people engage in commonly in natural contexts. Equally important, it allows for multiple different kinds of judgments to be made in response to a single problem cue—a valid judgment can be made that one variable plays a causal role, based on appropriate evidence, while at the same time causal or noncausal judgments are made regarding other variables that are invalid due to lack of the necessary evidence. It is this characteristic that has allowed us to examine the question of how the propensity to make one kind of response (valid inference) is related to the propensity to make another kind of response (invalid inference).

If the two response modes we have identified are independent, at a minimum we need a model in which their distinct functioning is represented. Rather than increasing strength of one mode, in a given problem context, in any way *causing* decreasing strength of the other (or decreasing strength of one causing increasing strength of the other), two distinct challenges must be represented. One involves constructing, accessing, and implementing one mode. The other involves gaining awareness of, monitoring, and inhibiting the other mode when it is inappropriate.

Our results are consistent with growing attention in the study of cognitive development to the role of response inhibition (Harnishfeger & Bjorklund, 1993; Kuhn, 2006; Kuhn & Franklin, 2006; Williams, Ponesse, Schacher, Logan, & Tannock, 1999). Traditionally, the focus in cognitive development research has been on the attainment of new forms of cognition. Recognition based on microgenetic work of the coexistence of multiple forms highlights the need to gain control of and relinquish the less sophisticated or adaptive mode of operation, as well as to attain and consolidate the more advanced form—two distinct kinds of change, both of which are facilitated by practice (Brace, Morton, & Munakata, 2006; Kuhn et al., 1995; Kuhn & Franklin, 2006; Kuhn & Pease, 2006; Siegler, 2006). But engagement and practice by themselves are not sufficient. A model that incorporates the dual challenges of production and inhibition requires a metalevel operator distinct from operations that occur at the performance level (Kuhn, 2001). Constructing, implementing, and monitoring the more advanced operation is a distinct task from inhibiting the less advanced response. Each of these tasks, we would argue, requires a metalevel operator that governs the performance operators. If so, further specifying the nature of this metalevel operation becomes an important objective.

Our findings are also relevant to the growing literature in cognitive psychology on dual-process systems (Evans, 2003; Evans & Over, 1996; Sloman, 1996). The two kinds of judgments that our task yields may not map perfectly onto the theoretical constructs of heuristic and analytic processing modes. In particular, a small proportion of responses we classified as invalid judgments arguably might have entailed some degree of analytic processing that went astray and failed to yield a valid judgment. (The reverse error, classifying as valid a judgment that was produced heuristically, is highly unlikely.) Broadly, however, the production of valid judgments can be hypothesized to require an analytic operator, and the inhibition of invalid judgments can be hypothesized to not require an analytic operator and to arise from a heuristic system.

In reviewing the dual-processing literature, Evans (2003) emphasizes the need to better understand how the two systems interact. Several authors have addressed the question at a theoretical level. Taking the position that the two are closely linked, Klaczynski (2001, 2004, 2005), for example, proposes that the analytic system serves two functions. It does the cognitive work necessary to generate and execute the higher order response and in addition it inhibits the alternative heuristic response. Stanovich (1999, 2004), in contrast, subscribes to the alternative possibility that production of an analytic response does not increase or decrease the probability of an additional heuristic response to the same situation, and, similarly, a heuristic response does not affect the probability of an additional analytic response. He describes the heuristic systems as "not under the control of the analytic processing system" (2004, p. 37) and able to "sometimes execute and provide outputs that are in conflict with the results of a simultaneous computation being carried out by analytic processing" (p. 37), although he does later note that the analytic system is capable in certain situations of "overriding" the heuristic system. Given the modest amount of empirical evidence that has been brought to bear on dual-systems models relative to the theoretical interest they have engendered, the question we have identified—whether a formulation like Klaczynski's, in which the analytic system controls and inhibits the heuristic system, or one like Stanovich's, in which the two systems are largely independent, is more correct—thus seems a fundamental one to address via empirical investigation. The work described here is one such example and one that clearly favors one alternative over the other.

Another aspect of the present work that warrants note is its social dimension. Cognition is fundamentally and most often a social activity that takes place in a social rather than an isolated context and is not only influenced by but indeed constructed within this context. In the educational literature, the benefits of "cooperative learning"—which means essentially having children work in small groups—has long been regarded as a beneficial practice, despite the only modest amount of research evidence available regarding how students interact in such groups and what kinds of cognitive processes, beneficial or not, are involved (Damon, 1984: Damon & Phelps, 1989; Dimant & Bearison, 1991; Resnick, Levine, & Teasley, 1991; Resnick & Nelson-LeGall, 1997). As noted earlier, we had participants work in pairs because of its presumed facilitative effects, rather than to study the social process per se, and also because this social context better resembles the natural one in which cognition develops. In the specific case of the task employed here, however, we do have evidence of the superior progress made in a pair versus solitary condition. In an earlier study, students worked simultaneously over a period of months on one content version of the task alone and on another content version with a partner; intraindividual comparisons showed the majority of participants making more progress on the task they were engaged in with a partner (Kuhn, 2001).

Although much more evidence is needed, the present results can be taken as good news in the sense that a partner appeared to influence a child to function at a higher level more often than the partner influenced the child to function at a lower level. Although we did not observe partners' social interaction itself except anecdotally, the better idea appears to have more often won out. Moreover, our results suggested that partners had an important influence on the second of the two processes postulated in the dual-process model and the one that in general has received much less attention: inhibiting the less effective mode of functioning (and hence, as we have noted, serving as further evidence of independent operation of the two processes). Although social process data must be examined more extensively before broad conclusions can be drawn, our findings suggest that the more valuable influence of a social context on thinking may lie less in invoking new ideas than it does in making evident the weaknesses of existing ones.

Finally, we need to put the findings we have described in an educational context. Two broad implications warrant noting. First, strategy development is more than a simple matter of acquiring expertise. There are now many examples in the literature of students who acquire strategic skill that does not benefit them. For many, sometimes multiple reasons, they do not utilize the skill they have acquired. A metalevel manager must be invoked and investigated, as it is at this level that performance is determined. As we have undertaken to illustrate here, this manager must monitor and control multiple potential actions, not just one. Second, in real-life educational settings, these processes do not take place in a vacuum. There are external, as well as internal, influences on a student's strategy production, as well as strategy inhibition. This is likely a good thing. It is in a rich social context of deciding what to do that deliberation over alternatives is most likely to come into play.

NOTES

1. Specifically, the variable of captain's age (young or old) yields a distribution of outcomes, rather than a single consistent outcome. The most frequent outcome (60% of instances) is level 1 for the young captain and level 2 for the old captain. However, in 20% of instances, the young captain yields a level 0 outcome and in 20% a level 2 outcome. Similarly In 20% of cases the old captain yields a level 1 outcome and in 20% a level 3 outcome. Thus, students must generate multiple instances and compare these distributions (for young and old captain) in order to identify the effect. Comparison of only two instances may be misleading.
2. The interacting variables are snake activity and gas level. Snake activity has an effect only when gas level is heavy.
3. Included in this category are three participants (two at the pretest and one at the posttest) who showed all possible valid inferences and only a single additional invalid inference made in the context of a large number of correct judgments of indeterminacy (that the evidence was inadequate to make an inference regarding that variable). These isolated incorrect judgments, it was reasoned, could be attributed to momentary inattention on the participant's part or to a data recording error.
4. This is so even though constraints exist that dictate some degree of inverse correlation between the two values. If, on a typical occasion, an individual makes judgments about four instances, each involving five variables, there exist 20 opportunities to make a judgment. Yet in any single one of these 20 cases, the individual cannot make both a valid judgment and an invalid one.
5. Substitution of the conventional parametric Pearson r statistic does not

change this outcome. The *r* coefficient reached significance neither for the pretest data nor for the posttest data.

6. The participant's level of functioning at a given session was taken as the participant's individual level at the individual assessment closest in time to this session. This was the participant's pretest level for sessions occurring during the 2 months immediately following the pretest (following which there was an extended holiday break) and the participant's posttest level for sessions occurring during the 3 months preceding and following the posttest.

7. Although pairing was done randomly, the somewhat higher proportion of instances in which a participant works with a higher level peer can be explained by the fact that the higher functioning participants overall had slightly better attendance and also tended to complete a greater number of instances per session.

8. For three participants in the case of valid inferences and three participants in the case of invalid inferences, the gamma statistic could not be computed because of lack of variance in one or the other variable. The sample size for these analyses is therefore 31 rather than 34.

9. Note, this result does not contradict the finding reported above that significant associations with partner level were more frequent for valid inferences than invalid inferences. A number of factors could influence the gamma statistic of association for each participant, notably the distribution (and hence variance) of the three kinds of partner mismatch (higher, lower, equivalent). The number of times a participant was matched with each kind of partner was a matter of chance. Hence, some individuals had limited variance across the three types. What is notable about these gamma coefficients, then, is the number of participants for which they are significant, rather than those for which they are not. What the ANOVA results indicate, in contrast, is that when a partner mismatch occurred it was more likely to influence the participant in the case of invalid than valid inferences.

REFERENCES

Alloy, L., & Tabachnik, N. (1984). Assessment of covariation by humans and animals: The joint influence of prior expectations and current situational information. *Psychological Review, 91,* 112–149.

Brace, J., Morton, J. B., & Munakata, Y. (2006). When actions speak louder than words: Improving children's flexibility in a card-sorting task. *Psychological Science, 17,* 665–669.

Damon, W. (1984). Peer education: The untapped potential. *Journal of Applied Developmental Psychology, 5,* 331–43.

Damon, W., & Phelps, E. (1989). Strategic uses of peer learning in children's education. In T. Berndt & A. Ladd (Eds.), *Peer relationships in child development* (pp. 135–157). New York: Wiley.

Dimant, R., & Bearison, D. (1991). Development of formal reasoning during successive peer interactions. *Developmental Psychology, 27,* 277–284.

Evans, J. St. (2003). In two minds: Dual-process accounts of reasoning. *Trends in Cognitive Science, 7,* 454–459.

Evans, J. St., & Over, D. (1996). *Rationality and reasoning.* Hove, UK: Psychology Press.

Harnishfeger, K., & Bjorklund, D. (1993). The ontogeny of inhibition mechanisms: A renewed approach to cognitive development. In M. Howe & R. Pasnak (Eds.), *Emerging themes in cognitive development: Vol. 1. Foundations,* pp. 28–49. New York: Springer-Verlag.

Klaczynski, P. (2001). The influence of analytic and heuristic processing on adolescent reasoning and decision making. *Child Development, 72,* 844–861.

Klaczynski, P. (2004). A dual-process model of adolescent development: Implications for decision making, reasoning, and identity. In R. Kail (Ed.), *Advances in child development and behavior* (Vol. 31, pp. 73–123). San Diego: Academic Press.

Klaczynski, P. (2005). Metacognition and cognitive variability: A dual-process model of decision making and its development. In J. Jacobs & P. Klaczynski (Eds.), *The development of decision making in children and adolescents.* Mahwah, NJ: Erlbaum.

Kuhn, D. (1995). Microgenetic study of change: What has it told us? *Psychological Science, 6,* 133–139.

Kuhn, D. (2001). Why development does (and doesn't) occur: Evidence from the domain of inductive reasoning. In R. Siegler & J. McClelland (Eds.), *Mechanisms of cognitive development: Neural and behavioral perspectives.* Mahwah, NJ: Erlbaum.

Kuhn, D. (2006). Do cognitive changes accompany developments in the adolescent brain? *Perspectives on Psychological Science, 1,* 59–67.

Kuhn, D. (2007). Reasoning about multiple variables: Control of variables is not the only challenge. *Science Education, 91,* 710–726.

Kuhn, D., & Dean, D. (2005). Is developing scientific thinking all about learning to control variables? *Psychological Science, 16,* 866–870.

Kuhn, D., & Franklin, S. (2006). The second decade: What develops (and how)? In D. Kuhn & R. Siegler (Eds.) & (W. Damon & R. Lerner (Series Eds.), *Handbook of child psychology: Vol. 2. Cognition, perception, and language* (6th ed., pp. 953–993). Hoboken NJ: Wiley.

Kuhn, D., Garcia-Mila, M., Zohar, A., & Andersen, C. (1995). Strategies of knowledge acquisition. *Society for Research in Child Development Monographs, 60*(4, Serial No. 245).

Kuhn, D., Katz, J., & Dean, D. (2004). Developing reason. *Thinking and Reasoning, 10,* 197–219.

Kuhn, D., & Pease, M. (2006). Do children and adults learn differently? *Journal of Cognition and Development, 7,* 279–293.

Kuhn, D., & Pease, M. (2008). What needs to develop in the development of inquiry skills? *Cognition and Instruction, 26,* 512–559.

Kuhn, D., & Phelps, E. (1982). The development of problem-solving strategies. In H. Reese (Ed.), *Advances in child development and behavior* (Vol. 17). New York: Academic Press.

Kuhn, D., Schauble, L., & Garcia-Mila, M. (1992). Cross-domain development of scientific reasoning. *Cognition and Instruction, 9,* 285–332.

Lehrer, R., & Schauble, L. (2006). Scientific thinking and scientific literacy: Supporting development in learning contexts. In W. Damon & R. Lerner (Series Eds.) & K. A. Renninger & I. Sigel (Vol. Eds.), *Handbook of child psychology* (6th ed., Vol. 4). Hoboken NJ: Wiley.

Resnick, L., Levine, H., & Teasley, S. (1991). *Perspectives on socially shared cognition.* Washington, DC: American Psychological Association.

Resnick, L., & Nelson-Le Gall, S. (1997). Socializing intelligence. In L. Smith, J. Dockrell, & P. Tomlinson (Eds.), *Piaget, Vygotsky and beyond.* London: Routledge.

Schauble, L. (1990). Belief revision in children: The role of prior knowledge and strategies for generating evidence. *Journal of Experimental Child Psychology, 49,* 31–57.

Schauble, L. (1996). The development of scientific reasoning in knowledge-rich contexts. *Developmental Psychology, 32,* 102–119.

Siegel, S., & Castellan, J. N. (1988). *Nonparametric statistics for the behavioral sciences* (2nd ed.). New York: McGraw-Hill.

Siegler, R. S. (1996). *Emerging minds: The process of change in children's thinking.* New York: Oxford University Press.

Siegler, R. (2006). Microgenetic studies of learning. In W. Damon & R. Lerner (Series Eds.) & D. Kuhn & R. Siegler (Vol. Eds.), *Handbook of child psychology: Vol. 2. Cognition, perception, and language* (6th ed., pp. <x–<x). Hoboken NJ: Wiley.

Sloman, S. (1996). The empirical case for two systems of reasoning. *Psychological Bulletin, 119,* 3–22.

Stanovich, K. (1999). *Who is rational? Studies of individual differences in reasoning.* Mahwah, NJ: Erlbaum.

Stanovich, K. (2004). *The robot's rebellion.* Chicago: University of Chicago Press.

Williams, B., Ponesse, J., Schacher, R., Logan, G., & Tannock, R. (1999). Development of inhibitory control across the life span. *Developmental Psychology, 35,* 205–213.

Zimmerman, C. (2007). The development of scientific thinking skills in elementary and middle school. *Developmental Review, 27,* 172–223.

7

Fostering Scientific Reasoning with Multimedia Instruction

Richard E. Mayer

Scientific explanation is at the heart of science. In short, a major goal of science is to explain how things work, including physical systems (such as how lightning storms develop), biological systems (such as how the human respiratory system works), and mechanical systems (such as how an electric motor works). If a major goal of science is to explain how things work, then a major goal of science education is to help students be able to reason about explanations of how things work. In this chapter, I examine four issues:

1. What is scientific reasoning?
2. What knowledge do students need for scientific reasoning?
3. Which cognitive processes during learning lead to scientific reasoning?
4. Which kinds of instructional methods foster cognitive processing during learning that leads to scientific reasoning?

WHAT IS SCIENTIFIC REASONING?

Consider the following scenario. Alice is interested in electric motors, so she finds a multimedia lesson that explains how electric motors work.

160

The lesson begins with a frame showing an electric motor with each of the main parts labeled: battery, wires, commutator, wire loop, and magnets. When Alice clicks on any part, a list of frequently asked questions appears. When Alice clicks on any of the questions, an onscreen agent named Dr. Phyz appears and offers an answer as he moves about the animation in the screen (such as shown in Figure 7.1). By clicking on each of the questions for each of the parts as many times as she likes, Alice can systematically build a step-by-step chain of how a change in one part of the system causes a change in the next part and so on. The pace is under her control so she can make sure she understands one link in the chain before moving on to the next one. Later, Alice reports that she liked the lesson and she is even able to remember parts of what Dr. Phyz said. More important, she can also answer transfer questions that require scientific reasoning about the electric motor. This pattern of good performance in retention and transfer is an indication of meaningful learning.

In contrast, Barbara finds a different version of the lesson. The lesson consists of a continuous narrated animation in which an onscreen agent named Dr. Phyz explains the role of the battery, wires, commutator, wire loop, and magnets. The lesson uses exactly the same words and ani-

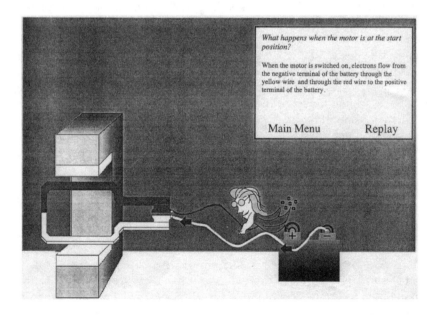

FIGURE 7.1. A frame from a multimedia lesson on how electric motors work. From Mayer, Dow, and Mayer (2003). Copyright 2003 by the American Psychological Association. Reprinted by permission.

mation as the interactive version that Alice saw. In both lessons the goal is to explain the cause-and-effect system in which moving electrons and magnetic fields interact to cause a wire loop to move. Even though the lesson is almost 10 minutes long, Barbara enjoys her learning experience, and she even remembers parts of what Dr. Phyz said. However, when she is asked questions that require scientific reasoning, she performs poorly. This pattern of good retention performance and poor transfer performance reflects rote learning.

When Mayer, Dow, and Mayer (2003) conducted a short experiment to compare learning about electric motors from an interactive narrated animation (like Alice's lesson) or a continuous narrated animation (like Barbara's lesson), they found that college students performed better on scientific reasoning questions with the interactive lesson rather than with the continuous lesson. Although the lessons lasted less than an hour, there were clear differences in the type of learning that occurred. The goal of this chapter is to pinpoint some instructional methods that lead to meaningful learning rather than rote learning, that is, that lead to superior performance on questions requiring scientific reasoning.

In this chapter, I focus on one particular aspect of scientific reasoning, exemplified by being able to understand Dr. Phyz's explanation of electric motors. For our purposes, let's begin with the idea that understanding a scientific explanation of how a system works requires building a *mental model* of the system. A mental model is a person's representation of a cause-and-effect system, in which a change in the state of one part causes a change in the state of another part and so on (Mayer et al., 2003; Mayer, Mathias, & Wetzel, 2002). For example, part of the learner's mental model of the electric motor may be: When the motor is switched from off to on, electrons flow from the negative terminal of the battery through the yellow wire and through the red wire to the positive terminal of the battery. Scientific reasoning occurs when someone mentally runs a mental model in order to solve a problem, that is, by manipulating a mental model in a principled way.

How can we assess the learner's scientific reasoning? Table 7.1 lists four kinds of questions that are intended to require scientific reasoning about electric motors, that is, questions in which learners are required to run their mental models of how an electric motor works. *Troubleshooting questions* ask the learner to determine why the system might not be functioning properly. *Redesign questions* ask the learner to modify the system to meet some new requirement. *Principle induction questions* ask the learner to determine the principle underlying a causal link. *What-if questions* ask learners to infer the consequences of a specific change in the system. We have used versions of these kinds of questions in dozens of experiments in our attempt to assess how various instructional manip-

TABLE 7.1. Examples of Four Types of Scientific Reasoning Questions

Question type	Example
Troubleshooting	"Suppose you switch on an electric motor, but nothing happens. What could have gone wrong?"
Redesign	"What could you do to reverse the movement of the electric motor, that is, to make the wire loop move in the opposite direction?"
Principle induction	"Why does the wire loop move?"
What-if	"What happens if you move the magnets further apart?"

ulations affect meaningful learning (Mayer, 2001, 2005). The learners commonly were college students in a lab setting, although in some cases the learners were high school students in a classroom setting, and the tests generally were given immediately after a short lesson.

To determine a score on scientific reasoning, we tally the number of acceptable solutions to each problem. For example, for the troubleshooting question about an electric motor ("Suppose you switch on an electric motor, but nothing happens. What could have gone wrong?") acceptable answers are the wire loop is stuck, the wire is severed or disconnected from the battery, the battery fails to produce voltage, the magnetic field does not intersect the wire loop, or the wire loop does not make contact with the commutator. An unacceptable answer is something is wrong with the magnet. In general, students are able to produce few of the possible acceptable answers.

WHAT DO STUDENTS NEED TO KNOW?

If our educational goal is to promote scientific reasoning, what do students need to know to be able to solve scientific reasoning problems such as those in Table 7.1? Based on an adaptation of taxonomies of learning outcome (Anderson et al., 2001), Table 7.2 lists five kinds of knowledge that appear to be needed for scientific reasoning: facts, concepts, procedures, strategies, and beliefs. *Facts* are basic descriptions of the characteristics of elements. In particular, the Dr. Phyz lesson introduces facts that are relevant to the functioning of the system, such as knowing that electricity flows from negative to positive terminals. *Concepts* refer to "interrelations among elements within a larger structure that enable them to function together" (Anderson et al., 2001, p. 29). In particular, the Dr. Phyz lesson focuses on helping students build a mental model of a causal system, that is, knowing the cause-and-effect chain involved in how an electric motor works. *Procedures* refer to algorithms for how to

TABLE 7.2. Examples of Five Types of Knowledge Required
for Scientific Reasoning

Type of knowledge	Example
Facts	Knowing that the rate of electrical flow is measured in amps or that a battery is used to power the flow of electricity.
Concepts	Having a mental model of the causal and effect chain of how an electric motor works.
Procedures	Knowing arithmetic and algebraic rules for how to compute the rate of electricity flow based on a formula.
Strategies	Knowing how to run a mental model in order to answer a question and being able to determine whether a solution plan is working.
Beliefs	Thinking of oneself as capable of solving scientific reasoning problems.

do something, such as how to carry out arithmetic computations when using a formula. When scientific reasoning requires quantitative thinking, arithmetic and algebraic procedures are needed. *Strategies* are general methods for planning and monitoring how to accomplish some task, such as knowing how to mentally run or manipulate your mental model of the electric motor to answer questions. *Metastrategies* are special strategies used for monitoring performance and for coordinating all the kinds of knowledge, such as determining that you need to use your mental model of electric motors in order to answer a question you received. Finally, *beliefs* include the idea that scientific material is or is not understandable, such as believing that you can understand how electric motors work if you try.

This analysis suggests that there is more to learning than acquiring facts and procedures. In particular, meaningful learning—that is, learning that leads to successful scientific reasoning—also requires developing concepts (i.e., a mental model of the electric motor), strategies (i.e., the ability to manipulate and run the mental model), and beliefs (i.e., the idea that it is possible to understand how an electric motor works).

WHAT COGNITIVE PROCESSING DURING LEARNING LEADS TO SCIENTIFIC REASONING?

Figure 7.2 summarizes a cognitive theory of multimedia learning, which highlights five cognitive processes during learning: selecting words, selecting pictures, organizing words, organizing pictures, and integrating (Mayer, 2001, 2005; Mayer & Moreno, 2003). On the left side, we begin with a multimedia lesson consisting of words and pictures (such as a nar-

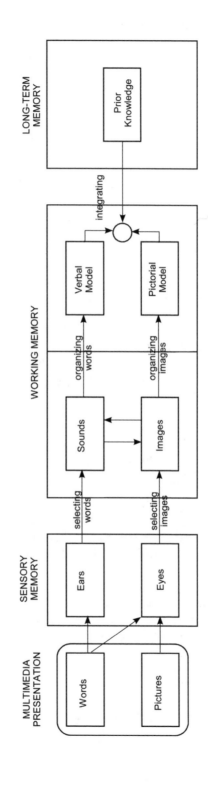

FIGURE 7.2. A cognitive theory of multimedia learning. From Mayer, Heiser, & Lonn (2001). Copyright by the American Psychological Association. Reprinted by permission.

165

rated animation). The spoken words enter your cognitive system through your ears and are held in auditory sensory memory. The pictures enter your cognitive system through your eyes and are held in visual sensory memory. The information in the auditory and visual sensory memories fades rapidly, but as you pay attention part of the information can be transferred to working memory (as is indicated by the "selecting words" and "selecting pictures" arrows). In working memory, processing capacity is limited, but you can use some of the capacity to mentally organize the words into a coherent structure and mentally organize the pictures into a coherent structure (as indicated by the "organizing words" and "organizing pictures" arrows). Finally, you can integrate the pictorial and verbal models with each other and with relevant information from long-term memory (as indicated by the "integrating" arrow).

According to the cognitive theory of multimedia learning, meaningful learning occurs when learners successfully engage in all five of these cognitive processes. Meaningful learning enables the construction of a runnable mental model that can be used for scientific reasoning. In contrast, rote learning occurs when learners engage mainly in selecting relevant words and pictures. In this case the learner selects parts of the words and pictures to be stored in long-term memory, but does not integrate and organize them into a coherent mental model. Thus, the learner may perform well on retention tests—in which the learner is asked to remember parts of the presentation—but not on scientific reasoning tasks—in which the learner needs to run or manipulate a causal model. There is encouraging evidence that students can learn strategies for guiding their cognitive processing during learning (Pressley & Harris, 2006; Pressley & Woloshyn, 1995).

WHICH INSTRUCTIONAL METHODS PRIME COGNITIVE PROCESSING THAT LEADS TO SCIENTIFIC REASONING?

The next step in promoting scientific reasoning is to determine the instructional methods that prime the cognitive processes of selecting, organizing, and integrating during learning. In short, an important goal of instructional research is to determine how to help students learn in ways that will allow them to transfer what they have learned to new situations—including scientific reasoning. As summarized in Table 7.3, I examine some exemplary techniques for promoting meaningful learning of scientific explanations based on research conducted by my colleagues and me at the University of California, Santa Barbara: techniques for selecting (coherence principle and contiguity principle), techniques for

TABLE 7.3. Instructional Techniques for Promoting Meaningful Learning

Technique	Definition
Techniques for selecting	
Coherence principle	People learn better from a multimedia lesson when extraneous words and pictures are excluded.
Contiguity principle	People learn better from a multimedia lesson when words are placed next to corresponding pictures.
Techniques for organizing	
Signaling principle	People learn better from a multimedia lesson when the organization is highlighted.
Segmenting principle	People learn better from a multimedia lesson when the lesson is presented in learner-paced segments.
Techniques for integrating	
Multimedia principle	People learn better from words and pictures than from words alone.
Pretraining principle	People learn better from a multimedia lesson when they know the names and characteristics of key components.

organizing (signaling principle and segmenting principle), and techniques for integrating (pretraining principle and multimedia principle).

Techniques for Selecting Coherence and Contiguity Principles

First, how can we help students select the relevant words and pictures from a multimedia lesson for further processing? Two useful techniques are what I call the *coherence principle* and the *contiguity principle*. The coherence principle is that people learn better from a multimedia lesson when extraneous material is excluded rather than included. When extraneous material is excluded, learners are less likely to select irrelevant information for further processing and more likely to select relevant information (as indicated by the "selecting" arrows in Figure 7.2). In addition, they are less likely to waste their limited cognitive processing capacity on extraneous processing, so they have more capacity available for the appropriate cognitive processing during learning.

For example, consider a multimedia lesson that explains the process of lightning formation. The lesson consists of a narrated animation, depicting 16 steps in the causal chain, and runs for about 2½ minutes. Suppose we then test scientific reasoning by asking students to answer the types of questions in Table 7.1 (e.g., a troubleshooting question for the lightning lesson is, "Suppose you see clouds in the sky but no lightning. Why not?"). What happens if we spice up the lesson by inserting a few short video clips of lightning storms, or by inserting interesting facts or anecdotes about incidents involving lightning? We found that adding interesting but irrelevant material tends to decrease students' performance on tests of scientific reasoning. This finding was consistent across a series of 13 experimental tests carried out in our lab involving lessons on how lightning forms (Harp & Mayer, 1997, Experiment 1; Harp & Mayer, 1998, Experiments 1, 2, 3, and 4; Mayer, Bove, Bryman, Mars, & Tapangco, 1996, Experiments 1, 2, and 3; Mayer, Heiser, & Lonn, 2001, Experiment 3; Moreno & Mayer, 2000, Experiment 1), how brakes work (Moreno & Mayer, 2000, Experiment 2), and how ocean waves work (Mayer & Jackson, 2005, Experiments 1 and 2). The median effect size favoring the concise lesson was 0.98, which is a large effect. When the goal is to promote scientific reasoning about a causal system, you should eliminate material that is not essential for explaining how the system works.

Another way to guide the learner's attention is the contiguity principle—the idea that people learn better when printed words are placed next to the part of the graphic that they describe on a page or screen. For example, consider an annotated animation on lightning formation, in which captions at the bottom of the screen describe what is happening in the animation. A problem with this format is that learners do not know where to look in the animation to see what is being described in the caption. The result is that they may engage in a lot of visual scanning—looking at portions of the animation that are not relevant to the instructional goal. In this way they tend to select pictures that are not relevant and thereby make it more difficult to construct a mental model of the system. In order to help guide the learner's attention, we can place the printed description next to the corresponding part of the animation. For example, the printed text, " ... negative particles fall to the bottom of the cloud ... " should be placed next to the bottom of cloud in the animation as the negative particles are moving to the bottom. In this way, when the learner reads the relevant words, the learner is also likely to view relevant pictures (indicated by the "selecting" arrows), and make a mental connection between them (indicated by the "integrating" arrow).

In a series of five experiments involving multimedia lessons on lightning (Mayer, Steinhoff, Bower, & Mars, 1995, Experiments 1, 2, and 3; Moreno & Mayer, 1999, Experiment 1) and brakes (Mayer, 1989, Experiment 2), we found that students performed better on transfer tests when they learned from lessons in which printed words were placed next to the corresponding part of the graphic rather than at the bottom of the graphic. The median effect size was 1.12, which is a large effect. Similar results were reported by Chandler and Sweller (1991, Experiment 1), Sweller, Chandler, Tierney, and Cooper (1990, Experiment 1), and Tindall-Ford, Chandler, and Sweller (1997, Experiment 1). When a lesson consists of printed words and graphics—either on a screen or on a page—learners engage in more appropriate cognitive processing when the words are placed near the graphics they describe.

Techniques for Organizing: Signaling and Segmenting Principles

The next two techniques listed in Table 7.3, *signaling* and *segmenting*, are intended to help learners mentally organize relevant aspects of the incoming information into a coherent structure. First, consider a narrated animation on how airplanes achieve lift in which the explanation is complex and the script contains many extraneous facts. How can we help the learner attend to the relevant material and organize it into a causal chain? If we can't eliminate the extraneous material (as called for in the coherence principle), the next best approach is to use cues that highlight the important information and show how it should be organized (as called for in the signaling principle). Signaling includes adding an introductory outline statement, such as a list of the three main steps in lift; adding headings, such as each of the three main steps; and emphasizing the key principles through verbal intonation, such as "because it is curved, the surface on the **top** of the wing is **longer** than on the **bottom** ..."(in which bolded words were emphasized). In signaling, no new content material is added, but the key material is highlighted and organized for the learner. After receiving a narrated animation lasting about 4 minutes, students were asked to solve the types of transfer problems described in Table 7.1. For example, a redesign question is: "How could an airplane be designed to achieve lift more rapidly?"

Mautone and Mayer (2001) found that students performed better on the transfer test after receiving the signaled version rather than the nonsignaled version. Overall, signaling improved scientific reasoning performance on a series of three experimental tests involving multimedia lessons on airplane flight (Mautone & Mayer, Experiments 3a and 3b) and lightning (Harp & Mayer, 1998, Experiment 3a). The median effect size was 0.60, which is in the medium to large range. When the goal is to guide how students select and organize presented material, signaling can be an effective technique.

Next consider a situation in which students receive a continuous presentation, such as a narrated animation on lightning formation. The lesson consists of 16 main steps in the causal chain, but the material is presented at a fast pace without much time for learners to see the connection from one step to the next. What can be done to help learners identify the main steps and mentally organize them into a causal chain? A technique intended to help guide cognitive processing during learning in this situation is segmenting. In segmenting, we break a continuous lesson into smaller segments—each containing one main link in the causal chain—and we allow the learner to control the start of each new segment. For example, in the lighting lesson, a segment may consist of about 10 seconds of animation and one or two sentences of narration, after which a "CONTINUE" button appears on the screen. When the learner clicks on the button, the next segment is presented followed by a "CONTINUE" button, and so on.

Mayer and Chandler (2001) found that students who learned with a segmented lesson performed better on solving scientific reasoning problems (like in Table 7.1) than did students who learned with a continuous lesson. Overall, in a series of three experimental tests, segmenting a multimedia lesson improved learning of explanations about lightning (Mayer & Chandler, 2001) and about electric motors (Mayer et al., 2003, Experiments 2a and 2b). The median effect size favoring segmented rather than continuous presentation was 0.98, which is a large effect. When the goal is to help learners select and organize relevant material, segmenting can be an effective technique.

Techniques for Integrating: Multimedia and Pretraining Principles

How can we help learners understand a scientific explanation more deeply? Two techniques listed in Table 7.3 are to add appropriate graphics (i.e., *multimedia principle*) and to begin with familiar concepts (i.e., *pretraining principle*). The multimedia principle is that people learn more deeply from words and pictures than from words alone. According to the cognitive theory of multimedia learning, students learn more deeply when they are able to integrate their pictorial and verbal representations. Presenting corresponding words and pictures is intended to facilitate this process of integrating pictorial and verbal representations.

For example, consider the following explanation of how a bicycle tire pump works: "When the handle is pulled up, the piston moves up, the inlet valve opens, the outlet valve closes, and air enters the lower part of the cylinder. When the handle is pushed down, the piston moves down, the inlet valve closes, the outlet valve opens, and air moves out through the hose." Does this explanation enable students to engage in scientific reasoning such as being able to answer the kinds of questions listed in

Table 7.1? For example, a troubleshooting question is: "Suppose you pull up and push down several times but no air comes out of the hose. What could have gone wrong?" Mayer and Anderson (1992) report that students who received a spoken explanation of how the pump works performed relatively poorly on answering scientific reasoning questions like this one. In contrast, scientific reasoning performance was much better when they added a short concurrent animation depicting the actions described in the spoken explanation. In short, students learned better with words and pictures than with words alone.

Overall, in a series of ten experimental comparisons involving explanations of pumps (Mayer & Anderson, 1991, Experiment 2a; Mayer & Anderson, 1992, Experiment 1; Mayer & Gallini, 1990, Experiment 2), brakes (Mayer, 1989, Experiments 1 and 2; Mayer & Anderson, 1992, Experiment 2; Mayer & Gallini, 1990, Experiment 1), generators (Mayer & Gallini, Experiment 3), and lightning (Mayer et al., 1996, Experiment 2; Moreno & Mayer, 2002, Experiment 1), there was consistent evidence for the multimedia principle. Students who learned from listening to or reading words alone performed more poorly on scientific reasoning transfer tests than did students who also received corresponding animation or illustrations. The median effect size favoring words and pictures was 1.50, which is a large effect. In addition, numerous other researchers have also obtained the same pattern of results concerning scientific explanations for inexperienced learners (Fletcher & Tobias, 2005). In summary, when the goal is to foster deep processing including integrating knowledge, using multimedia presentations can be an effective technique. Of course, all graphics are not equally effective so research is needed to determine the features of effective multimedia presentations.

The final technique listed in Table 7.3 is pretraining, in which the learner is familiarized with key concepts before the lesson is presented. The goal of pretraining is make sure that the learner activates appropriate prior knowledge when presented with the lesson. For example, consider a narrated animation on how a car's braking system works. One of the lines in the narration contains the words, " … a piston moves forward in the master cylinder.… " If the learner does not know what a piston is or how it works, this part of the presentation will be confusing. The learner may search her long-term memory, but not be able to find useful information about pistons. Mental effort used on trying to figure out what these words mean is wasted, and detracts from the main effort to build a mental model of the braking system. In contrast, suppose we provide pretraining concerning how each of the key components works. Learners are shown a graphic of the piston in the master cylinder and shown how the piston can move forward and back. In this way, the learner builds useful knowledge about the characteristics of each component. Then, when presented with a narrated animation, the learner can relate each term to relevant prior knowledge from long-term memory—as indicated by the "integrating" arrow in Figure 7.2.

Mayer, Mathias, and Wetzell (2002) found that students who received this kind of pretraining performed better on scientific reasoning transfer tests than did students who did not receive the pretraining. Pretrained learners were better able to answer questions of the types like those listed in Table 7.1, such as the troubleshooting question, "Suppose you press on the brake pedal in your car but the brakes do not work. What could have gone wrong?" Overall, in five experiments involving brakes (Mayer, Mathias, & Wetzell, 2002, Experiments 1 and 2), pumps (Mayer, Mathias, & Wetzell, 2002, Experiment 3), and geology (Mayer, Mautone, & Prothero, 2002, Experiments 2 and 3), students who received pretraining in the names and characteristics of the key concepts performed better on scientific reasoning questions than did students who had not received pretraining. The median effect size was 0.92, which is considered a large effect. Pollock, Chandler, and Sweller (2002, Experiments 1 and 3) obtained similar results in a lesson involving electrical engineering. In addition, classic research on advance organizers shows that students understand scientific explanations more deeply when they are preceded by a concrete advance organizer—words and/or graphics presenting an analogous system (Mayer, 2008). Overall, the pretraining principle is based on the idea that sometimes students need help in making connections between what is presented and what they already know.

CONCLUSION

In conclusion, this chapter examines how to improve scientific reasoning. In particular, this chapter focuses on a specific goal of science instruction: helping students understand scientific explanations. A *scientific explanation* provides a step-by-step presentation of a causal chain in order to help the student understand how a causal system works. The learner must build a mental model of the system and be able to manipulate that model when asked scientific reasoning questions, such as troubleshooting questions. Building a runnable mental models requires the learner to engage in appropriate cognitive processing during learning—including attending to the relevant information in the lesson, mentally organizing the material, and integrating it with other knowledge.

In this chapter, I examined six exemplary techniques for fostering appropriate cognitive processing during learning from multimedia lessons and summarized research showing that each resulted in improvements in students' performance on tests of scientific reasoning. The six principles listed in Table 7.3 should not be taken as unalterable laws, but rather should be applied in ways that are consistent with the cognitive theory of multimedia learning. They work when they influence the learner's cognitive processing—selecting, organizing, and integrating—so it is important to determine the conditions under which they are most effective. For example, some techniques that are effective for learners who lack much knowledge about the domain (i.e., as in examined in this chapter) may not be effective for learners who have greater knowledge about the domain (Kalyuga, 2005).

Overall, there is reason for optimism concerning the potential for educational psychology to improve student learning. My hope is that this chapter provides a modest contribution to that lofty goal. In particular, I have examined research-based instructional methods for improving multimedia science lessons that produce large increases in student performance on scientific reasoning tasks—with many effect sizes above 1. Although the research I reviewed in this chapter mainly involves short-term studies with college students in laboratory settings, there is preliminary evidence that some of the principles also apply in more authentic educational settings (Harskamp, Mayer, Suhre, & Jansma, 2007). Overall, this work represents an attempt to apply the science of learning, that is, to develop principles for instruction that are consistent with and contribute to a theory of how people learn.

ACKNOWLEDGMENT

Preparation of the chapter was supported by a grant from the Office of Naval Research.

REFERENCES

Anderson, L. W., Krathwohl, D. R., Airasian, P. W., Cruickshank, K. A., Mayer, R. E., Pintrich, P. R., et al. (2001). *A taxonomy for learning, teaching, and assessing: A revision of Bloom's taxonomy of educational objectives.* New York: Longman.

Chandler, P., & Sweller, J. (1991). Cognitive load theory and the format of instruction. *Cognition and Instruction, 8,* 293–332.

Fletcher, J. D., & Tobias, S. (2005). The multimedia principle. In R. E. Mayer (Ed.), *The Cambridge handbook of multimedia learning* (pp. 117–134). New York: Cambridge University Press.

Harp, S. F., & Mayer, R. E. (1997). The role of interest in learning from scientific text and illustrations: On the distinction between emotional interest and cognitive interest. *Journal of Educational Psychology, 89,* 92–102.

Harp, S. F., & Mayer, R. E. (1998). How seductive details do their damage: A theory of cognitive interest in science learning. *Journal of Educational Psychology, 90,* 414–434.

Harskamp, E., Mayer, R. E., Suhre, C., & Jansma, J. (2007). Does the modality principle for multimedia learning apply to science classrooms? *Learning and Instruction, 17,* 465–477.

Kalyuga, S. (2005). Prior knowledge principle in multimedia learning. In R. E. Mayer (Ed.), *The Cambridge handbook of multimedia learning* (pp. 325–338). New York: Cambridge University Press.

Mautone, P. D., & Mayer, R. E. (2001). Signaling as a cognitive guide in multimedia learning. *Journal of Educational Psychology, 93,* 377–389.

Mayer, R. E. (1989). Systematic thinking fostered by illustrations in scientific text. *Journal of Educational Psychology, 81,* 240–246.

Mayer, R. E. (2001). *Multimedia learning.* New York: Cambridge University Press.

Mayer, R. E. (Ed.). (2005). *The Cambridge handbook of multimedia learning.* New York: Cambridge University Press.

Mayer. R. E. (2008). *Learning and instruction* (2nd ed.). Upper Saddle River, NJ: Pearson Merrill Prentice Hall.

Mayer, R. E., & Anderson, R. B. (1991). Animations need narrations: An experimental test of a dual-coding hypothesis. *Journal of Educational Psychology, 83,* 484–490.

Mayer, R. E., & Anderson, R. B. (1992). The instructive animation: Helping students build connections between words and pictures in multimedia learning. *Journal of Educational Psychology, 84,* 444–452.

Mayer, R. E., Bove, W., Bryman, A., Mars, R., & Tapangco, L. (1996). When less is more: Meaningful learning from visual and verbal summaries of science textbook lessons. *Journal of Educational Psychology, 88,* 64–73.

Mayer, R. E., & Chandler, P. (2001). When learning is just a click away: Does simple user interaction foster deeper understanding of multimedia messages? *Journal of Educational Psychology, 93,* 390–387.

Mayer, R. E., Dow, G. T., & Mayer, S. (2003). Multimedia learning in an interactive self-explaining environment: What works in the design of agent-based microworlds? *Journal of Educational Psychology, 93,* 806–813.

Mayer, R. E., & Gallini, J. K. (1990). When is an illustration worth ten thousand words? *Journal of Educational Psychology, 82,* 715–726.

Mayer, R. E., Heiser, H., & Lonn, S. (2001). Cognitive constraints on multimedia learning: When presenting more material results in less understanding. *Journal of Educational Psychology, 93,* 187–198.

Mayer, R. E., & Jackson, J. (2005). The case for coherence in scientific explanations: Quantitative details can hurt qualitative understanding. *Journal of Experimental Psychology: Applied, 11,* 13–18.

Mayer, R. E., Mathias, A., & Wetzell, K. (2002). Fostering understanding of multimedia messages through pre-training: Evidence for a two stage model of mental model construction. *Journal of Experimental Psychology: Applied, 8,* 147–154.

Mayer, R. E., Mautone, P., & Prothero, W. (2002). Pictorial aids for learning by doing in a multimedia geology simulation game. *Journal of Educational Psychology, 94*, 171–185.

Mayer, R. E., & Moreno, R. (2003). Nine ways to reduce cognitive load in multimedia learning. *Educational Psychologist, 38*, 43–52.

Mayer, R. E., Steinhoff, K., Bower, G., & Mars, R. (1995). A generative theory of textbook design: Using annotated illustrations to foster meaningful learning of science text. *Educational Technology Research and Development, 43*, 31–43.

Moreno, R., & Mayer, R. E. (1999). Cognitive principles of multimedia learning: The role of modality and contiguity. *Journal of Educational Psychology, 91*, 358–368.

Moreno, R., & Mayer, R. E. (2000). A coherence effect in multimedia learning: The case for minimizing irrelevant sounds in the design of multimedia messages. *Journal of Educational Psychology, 92*, 117–125.

Moreno, R., & Mayer, R. E. (2002). Learning science in virtual reality multimedia environments: Role of methods and media. *Journal of Educational Psychology, 94*, 598–610.

Pollock, E., Chandler, P., & Sweller, J. (2002). Assimilating complex information. *Learning and Instruction, 12*, 61–86.

Pressley, M., & Harris, K. (2006). Cognitive strategies instruction: From basic research to classroom instruction. In P. A. Alexander & P. H. Winne (Eds.), *Handbook of educational psychology* (pp. 265–286). Mahwah, NJ: Erlbaum.

Pressley, M., & Woloshyn, V. (1995). *Cognitive strategy instruction that really improves children's academic performance* (2nd ed.). Cambridge, MA: Brookline Press.

Sweller, J., Chandler, P., Tierney, P., & Cooper, M. (1990). Cognitive load and selective attention as factors in the structuring of technical material. *Journal of Experimental Psychology: General, 119*, 176–192.

Tindall-Ford, S., Chandler, P., & Sweller, J. (1997). When two sensory modes are better than one. *Journal of Experimental Psychology: Applied, 3*, 257–287.

8

The Importance of Metacognition for Conceptual Change and Strategy Use in Mathematics

Martha Carr

In explaining the development of mathematics strategies and mathematics achievement, the focus has tended to be on the development and organization of conceptual knowledge (e.g., Lampert, 1986; Steffe, Cobb, & von Glaserfeld, 1988). Although the quality of conceptual knowledge is important for explaining performance in mathematics, metacognitive knowledge and skills play an important role in determining how well and how quickly students will learn. The ability of individuals to assess the state of their knowledge has been found to support the emergence of more advanced conceptual knowledge (e.g., Kuhn, 2002). In addition, good problem solving in mathematics requires metacognitive skills and knowledge (Borkowski, 1992; Carr & Biddlecomb, 1998; De Corte, Verschaffel, & Op't Eynde, 2000; Schoenfeld, 1983). As early as kindergarten, metacognitive knowledge is a better predictor of mathematics performance on a word problem test than a measure of general ability (Mevarech, 1995). As we learn more about how metacognition influences learning, it becomes increasingly evident that mathematics curricula need to include metacognitive instruction as a means of improving the quality and speed of learning.

Metacognitive skills and knowledge take a number of different forms including declarative knowledge about strategies, tasks, and the self as learner; metacognitive reflection and monitoring that occurs during problem solving; and more general metacognitive understanding of the need to be strategic and the role of effort in learning (Pressley, Borkowski, & Schneider, 1987). According to Pressley et al. (1987), these metacognitive skills and knowledge combine with good conceptual and procedural knowledge to regulate problem solving for optimal performance. Metacognitive knowledge and skills are not the only factors that affect learning, but without metacognition learning becomes difficult and slow, as students rely on others to guide problem solving.

Metacognitive knowledge and skills are unique in the cognitive system in that they are both forms of declarative and procedural knowledge and a mechanism by which both forms of knowledge may be modified. Metacognitive knowledge and skills, for example, support the use of existing strategies because when students possess declarative metacognitive knowledge they know when, why, and how to use strategies. Metacognitive monitoring and reflection support the emergence of new strategies when students modify an existing strategy in response to a new situation (Crowley, Shrager, & Siegler, 1997). The outcome of these discoveries, in turn, supports the emergence of more sophisticated metacognitive knowledge and more efficient monitoring (see Figure 8.1).

This chapter focuses on what we know about how conceptual change in mathematics occurs as a function of metacognition and the role of metacognition in the development and use of strategies during problem solving. Explicit instruction of declarative and procedural metacognitive knowledge is argued to be critical for both conceptual change and the development of strategies. Recommendations are made for a renewal of research focusing on the learning of mathematics as a reflective process.

METACOGNITION AND CONCEPTUAL CHANGE IN MATHEMATICS

Much of the theory on conceptual change points to the importance of metacognition (e.g., Dole & Sinatra, 1998; Piaget, 1976). Learning is facilitated when a student is able to reflect on the difference between what he or she thinks is true and new information either verifying or discounting that belief (Kuhn, 2002). This process allows for inconsistencies in current beliefs to be made evident and for new beliefs to be constructed based on new information (Vosniadou & Verschaffel, 2004). Reflection through writing can also promote the construction of conceptual knowledge in a new domain, such as calculus (Cooley, 2002). It is through

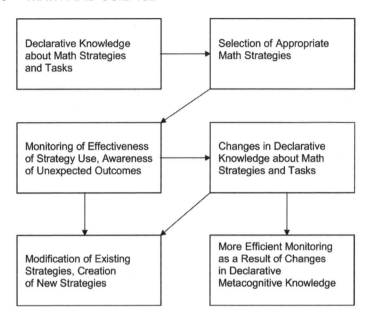

FIGURE 8.1. The interaction between declarative and procedural metacognitive knowledge.

reflection that increasingly complex and coherent theories develop as students integrate new information with what they already know.

The research in mathematics education suggests that many of the difficulties students have learning mathematics are a result of conflicts between their current beliefs and new information being taught (Stafylidou & Vosniadou, 2004). For instance, students have difficulty with fractions because they approach the learning of fractions believing that the outcome of multiplication results in a larger number, but this conflicts with evidence indicating that the multiplication of fractions produces smaller numbers (Stafylidou & Vosniadou, 2004). The solution to such conflicts is not to replace old with new knowledge, but to promote the construction of a more complex and abstract representation that includes both new and old beliefs in a coherent and cohesive structure (Merenluoto & Lehtinen, 2004). In the case of multiplication, students need to construct a representation that explains how multiplication for whole numbers and fractions is related. Work by Merenlouto and Lehtinen (2002) indicates that high school students who use metacognitive strategies to integrate their concepts of rational and natural numbers have a better understanding of those concepts. Likewise, the ability to monitor has been found to make it easier for students to develop an appropriate conceptual understanding of ratios as a single unit, as opposed to two separate units or composites (Lamon, 1993).

A number of factors limit the development of metacognitive knowledge and skills, and conceptual change. Students with larger working memories are more self-aware and able to reflect on themselves as learners (Demetriou & Kazi, 2001). In elementary school, students' declarative metacognitive knowledge about their problem-solving skills is linked with their working memory capacity (Panaoura, 2006). In addition, growing up in a low-income home appears to hinder the emergence of declarative metacognitive knowledge about mathematics. Pappas, Ginesburg, and Jiang (2003) found that preschool children from low socioeconomic status (SES) homes had poorer declarative metacognitive knowledge in comparison to children from middle SES homes. Specifically, low SES preschool-age children were less able than middle-income preschoolers to explain their problem solving processes and what they know about mathematics. Factors such as working memory and low SES status likely make it difficult for students to develop the declarative metacognitive knowledge needed to support conceptual change.

We have evidence that metacognitive reflection is important for conceptual change and that declarative metacognitive knowledge, as a form of conceptual knowledge, is influenced by working memory and SES. Much more work, however, needs to be done on the relationship between reflection and the emergence of more complex and abstract mathematical knowledge. We also need to know more about how students' knowledge about themselves as learners and about strategy use emerges out of their mathematical experiences. Given the abstract nature of mathematics and some of the major conceptual shifts that must take place in order for students to progress in mathematics, research on teaching methods designed to enhance reflection should result in improved conceptual change in students' mathematical knowledge.

METACOGNITION AND MATHEMATICS PROBLEM SOLVING

A substantial body of research points to the importance of metacognitive knowledge and skills for problem solving. It distinguishes high from low achievers, students with disabilities from average students, and experts from novices. As with the research on conceptual change, much of the research on problem solving has focused on the role of metacognitive procedural knowledge, including planning, evaluation, monitoring, and self-calibration, in problem solving. Declarative metacognitive knowledge, however, discriminates high- from low-achieving students and seems to be a developmental precursor to metacognitive procedural knowledge. Thus, each form of metacognition appears to play a key role in problem solving.

A significant difference between expert and novice mathematicians and between high- and low-performing students is in their use of metacognitive skills during problem solving. Whereas novices tend to read the problem and then use trial-and-error methods to solve it, experts devote considerable time to analyzing the problem, planning, and verifying the results of their chosen strategy (Schoenfeld, 1987). When good and poor mathematics students are compared, a similar profile emerges. Lucangeli, Cornoldi, and Tellarini (1998) and Lucangeli and Cornoldi (1997) found that students who were good in mathematics were better at predicting outcomes, planning ahead, monitoring, and evaluating their work on arithmetical reasoning and problem-solving tasks. Other research indicates that students who are better able to calibrate their evaluations of their mathematics performance to reflect actual performance have higher mathematics achievement (Desoete & Roeyers, 2006). Metacognitive procedural knowledge also discriminates between third-grade students who are more flexible in their mathematics problem solving and children who use inflexible, rote procedures (Heirdsfield & Cooper, 2004).

The ability to use metacognitive skills, such as monitoring and planning, during problem solving is influenced by the students' state of current conceptual understanding. Students require some conceptual knowledge on which to base judgments about the accuracy of their conclusions and the success of their problem solving (Nietfeld & Schraw, 2002). Heirdsfield and Cooper (2002), for example, found that preschool-age children with better number sense were more likely to accurately predict whether they could solve a problem and recognized when they were going off track in their computation. Metacognitive knowledge, monitoring, and domain-specific conceptual knowledge intersect in what Siegler and Crowley (1994) refer to as "goal sketches." Goal sketches are used when students monitor their problem solving to evaluate whether the outcome is within set boundaries for possible outcomes. For example, when adding two numbers, students have a goal sketch of the answer being larger than either of the two numbers being added. As students acquire a richer conceptual knowledge, their goal sketches will become more accurate as an estimate of the solution, allowing them to better calibrate their actions for better performance.

A number of studies have linked declarative metacognitive knowledge to better problem solving and mathematics achievement. Elementary-school-age students who are better able to explain why and when they should use arithmetic strategies are better at solving basic computation problems (Carr & Jessup, 1995). Middle school students who can describe when and how to use strategies likewise are more likely to be successful in solving word problems (Teong, 2002). Declarative metacognitive knowledge seems to be particularly important for newly emerging mathematics strategies as opposed to older, familiar strategies (Carr, Alexander, & Folds-Bennett, 1994). This suggests that declarative metacognitive knowledge might help students who are just beginning to experiment with a new strategy to better select problems on which to use the strategy and to be more accurate in its use.

The development of declarative metacognitive knowledge appears to precede the development of metacognitive procedural knowledge and is thought to support the emergence of procedural metacognitive knowledge (Mcdonald, 1990). Younger children tend to develop declarative metacognitive knowledge before they develop procedural metacognitive knowledge. For example, Lester and Garofalo (1982) found that third- and fifth-grade students had declarative metacognitive knowledge about mathematics strategies in that they were able to report different counting strategies, but they did not routinely analyze problem information, monitor progress, or evaluate results. In older students, both forms of metacognition have emerged and are correlated. Perrenet and Wolters (1994), for example, found eighth-grade students' metacognitive declarative knowledge to be correlated with the use of metacognitive procedures for checking and correcting solutions on linear equation problem solving. The limited declarative metacognitive knowledge of students from low SES homes (Pappas et al., 2003) reflects a generally poor vocabulary that is thought to limit students' ability to interpret and translate mathematics problems (Cardelle-Elwar, 1995).

Differences in metacognition and developmental delays in mathematics strategies characterize students with mathematics disabilities as well (Geary & Brown, 1991; Montague & Bos, 1990). Montague and Bos (1990) compared eighth-grade students with a mathematics learning disability to high-, average-, and low-achieving students in mathematics. The students were compared on cognitive and metacognitive characteristics related to mathematical problem solving, including assessments of mathematical achievement, mathematical reasoning, mathematical problem solving, declarative metacognitive knowledge about strategies, and control of strategies. The difficulties that low achieving students and students with mathematics disabilities had with problem solving were found to be less related to computation errors than to the ability to predict outcomes and select the correct procedure. Students with learning disabilities were also found to have less declarative metacognitive knowledge about problem-solving strategies, making it difficult for them to regulate strategy use. Other research indicates that when differences in cognitive abilities, including IQ and performance on mathematics tests, are controlled, elementary-school-age students with mathematics disabilities are less skilled than average-ability students in declarative metacognitive knowledge about problem solving and in the regulation of problem-solving strategies (Slife, Weiss, & Bell, 1985). For these students, the ability to select appropriate strategies to solve problems and a poor understanding of strategies limits their ability to progress in mathematics.

The results of the work on metacognition and problem solving indicate that both forms of metacognition are characteristic of good problem solving. As proposed by Pressley et al. (1987), good problem solving is the outcome of the interaction of declarative and procedural metacognitive knowledge and mathematical conceptual knowledge. This process may be hindered when students have learning disabilities that affect a number of cognitive systems, including metacognitive procedural and declarative knowledge. Whereas we know little about how to instruct metacognitive knowledge and skills for better conceptual change, there is a substantial body of knowledge related to the instruction of metacognition for better problem solving and mathematics achievement.

HOW SHOULD METACOGNITION BE INSTRUCTED?

Mathematics is frequently taught by having children memorize procedures. There is ample research in a number of domains showing that this does not work. First, the fact that students have learned a procedure does not mean that they know why and when they should use it (e.g., O'Sullivan & Pressley, 1984). Nor does the rote learning and application of procedures mean that students understand how they work (e.g., Pressley, Levin, & Ghatala, 1984). Rote learning of procedures, more importantly, results in students failing to understand how the procedure can be altered and transferred (e.g., Pressley, Harris, & Marks, 1992). Within the domain of mathematics, students who rely on memorization of procedures and facts do more poorly than students who use metacognitive strategies to learn mathematics, even in Asian countries that are thought to emphasize rote memorization strategies in mathematics instruction (Chiu, Chow, & McBride-Chang, 2007).

When mathematics is taught as a set of rote procedures a number of problems emerge. One problem occurs when poor conceptual knowledge makes it difficult for children to carry out procedures accurately. For example, when children first begin to do double and triple digit arithmetic, they often develop buggy algorithms as a result of a poor understanding of place value (Fuson, 1992). The solutions that result from these buggy algorithms are often wildly off base and children are not aware of the discrepancy between their answer and the correct answer.

A second problem is the tendency of students to fail to reflect on the adequacy of the procedures used for solving mathematics problems, why these procedures are selected for use, and whether the outcome makes any sense (Schoenfeld, 1985). Schoenfeld (1987) described a study in which secondary students determined how many buses were needed to transport 1,128 soldiers to a training site when each bus held 36 soldiers. Forty-seven percent of the students did not correctly answer the questions because they did not round the remainder up to the next number. In the real world, this would have resulted in too few buses and a major transportation problem. Their answers may have been computationally correct, but incorrect when applied to a real-world problem. One reason why these problems emerge is that students lack the general metacognitive understanding that mathematics should make sense, and therefore they make no effort to determine whether it does (Silver, Shapiro, & Deutsch, 1993).

It is clear that children need to understand mathematics as more than the rote application of procedures and memorization of facts. In response to this problem, recent research on mathematics instruction has explored a number of techniques for promoting understanding over rote learning. The techniques, presented in Table 8.1, share a common characteristic in that they all focus on teaching children to reflect on their problem solving and on their conceptual knowledge during learning. This can be accomplished in a number of ways. Studies utilizing direct instruction of strategies and metacognitive knowledge have been found to improve students' procedural skills and their mathematics achievement. Teaching methods that involve more explanation and questioning are characteristic of higher performing classrooms, likely because asking children to explain prompts children to look for and construct declarative metacognitive knowledge (Perry, 2000). Curriculum that involves explanation through social discourse and co-construction of mathematical knowledge likewise allows students to construct a good understanding of the mathematics they are learning (Leinhardt & Steele, 2005). There is no evidence that a single method is better than the others. de Jager, Jansen, and Reezigt (2005), for example, compared direct instruction and cognitive apprenticeship models of instruction in seventh-grade children and found that the two methods worked equally well in improving metacognitive skills and knowledge. The bulk of the work on instruction designed to teach metacognitive skills and to improve performance, however, has utilized direct instruction of strategies and metacognition. Thus, the research literature supports the use of explicit instruction of metacognition and strategies.

That research shows that direct instruction of declarative and procedural metacognitive knowledge improves both mathematics achieve-

TABLE 8.1. Metacognitive Instructional Techniques for Promoting Mathematics Learning

Technique	Definition and examples
Explicit instruction (declarative)	Providing direct or explicit instruction on strategies in combination with metacognitive declarative knowledge. For example, telling children why strategies work, when they should and should not be used; telling children which strategies should be used for which tasks; explaining the limitations of strategies for some tasks.
Explicit instruction (procedural)	Providing direct or explicit instruction on how to monitor during problem solving. For example, telling children about the need to plan before beginning the process of problem solving, to set goals for different planning steps, and to stop during problem solving to determine whether they are achieving a set goal; discussing what to do when problem solving is not going as planned.
Self-explanation prompts	Activities that involve asking children to explain the task and the factors that affect their ability to do a task or their problem solving. For example, asking a child to explain how she solved a problem or how she plans to solve a problem.
Social interaction	Following direct instruction of metacognitive declarative or procedural knowledge, children are directed to work in groups to construct solutions to problems. For example, giving children questions about their understanding of a complex word problem or how to set up the word problem; then having the children work in groups to solve the complex problem using the questions to guide discussion.

ment and metacognition. It enhances the effectiveness of collaborative learning by promoting more complex thinking during discussions, and it improve mathematics achievement in populations that typically do poorly in mathematics: children with learning disabilities and children from low-income homes. Not all students, however, respond in the same way to metacognitive instruction, with some students showing considerable change and others little change (Thomas & McRobbie, 2001).

Although direct instruction has been linked to the rote memorization of mathematics procedures, it can be successfully used to teach mathematics strategies and procedures if students are directed to be reflective during problem solving. The usefulness of direct instruction of mathematics strategies is evident in the work of Charles and Lester (1984), who taught mathematics strategies for word problems in combination with metacognitive monitoring skills. The metacognitive monitoring skills used to assess the progress of problem solving were based on the principles of problem solving outlined by Polya (1957). The fifth- and seventh-grade students who participated in the treatment group were sig-nificantly more likely to better understand the word problems they were presented, more likely to develop a better planned response to the word problem, and more likely to get the correct answer. In another study, Des-oete, Roeyers, and De Clercq (2003) assigned 237 third-grade students to one of five conditions. One condition included metacognitive instruction designed to improve prediction and direct instruction on algorithms. The other conditions either provided instruction on algorithms only; instruc-tion designed to improve motivation and basic math skills; instruction on simple mathematics problem solving; or instruction on spelling instruc-tion (control group). Students in the condition that received instruction on metacognition and algorithms showed significant gains in metacogni-tive skills in comparison to the other four nonmetacognitive instruction groups. They also showed significant gains in the trained mathematics skills and knowledge, including number reading, procedural calculation, language comprehension of word problems, and mental representation skills. Furthermore, when students were followed up 6 weeks later, the metacognition and algorithm group continued to show better perfor-mance. The instruction did not, however, transfer to tasks not included in the instruction.

Other studies have found that metacognitive instruction improves the transfer of learned skills to new and different tasks. Fuchs et al. (2003) compared the impact of three types of instruction on students' metacognitive procedural knowledge and transfer: direct instruction on metacognitive procedural skills (e.g., setting goals, assessing progress to goal) and transfer (e.g., identifying how learned skills can be used in other settings), direct instruction for transfer only, and a control group. It was found that children who received either the transfer-only instruction or the transfer plus metacognitive procedural knowledge instruction out-performed the control group on near transfer tasks. The metacognitive procedural knowledge plus transfer group showed superior performance to the other groups on far transfer and metacognitive procedural knowl-edge at posttest. In another study by Tajika, Nakatsu, Nozaki, Neumann, and Maruno (2007), a group of sixth-grade students were taught to use a self-explanation strategy in which children explained their problem solving. The instruction was designed to promote reflection on concep-tual knowledge. Other groups were either shown how to use worked examples to learn the topic (no metacognitive instruction) or received no instruction (control group). The students who were given the self-explanation strategy outperformed students in the other two groups on both the ratio word problem test and on the transfer test. Furthermore, students who generated more self-explanations, and who likely devel-oped a deeper understanding of worked-out examples as a result, did better than students who generated fewer explanations on the task. The results of these studies suggest that transfer occurs when it is directly targeted for instruction or when the students are asked to be reflective in problem solving.

Furthermore, the use of self-explanation, in which children explain the task or their problem solving, has been found to promote understanding and conceptual change (Chi & VanLehn, 1991). Hiebert and Wearne (1993) had second-grade students describe and explain the arithmetic strategies they had constructed on their own. In comparison to children being taught procedures for solving double digit arithmetic problems (traditional format), children using the constructivist approach that included questions and explanation performed better on the end-of-year test. Likewise, the inability to generate a self-explanation is related to difficulty solving problems. For instance, Silver et al. (1993) found that middle school students who had difficulty solving an augmented-quotient division-with-remainders problem also had difficulty in providing written accounts of their mathematical thinking and reasoning. The ability to make problem solving explicit likely brings inconsistencies in beliefs to the surface, making it easier for the student to identify problems. When children are unable to verbalize their reasoning, this process is curtailed.

Self-explanation also supports better problem solving. Schoenfeld (1987) had college-age students periodically ask themselves during problem solving what they were doing, why they were doing it, and whether it was helping. He found that the use of self-explanation resulted in better control during problem solving and better outcomes. Other instructional programs, such as cognitive apprenticeships, in which children are encouraged to construct and discuss their problem solving, have been found to improve conceptual understanding (Leinhardt & Steele, 2005). Unfortunately, no research has explicitly examined metacognitive processes and skills within the cognitive apprenticeship instructional model.

Direct instruction of metacognitive skills and knowledge, however, has been found to improve the effectiveness of cooperative learning groups. In one study, by Mevarech and Kramarski (1997) a group of seventh-grade students were given metacognitive instruction in which they were made explicitly aware of the problem-solving process and the need to self-regulate. They were instructed to ask three kinds of metacognitive questions: comprehension questions (describe in your own words and decide what type of problem it is), strategic questions (justify the strategy for problem solving), and connection questions about how the problem is different from and similar to prior problems during problem solving. The students used these metacognitive skills as they worked in cooperative groups on algebra and mathematical reasoning tasks. When compared with their classmates who did not receive the instruction, students given the instruction did significantly better on measures of their understanding of algebra and mathematical reasoning. Other work by Mevarech, Tabuk, and Sinai (2006) indicated that the addition of metacognitive instruction to cooperative learning resulted in better comprehension of the problem and better planning of the solution when compared with a group only receiving cooperative learning. Kramarski (2004) found that when metacognitive instruction was combined with cooperative learning, it improved eighth-grade students' graph interpretation and the ability to transfer the skills to a different graphing task. Qualitative analyses of group interactions indicated that the metacognitive instruction supported better social construction of knowledge through more elaborative interactions that involved activating metacognitive knowledge in comparison to the cooperative-only group. Students in the cooperative learning-only groups tended to work by themselves more and had discussions that were more technical than conceptual.

Children with learning disabilities have routinely been found to benefit from explicit instruction (Levin, 1976; Pressley, 1982), and a number of studies examining the impact of direct instruction of mathematics strategies and metacognition has produced similar results. Lucangeli et al. (1998) studied the impact of metacognitive training on the performance of normally achieving and learning-disabled children. They found that instruction on metacognition improved mathematics achievement of both average students and students with learning disabilities in mathematics. Montague (1992) found that metacognitive strategy instruction in the form of self-instruction, self-monitoring, and self-questioning resulted in improved word problem solving for middle school children with math disabilities. Cardelle-Elawar (1992) investigated the impact of metacognitive instruction designed to improve low-performing sixth-grade students' knowledge of their mental processes, to increase their reflection on their own thinking during problem solving, and to improve their understanding of learning processes. The intervention produced higher achievement and motivation for mathematics in the treatment group when compared to a control group.

Cardelle-Elawar (1995) examined the impact of teacher-implemented metacognitive instruction on low-performing, primarily low SES elementary and middle school children in mathematics. The instruction on metacognition involved teaching students about their own mental processes, discussing how to problem-solve, and orienting students to reflect on their own thinking processes during problem solving. This instruction on metacognition was explicit in that it involved lectures and demonstrations by the classroom teachers, open classroom discussions, and simulated exercises. In comparison to a control group that received traditional instruction in mathematics focusing on procedures, written assignments, and corrections, the treatment group's mathematics achievement and motivation were significantly higher at posttest. Metacognitive instruction for this group may have been particularly effective in that it increased students' vocabulary related to cognitive processes and states in addition to providing explicit instruction about monitoring during problem solving.

Several frameworks have guided this research. One framework, developed by Garofalo and Lester (1985) is based on the work of Polya (1957). The original framework by Polya included four phases of problem solving, including understanding, planning, carrying out the plan, and looking back. The metacognitive components added by Garofalo and Lester included having the students assess their familiarity with task and difficulty level, identify their goals and subgoals, monitor their progress during problem solving, and evaluate the outcomes and problem execution. Garofalo and Lester's model put more emphasis on the metacognitive aspects of instruction on problem solving with the goal of avoiding the rote application of procedures. Another framework by Mayer (1987) assumed that four skills are needed for good problem solving: (1) the ability to translate the problem, (2) the ability to integrate the different parts of the problem into a viable solution, (3) the ability to plan and monitor the problem-solving process, and (4) the ability to accurately execute the procedures for the solution. Both frameworks assume procedural metacognitive knowledge to be pivotal for good problem solving. They place less emphasis on declarative metacognitive knowledge as a part of the problem-solving process, but this form of metacognition is implicit in the task and necessary for the procedural metacognitive knowledge.

Research evidence supports the explicit instruction of mathematics strategies, problem-solving skills, and metacognition. The focus has tended to be on procedural metacognitive knowledge, but to teach procedural metacognitive knowledge the vocabulary related to cognitive processes must be developed and used. It is difficult to talk about reflection or strategy selection if students do not have a vocabulary related to declarative metacognitive knowledge. What we do not know at this point is how well these techniques worked when they are used in average classrooms with average teachers. That knowledge awaits large-scale, randomized studies.

WHAT WORKS AND WHY?

Several recommendations based on research evidence can be made to teachers who are looking for classroom activities designed to enhance metacognition and improve mathematics achievement. It is clear from the research literature that when students are active learners and generators of knowledge, they are more likely to learn. Instructing students to use self-explanation seems to be particularly effective for improving performance, particularly for low-performing students. There is no evidence that students need to construct metacognitive strategies, such as self-explanation, independently of the teacher in order for them to understand and be able to use these strategies. These strategies can be directly taught to students by teachers. In addition, the acquisition of declarative metacognitive knowledge is likely to increase students' opportunities to construct and use efficient strategies.

Build Declarative Metacognitive Knowledge

Although most studies have focused on the impact of procedural metacognitive knowledge on mathematics strategy use and achievement, what students know about their cognitive systems and mathematics strategies likely supports the emergence and use of procedural metacognitive knowledge. The research evidence suggests that students first develop a vocabulary in the form of declarative metacognitive knowledge about themselves as learners and about the mathematics strategies they use, before they develop the capacity to reflect and monitor. What students know about themselves as learners and about strategies likely mediates the processes of reflection and monitoring during problem solving. A student is unlikely to be able to determine whether a strategy is working if he or she has little understanding of the strategy or the tasks to which the strategy can be applied. Teachers can support the emergence of declarative metacognitive knowledge by explicitly discussing what influences memory and learning. They can explicitly discuss the different types of strategies that students use in mathematics and the benefits and drawbacks of different strategies. They can also explicitly discuss what it means to reflect on one's knowledge state and to monitor problem solving. The extent to which students understand themselves to be active learners is the extent to which they will be active in generating mathematical knowledge.

Use Explicit Instruction

Many students construct declarative and procedural metacognitive knowledge through their interactions with peers, teachers, and parents. Many students, however, come to school with poorly developed declarative and procedural metacognitive knowledge. This may occur because they do not discuss the mental processes and states that underlie learning in their homes or schools. It may also be that the experiences that would normally promote the construction of procedural and declarative metacognitive knowledge in most students does not do so in these students. Particularly for low-performing and learning-disabled students, the research suggests that what is not constructed through regular social interactions in the home and school can be successful taught using explicit instruction. Explicit instruction is particularly advantageous if students have limited working memory, poor vocabulary, and related poor conceptual knowledge or other cognitive deficits that might make the construction of metacognitive knowledge and skill more difficult.

Concerns that explicit, direct instruction results in the rote memorization of procedures and poor learning are understandable if mathematics is taught as rote procedures and facts, but this does not necessarily happen during explicit instruction. When children were explicitly instructed in the studies discussed in this chapter they were not only provided with the steps of a strategy, but they were also given the declarative and procedural metacognitive knowledge needed to maintain and transfer the strategy to new tasks. It is clear from this research that children can use knowledge gained through such explicit instruction flexibly, improving both their metacognitive knowledge and their knowledge of mathematics. Teachers should be encouraged to explicitly describe strategies and the metacognitive information needed to guide their use.

Use Self-Explanation to Support Reflection and Monitoring

A characteristic of programs that improve both mathematics achievement and metacognitive knowledge is the use of activities that orient the student to be an active, thoughtful problem solver, as opposed to a passive recipient of knowledge and skill. Self-explanation is one form of active, reflective problem solving that appears to be particularly effective in improving problem solving. Students can be taught to construct and use learning strategies through self-explanation and these strategies can result in higher achievement (Wong, Lawson, & Keeves, 2002). Self-explanation also promotes conceptual change by supporting the representation of new and old knowledge in working memory (Chi, De Leeuw, Chiu, & LaVancher, 1994). Self-reflection is thought to work as a verbal mediator that supports students' construction of problem representations during mathematics problem solving (Neuman & Schwarz, 2000). It appears to be an effective way to orient students to reflect on their own beliefs and how those beliefs compare to new information, promoting better learning. We need to know more about how self-explanation and similar strategies can be taught to improve mathematics achievement. We also need to know how useful this strategy is for students of different ages and abilities.

A number of studies examining the role of self-explanation in mathematics learning have pointed to its importance. Cross-cultural work indicates that students in Japan and Taiwan, who normally do better on mathematics achievement tests, receive many more explanations of mathematical concepts than their American counterparts (Perry, 2000). Instructional methods that utilize self-explanation result in increased mathematical understanding. This occurs when students' engagement in classroom discussions, in which they must explain and defend their understanding of mathematics, improves the richness of their mathematical knowledge (Lampert, 1986). Other work indicates that even when students are not completely correct in their explanation of a concept, they show improved learning when they are given a correct representation of the concept (Schwartz & Martin, 2004). These findings are in line with the research on self-explanation as a metacognitive instructional strategy.

WHAT IS DIFFERENT ABOUT MATHEMATICS?

Much of the research on metacognition has been on domain-general memory and reading strategies. Although the lack of conceptual knowledge can hinder a student's ability to use a memory strategy (e.g., Best, 1993), there is not as close a tie between conceptual knowledge and strategy use as in mathematics. The ability to use mathematics strategies tends to be much more reliant on the possession of necessary conceptual knowledge (Rittle-Johnson & Siegler, 1998; Steffe et al., 1988). What students know about counting and number constrains the types of computation strategies they can use (Geary, Bow-Thomas, & Yao, 1992). For example, the use of the decomposition strategy is dependent on students' understanding of the relational properties of number (Canobi, Reeve, & Pattison, 1998). Unlike reading or memory strategies, metacognitive strategy instruction in mathematics classrooms must consider the conceptual knowledge necessary for successful problem solving. The ability to decide which strategy to select and to monitor whether a strategy is working will be highly dependent on underlying conceptual knowledge about number.

Similarly, as children progress in mathematics, their conceptual knowledge undergoes radical shifts that require significant restructuring of mathematics concepts. Metacognitive reflection likely plays a pivotal role in the success of this process as students struggle to integrate information that is counterintuitive with existing beliefs. It is unlikely that this restructuring can occur without reflection during learning and monitoring during problem solving. Despite this, there is little research on the role of reflection in conceptual change in mathematics. Given the complexity of changes that need to occur for students to progress in mathematics, more research needs to be done on how reflection can influence conceptual change in mathematics.

The National Research Council (2001) concluded that expertise in mathematics is characterized by a constellation of interacting skills and knowledge, including a strong conceptual understanding, procedural fluency, strategic competence, metacognitive reasoning, and a productive disposition, including the view of mathematics as sensible and useful. We know little at this point about how these skills and knowledge interact to produce an increasingly expert understanding of mathematics. A focus of future research should be on documenting how these skills and knowledge support the others' development and the emergence of mathematical knowledge.

REFERENCES

Best, D. L. (1993). Inducing children to generate mnemonic organizational strategies: An examination of long-term retention and materials. *Developmental Psychology, 29*, 324–336.

Borkowski, J. G. (1992). Metacognitive theory: A framework for teaching literacy, writing, and math skills. *Journal of Learning Disabilities, 25*, 253–257.

Canobi, K. H., Reeve, R. A., & Pattison, P. E. (1998). The role of conceptual understanding in children's addition problem solving. *Developmental Psychology, 34*, 882–891.

Cardelle-Elawar, M. (1992). Effects of teaching metacognitive skills to students with low mathematics ability. *Teaching and Teacher Education, 8*, 109–121.

Cardelle-Elawar, M. (1995). Effects of metacognitive instruction on low achievers in mathematics problems. *Teaching and Teacher Education, 11*, 81–95.

Carr, M., Alexander, J., & Folds-Bennett, T. (1994). Metacognition and mathematics strategy use. *Applied Cognitive Psychology, 8*, 583–595.

Carr, M., & Biddlecomb, B. (1998). Metacognition in mathematics from a constructivist perspective. In D. J. Hacker, J. Dunloksy, & A. C. Graesser (Eds.), *Metacognition in educational theory and practice* (pp. 69–91). Mahwah, NJ: Erlbaum.

Carr, M., & Jessup, D. L. (1995). Cognitive and metacognitive predictors of mathematics strategy use. *Learning and Individual Differences, 7*, 235–247.

Charles, R. I., & Lester, F. K. J. (1984). An evaluation of a process-oriented instructional program in mathematical problem solving in grades 5 and 7. *Journal for Research in Mathematics Education, 15*, 15–34.

Chi, M. T. H., De Leeuw, N., Chiu, M.-H., & LaVancher, C. (1994). Eliciting self-explanations improves understanding. *Cognitive Science, 18*, 439–477.

Chi, M. T. H., & VanLehn, K. A. (1991). The content of physics self-explanations. *Journal of Learning Sciences, 1*, 69–105.

Chiu, M. M., Chow, B. W.-Y., & McBride-Chang, C. (2007). Universals and specifics in learning strategies: Explaining adolescent mathematics, science, and reading achievement across 34 countries. *Learning and Individual Differences, 17*, 344–365.

Cooley, L. (2002). Writing in calculus and reflective abstraction. *Journal of Mathematical Behavior, 21*, 255–282.

Crowley, K., Shrager, J., & Siegler, R. S. (1997). Strategy discovery as a competitive negotiation between metacognitive and associative mechanisms. *Developmental Review, 17*, 462–489.

De Corte, E., Verschaffel, L., & Op't Eynde, P. (2000). Self-regulation: A characteristic and a goal of mathematics education. In M. Boekaerts, P. R. Pintrich, & M. Zeidner (Eds.), *Handbook of self-regulation* (pp. 687–726). San Diego, CA: Academic Press.

Demetriou, A., & Kazi, S. (2001). *Unity and modularity in the mind and the self.* London: Routledge.

Desoete, A., & Roeyers, H. (2002). Off-line metacognition—A domain-specific retardation in young children with learning disabilities? *Learning Disability Quarterly, 25*, 123–139.

Desoete, A., & Roeyers, H. (2006). Metacognitive macroevaluations in mathematical problem solving. *Learning and Instruction, 16*, 12–25.

Desoete, A., Roeyers, H., & De Clercq, A. (2003). Can offline metacognition enhance mathematical problem solving? *Journal of Educational Psychology, 95*, 188–200.

Dole, J. A., & Sinatra, G. M. (1998). Reconceptualizing change in the cognitive construction of knowledge. *Educational Psychologist, 33*, 109–128.

Fuchs, L. S., Fuchs, D., Prentice, K., Burch, M., Hamlett, C. L., Owen, R., et al. (2003). Enhancing third-grade students' mathematical problem solving with self-regulated learning strategies. *Journal of Educational Psychology, 95*, 306–315.

Fuson, K. (1992). Research on whole number addition and subtraction. In D. A. Grouws (Ed.), *Handbook of research on mathematics teaching and learning* (pp. 243–275). New York: Macmillan.

Garofalo, J., & Lester, F. K. (1985). Metacognition, cognitive monitoring, and mathematical performance. *Journal for Research in Mathematics Education, 16*, 163–176.

Geary, D. C., Bow-Thomas, C., & Yao, Y. (1992). Counting knowledge and skill in cognitive addition: A comparison of normal and mathematically disabled children. *Journal of Experimental Child Psychology, 54*, 372–391.

Geary, D. C., & Brown, S. C. (1991). Cognitive addition: Strategy choice and speed-of-processing differences in gifted, normal, and mathematically disabled children. *Developmental Psychology, 27,* 398–406.

Heirdsfield, A. M., & Cooper, T. J. (2002). Flexibility and inflexibility in accurate mental addition and subtraction: Two case studies. *Journal of Mathematical Behavior, 21,* 57–74.

Heirdsfield, A. M., & Cooper, T. J. (2004). Factors affecting the process of proficient mental addition and subtraction: Case studies of flexible and inflexible computers. *Journal of Mathematical Behavior, 23,* 443–463.

Hiebert, J., & Wearne, D. (1993). Instructional tasks, classroom discourse and children's learning in second-grade arithmetic. *American Educational Research Journal, 2,* 393–425.

Kramarski, B. (2004). Making sense of graphs: Does metacognitive instruction make a difference on students' mathematical conceptions and alternative conceptions? *Learning and Instruction, 14,* 593–619.

Kuhn, D. (2002). A multi-component system that constructs knowledge: Insights from microgenetic study. In N. Granott & J. Parziale (Eds.), *Microdevelopment: Transition processes in development and learning* (pp. 109–130). New York: Cambridge University Press.

Lamon, S. J. (1993). Ratio and proportion: Children's cognitive and metacognitive processes. In T. P. Carpenter, E. Fennema, & T. A. Romberg (Eds.), *Rational numbers: An integration of research* (pp. 131–156). Hillsdale, NJ: Erlbaum.

Lampert, M. (1986). Knowing, doing and teaching multiplication. *Cognition and Instruction, 3,* 305–342.

Leinhardt, G., & Steele, M.D. (2005). Seeing the complexity of standing to the side: Instructional dialogues. *Cognition and Instruction, 23,* 87–163.

Lester, F. K., & Garofalo, J. (1982, March). *Metacognitive aspects of elementary school students' performance on arithmetic tasks.* Paper presented at the annual meeting of the American Educational Research Association, New York.

Levin, J. R. (1976). What have we learned about maximizing what children learn? In J. R. Levin & V. L. Allen (Eds.), *Cognitive learning in children: Theories and strategies* (pp. 105–134). New York: Academic Press.

Lucangeli, D., & Cornoldi, C. (1997). Mathematics and metacognition: What is the nature of the relationship? *Mathematical Cognition, 3,* 121–139.

Lucangeli, D., Cornoldi, C., & Tellarini, M. (1998). Metacognition and learning disabilities in mathematics. In T. E. Scruggs & M. A. Mastropieri (Eds.), *Advances in learning and behavioral disabilities* (Vol. 12, pp. 219–244). Greenwich, CT: JAI Press.

Mayer, R. E. (1987). Learnable aspects of problem solving: Some examples. In D. E. Berger, K. Pezdek, & W. P. Banks (Eds.), *Applications of cognitive psychology: Problem solving, education, and computing* (pp. 109–122). Hillsdale, NJ: Erlbaum.

Mcdonald, I. (1990). *Student awareness of learning.* Unpublished master's thesis. Melbourne, Australia: Monash University.

Merenluoto, K., & Lehtinen, E. (2002). Conceptual change in mathematics: Understanding the real numbers. In M. Limon & L. Mason (Eds.), *Recon-*

sidering conceptual change: Issues in theory and practice (pp. 233–258). Dordrecht, The Netherlands: Kluwer Academic.

Merenluoto, K., & Lehtinen, E. (2004). Number concept and conceptual change: Towards a systemic model of the processes of change. *Learning and Instruction, 14,* 519–534.

Mevarech, Z. R. (1995). Metacognition, general ability, and mathematical understanding. *Early Education and Development, 6*(2), 155–168.

Mevarech, Z. R., & Kramarski, B. (1997). IMPROVE: A multidimensional method for teaching mathematics in heterogeneous classrooms. *American Educational Research Journal, 34,* 365–394.

Mevarech, Z. R., Tabuk, A., & Sinai, O. (2006). Meta-cognitive instruction in mathematics classrooms: Effects on the solution of different kinds of problems. In A. Desoete & M. Veenman (Eds.), *Metacognition in mathematics education* (pp. 73–81). New York: Nova.

Montague, M. (1992). The effects of cognitive and metacognitive strategy instruction on mathematical problem solving of middle school students with learning disabilities. *Journal of Learning Disabilities, 25,* 230–248.

Montague, M., & Bos, C. (1990). Cognitive and metacognitive characteristics of eighth grade students' mathematical problem solving. *Learning and Individual Differences, 2,* 371–388.

National Research Council. (2001). The strands of proficiency. *Adding it up* (pp. 115–155). Washington, DC: National Academy Press.

Neuman, Y., & Schwarz, B. (2000). Substituting one mystery for another: The role of self-explanations in solving algebra word-problems. *Learning and Instruction, 10,* 203–220.

Nietfeld, J. L., & Schraw, G. (2002). The effect of knowledge and strategy training on monitoring accuracy. *Journal of Educational Research, 95,* 131–142.

O'Sullivan, J. T., & Pressley, M. (1984). Completeness of instruction and strategy transfer. *Journal of Experimental Child Psychology, 38,* 275–288.

Panaoura, A. (2006). The development of young pupils' self-representation and mathematical performance in relation to processing efficiency and working memory. *Educational Psychology, 26,* 643–676.

Pappas, S., Ginsburg, H. P., & Jiang, M. (2003). SES differences in young children's metacognition in the context of mathematical problem solving. *Cognitive Development, 18,* 431–450.

Perrenet, J. C., & Wolters, M. A. (1994). The art of checking: A case study of students' erroneous checking behavior in introductory algebra. *Journal of Mathematical Behavior, 13,* 335–358.

Perry, M. (2000). Explanations of mathematical concepts in Japanese, Chinese, and U.S. first- and fifth-grade classrooms. *Cognition and Instruction, 18,* 181–207.

Piaget, J. (1976). *The grasp of consciousness* (S. Wedgwood, Trans.). Cambridge, MA: Harvard University Press

Polya, G. (1957). *How to solve it.* Princeton, NJ: Princeton University Press.

Pressley, M. (1982). Elaboration and memory development. *Child Development, 53,* 296–309.

Pressley, M., Borkowski, J. G., & Schneider, W. (1987). Cognitive strategies:

Good strategy users coordinate metacognition and knowledge. In R. Vasta (Ed.), *Annals of child development* (Vol. 4, pp. 80–129). Greenwich, CT: JAI Press.

Pressley, M., Harris, K. R., & Marks, M. B. (1992). But good strategy instructors are constructivist! *Educational Psychology Review, 4,* 1–32.

Pressley, M., Levin, J. R., & Ghatala, E. S. (1984). Memory strategy monitoring in adults and children. *Journal of Verbal Learning and Verbal Behavior, 23,* 270–288.

Rittle-Johnson, B., & Siegler, R. S. (1998). The relationship between conceptual and procedural knowledge in learning mathematics: A review. In C. Donlan (Ed.), *The development of mathematical skills* (pp. 75–110). East Sussex, UK: Taylor & Francis.

Schoenfeld, A. H. (1983). Beyond the purely cognitive: Belief systems, social cognitions, and metacognitions as driving forces in intellectual performance. *Cognitive Science: A Multidisciplinary Journal, 7,* 329–363.

Schoenfeld, A. H. (1985). Metacognitive and epistemological issues in mathematical understanding. In E. A. Silver (Ed.), *Teaching and learning mathematical problem solving: Multiple research perspectives* (pp. 361–379). Hillsdale, NJ: Erlbaum.

Schoenfeld, A. H. (1987). What's all the fuss about metacognition? In A. H. Schoenfeld (Ed.), *Cognitive science and mathematics education* (pp. 189–215). Hillsdale, NJ: Erlbaum.

Schwartz, D. L., & Martin, T. (2004). Inventing to prepare for future learning: The hidden efficiency of encouraging original student production in statistics instruction. *Cognition and Instruction, 22,* 129–184.

Siegler, R. S., & Crowley, K. (1994). Constraints on learning in nonprivileged domains. *Cognitive Psychology, 27,* 194–226.

Silver, E. A., Shapiro, L. F., & Deutsch, A. (1993). Sense making and the solution of division problems involving remainders: An examination of middle school students' solution processes and their interpretations of solutions. *Journal of Research in Mathematics Education, 24,* 117–135.

Slife, B. R., Weiss, J., & Bell, T. (1985). Separability of metacognition and cognition: Problem solving in learning disabled and regular students. *Journal of Educational Psychology, 77,* 437–445.

Stafylidou, S., & Vosniadou, S. (2004). The development of students' understanding of the numerical value of fractions. *Learning and Instruction, 14,* 503–518.

Steffe, L. P., Cobb, P., & von Glaserfeld, E. (1988). *Construction of arithmetical meanings and strategies.* New York: Springer-Verlag.

Tajika, H., Nakatsu, N., Nozaki, H., Neumann, E., & Maruno, S. (2007). Effects of self-explanation as a metacognitive strategy for solving mathematical word problems. *Japanese Psychological Research, 49,* 222–233.

Teong, S. K. (2002). The effects of metacognitive training on mathematical word-problem solving. *Journal of Computer Assisted Learning, 19,* 46–55.

Thomas, G. P., & McRobbie, C. J. (2001). Using a metaphor for learning to improve students' metacognition in the chemistry classroom. *Journal of Research in Science Teaching, 38,* 222–259.

Vosniadou, S., & Verschaffel, L. (2004). Editorial: Extending the conceptual change approach to mathematics learning and teaching. *Learning and Instruction, 14,* 445–451.

Wong, R. M. F., Lawson, M. J., & Keeves, J. (2002). The effects of self-explanation training on students' problem solving in high-school mathematics. *Learning and Instruction, 12,* 233–262.

Part III

READING, WRITING, AND ACADEMIC PERFORMANCE

9

Determining and Describing Reading Strategies

Internet and Traditional Forms of Reading

Peter Afflerbach
Byeong-Young Cho

In 1995, Michael Pressley and the first author of this chapter published *Verbal Protocols of Reading: The Nature of Constructively Responsive Reading*. The book offers a compendium of accomplished readers' cognitive strategies as they read all manner of texts: journal articles, book chapters, paragraphs, content-area textbooks, newspaper editorials, technical manuals, poems, and stories. The accounts of reader strategies are synthesized from the professional literature, specifically 63 publications (chapters and articles from journals that include *Reading Research Quarterly, Poetics, Journal of Educational Psychology, Journal of Reading Behavior, Cognition and Instruction*, and *Text*). The studies reviewed used think-aloud protocols as a data source and contain accounts of the diverse and often complex strategies and sequences of strategies that talented readers use to construct meaning from text.

The encyclopedia of strategies created by Pressley and Afflerbach (1995) derives from a focus on accomplished readers, primarily as they read single texts in traditional (i.e., print) form. These expert readers use three general classes of strategies: identifying and learning text content, monitoring the act of reading, and evaluating different aspects of reading. Within each of these categories are strategies that generalize over acts of reading. The strategies are generic in that they are used by different readers in different reading situations, yet they are isomorphic in that they are modified with expert readers' application, in relation to the specific text and task. Representative strategies for identifying and learning text content include readers assigning importance to different parts of text, using prior knowledge to focus on particular words and terms in text, and developing summaries of text. Monitoring strategies include establishing goals and overseeing progress toward reaching them during reading, and identifying challenges to comprehension and working to fix them. The range of evaluating strategies includes establishing a critical stance, judging the accuracy of information contained in text, examining text for the presence or absence of evidence to support claims made, and the suitability of text and its contents to help the reader complete a task. The three general types of strategy may operate simultaneously and in rapid sequences, as when a reader reads a title of a newspaper editorial (calling up related prior knowledge to help identify important text information), makes a prediction based on this prior knowledge (setting up a monitoring task to judge the accuracy of the prediction), and notes that the author of the editorial is one who often makes strong claims without providing appropriate evidence to support them (reflecting an evaluation of the author). Expert readers use strategies, and combinations of these strategies, as they are best suited to a particular reading situation.

Pressley and Afflerbach (1995) determined that the strategies derived from expert readers' think-aloud protocols complement models of text comprehension, providing considerable detail and description of the nature of accomplished strategy use. For example, readers widely report a strategy use that includes focusing on parts of text deemed relevant, and combining information from across the text with prior knowledge to create a mental model of the text. Such strategies are representative of both the microprocesses and the macroprocesses of text comprehension described by Kintsch and his colleagues (Kintsch, 1998; van Dijk and Kintsch, 1983). Readers also report the use of strategies that fit well with Rosenblatt's (1938) ideas of readers involved in efferent and aesthetic reading transactions with text to construct meaning. Constructively responsive reading highlights the importance of readers' cognitive strategies and the construction of meaning as it is situated in relation to individual readers and their goals and characteristics.

In addition to specifying the strategic interactions of reader and text in models of comprehension, interest in describing and cataloging expert readers' strategies is also fueled by the idea that this knowledge can inform effective reading strategy instruction. It is important to identify particular strategies, series of strategies, and sequences of strategies, for this helps describe the path that students must take between the points of novice reader and expert reader (Bruner, 1985). Michael Pressley's collaborative work with teachers focused on building understanding of cognitive strategies, as described in constructively responsive reading, so that teachers could help students develop reading strategy expertise (Brown, Pressley, Van Meter, & Schuder, 1996; Pressley et al., 1992; Pressley, Wharton-McDonald, Mistretta, & Echevarria, 1998). The description of expert readers' strategies and detailed strategy information assists teachers as they explain and teach: what the strategy is, how it is used, why and when it is used, and how it might be introduced, learned, practiced, and mastered.

To sum up, Pressley and Afflerbach's (1995) model of constructively responsive reading provides fine-grained detail on the numerous strategies used by accomplished readers when reading traditional text. Constructively responsive reading informs both theory and practice related to reading strategies. However, constructively responsive reading is based on studies that were conducted before widespread Internet use, and it is not informed by research that describes Internet reading. That Internet reading and "traditional" reading strategies may be alike or dissimilar should not be surprising to any accomplished reader who works in both domains. Needed is work toward creating a detailed account of how "new" forms of reading, such as Internet reading, require strategies that resemble, differ from, or are the same as those used in more traditional reading. This work will have at least two benefits. It will update our theoretical models of reading comprehension and it will inform effective reading instruction.

READING IN NEW CONTEXTS: THE INTERNET

Since 1995, the Internet has seen exponential growth, with over 1.4 billion users worldwide in 2008 (Internet World Stats, 2008). Our elementary and secondary students are digital natives (Marsh, 2005; Palfrey & Gasser, 2008), born into the Internet age and possessing knowledge for navigating, communicating, and understanding that often exceeds the knowledge of the prior generation. There is much reading involved in use of the Internet, with texts of varied format, length, and provenance. Readers work in an environment in which different texts may compete for the attention of the reader. The Internet presents readers with unprecedented combinations of texts, graphics, video, audio, and interactive components, in an architecture that may be designed to guide and support or to mislead and distract the reader. Reading on the Internet often requires that readers select particular texts to read from a large universe of texts.

In this section we examine the nature of reading strategies reported by accomplished readers in studies conducted since the publication of *Verbal Protocols of Reading: The Nature of Constructively Responsive Reading* in 1995, and since the onset of the Internet age. We are especially interested in the degree to which reading in Internet environments demands and supports new reading strategies. We are also interested in how Internet reading shares a core of reading strategies with more "traditional" reading. Finally, we want to describe what the Internet demands of the strategic accomplished reader. We gain perspective on possible differences between Internet and traditional reading strategies by considering the description of constructively responsive reading (Pressley and Afflerbach, 1995). These strategies derive from research conducted prior to investigations of reading on the Internet, and they provide a first means of considering whether (and perhaps, how) reading is different in Internet and traditional settings. The list includes strategies such as evaluating the qualities of text; overviewing before reading (determining what is there and deciding which parts to process); looking for important information in text and paying greater attention to it than other information; relating important points in text to one another in order to understand the text as a whole; activating and using prior knowledge to interpret text; relating text content to prior knowledge (especially as part of constructing interpretations of text); inferring information not explicitly stated in text; determining the meaning of words not understood or recognized (when a word seems critical to meaning construction); and evaluating the qualities of text, with these evaluations in part affecting whether text has an impact on a reader's knowledge, attitudes, and behavior.

As we examine these strategic behaviors, we can consider our own experiences with Internet reading and reflect on how reading strategies change, are maintained, or are modified in that reading environment. All of the strategies may play central roles in constructing meaning from Internet texts, and this is one indicator of the universality of particular reading strategies. However, there may be strategies specific to Internet reading and critical to success that are not widely investigated or documented. Consider the following strategy:

- Overviewing before reading (determining what is there and deciding which parts to process).

In traditional text reading, overviewing often involves skimming a single text: a page or series of pages that are fixed in number, position, and content, in a passage, chapter, section, or other intact document. In contrast, *overviewing in Internet reading* may be markedly different: the text or series of texts to be encountered may be partially hidden, unknown to the reader and unanticipated. The means to search and locate subsequent texts might not yet be determined and there might be competing texts to be accessed through a series of mouse clicks that represent, at best, slightly educated guesses as to the relevance and comprehensibility of the texts. Overviewing texts before reading them takes on different parameters with Internet reading; even the accomplished reader may not be sure when to cease an overview and commence a reading.

Consider, also, a second constructively responsive reading strategy:

- Evaluating the qualities of text, with these evaluations in part affecting whether text has impact on reader's knowledge, attitudes, behavior, and so on.

Internet reading can include the reading of multiple texts, written by known or unknown authors, with clear or opaque purpose. Across an act of Internet reading, the reader may encounter a considerable number of texts, anticipated and chosen or not (e.g., pop-ups). Related acts of evaluating each text in the context of changing screens, scrolling text, back clicking, and uniform resource locator (URL) examination offer a contrast to more traditional (often single-text) reading. Evaluation is a key aspect of both traditional and Internet reading, but it may be more difficult when text emanates from an unknown source and when text is presented as a snippet, or with little or no attribution related to text source.

We hope that this cursory consideration suggests that there is a clear need to determine and describe reading strategies in Internet reading environments. Descriptions of the nature of Internet reading should be accompanied by careful comparative analysis of how, why, and when the strategies may differ from traditional reading. There are numerous claims for the existence of "new" strategies necessary for successful Internet reading (e.g., Coiro, 2003; Lankshear & Knobel, 2003; Leu, Kinzer, Coiro, & Cammack, 2004; Leu et al., 2008) as part of the demands of new literacies (Kress, 2003). One approach to determining the novelty of Internet reading strategies is to compare them with research-based accounts of reading strategies in more traditional reading. In the next section, we move from this initial comparison of our own experiences with traditional reading and reading on the Internet to a research-based comparison. We compare the existing catalog of accomplished readers' strategies described in constructively responsive reading (Pressley & Afflerbach, 1995) with findings from Internet reading research conducted in the last two decades. Our goal is to determine those strategies that are common across diverse acts of reading, those that are close relatives to previously cataloged and described strategies, and those strategies that are clearly unique to Internet reading.

Comparing Constructively Responsive Reading with Internet and Multiple-Text Reading

As Michael Pressley noted, the good strategy user is always aware of the context of reading. Afflerbach and Cho (2009) investigated constructively responsive reading on the Internet, which at a minimum represents change in the context of reading. They synthesized the results of think-aloud protocol studies that focus on Internet reading and describe reading strategies involved with Internet reading. In addition, they examined research on multiple text reading, as this work both anticipates reading multiple texts on the Internet and reflects considerable research attention over the last 20 years. The authors identified 14 studies that focus on multiple or intertextual reading and 32 studies that examine Internet and hypertext reading. Most studies used think-aloud protocols as a data source. This research comes from diverse publications, including *Instructional Science, Reading Research Quarterly, Webology, Journal of Educational Computing Research, Journal of Literacy Research, Mediapsychology, Journal of Educational Multimedia and Technology, Discourse Processes,* and *Library and Information Science Research,* and represents different traditions and shared interests in the investigation of Internet reading strategies.

Afflerbach and Cho (2008) used the methods of Pressley and Afflerbach (1995), in which each reading strategy identified and described in the individual studies was recorded on index cards. Then the authors sorted the strategies to determine their goodness of fit within the categories that comprise constructively responsive reading: identifying and learning text content, monitoring, and evaluating. We examined the strategies used when reading multiple texts, as this intertextuality serves as a bridge between certain traditional and Internet acts of reading. We next focused on the comparison of strategies reported by Internet readers with traditional reading strategies. This allows for consideration of whether or not new strategies are required by the novel contexts and demands of Internet reading. Also of interest was readers' modification of reading strategies for reading on the Internet, as compared with traditional strategies of reading printed texts.

Strategies for Reading Multiple Texts

When reading multiple documents, the reader must construct meaning for each individual text as well as a composite meaning constructed from the collection of texts. The reader uses between-text strategies as well as within-text strategies when reading multiple documents. The construction of intertextual meaning across texts is supported by linking strategies that include comparing, contrasting, and differentiating the information contained in single texts in relation to the other(s) (Braten & Stromso, 2003; Rouet, Britt, Mason, & Perfetti, 1996; Wolfe & Goldman, 2005). The strategic reader relates the currently read text to the texts previously read and extracts relevant information by referencing the currently read text to the recently read text. Further, the successful intertextual reader assembles ideas from the different texts into a coherent meaning structure (Hartman, 1995) and continuously elaborates cross-text mental representations, using various linking strategies (Wolfe & Goldman, 2005).

Internet reading is rife with situations where students read multiple texts, and these situations may demand complex strategy use. When reading multiple texts, Internet readers must apply strategies in a recursive and integrative manner to determine important ideas from the texts, to construct meaning, to monitor the reading process, to evaluate the constructed meaning, and to evaluate the effectiveness of their own strategic reading (Perfetti, Rouet, & Britt; 1999). To illustrate, as readers plan Internet search tactics, generate and use search terms, visit search engines, and seek text on the Internet, they often interact with multiple texts on the Internet (Tabatabai & Shore, 2005). They may "click through" to read several related articles or paragraphs. In this environment, readers must avoid becoming disoriented in the Internet hyperspace and focus on accessing and understanding multiple texts (Yang, 1997). Through monitoring, readers detect and fix problems that arise. Strategic readers evaluate information in individual texts related to the criteria of credibility, trustworthiness, or reasonableness (Kiili, Laurinen, & Marttunen, 2008).

Accomplished readers use comprehension strategies to piece information together from each text, contributing to the integrated construction of meaning for the entire set of texts (Salmeron, Canas, Kintsch, & Fajardo, 2005). Internet readers must construct a metarepresentation of the multiple texts they read in the course of searching for and locating all relevant texts. This metarepresentation may guide readers to perform subsequent readings and navigations on the Web. If readers determine that their Internet reading selections do not help them meet task demands, they can conduct additional searches and readings. When readers lack understanding of what is read, they can revisit webpages, using navigational functions, to reread (Coiro & Dobler, 2007). Taken together, the series of linking strategies is a central cognitive contribution to the comprehension of multiple texts.

In summary, reading multiple texts on the Internet and in traditional contexts share a common core of strategies for constructing meaning. Strategies for constructing meaning with individual texts are used in concert with strategies for remembering related text content, and for concurrently revising and fitting meanings together from across texts. Reading on the Internet often involves the intentional (but sometimes inadvertent) accessing and reading of multiple texts. Expert readers develop the means to navigate the multiple text environment, to benefit from the information contained in multiple texts, and also to avoid being overwhelmed by texts. Reading the multiple texts of the Internet demands that readers attend to simultaneous strategies of constructing meaning within and across texts, and this creates further demand for the management of these strategies through monitoring.

CONSTRUCTIVELY RESPONSIVE READING STRATEGIES AND THE INTERNET

The analysis of studies of Internet reading allows us to compare categories of reading strategy (Identifying and learning text content, monitoring, and evaluating), as well as iterations of strategy use. Through comparative analysis we determined that each of the above three categories is central to the successful construction of meaning of Internet texts. However, we also found a category of reading strategy that has no comparison group in traditional reading. We name this group of Internet reading strategies *realizing and constructing potential texts to read*. In this section, we describe Internet reading strategies and compare them with traditional reading strategies, noting differences and similarities. We provide a description of the strategies readers use to realize and construct potential texts to read.

Strategies for Identifying and Learning Text Content

Accomplished readers use diverse strategies to construct meaning, and many of these are dedicated to identifying and learning text content. Readers may preview the text, sizing up the task at hand, in relation to the goal (or goals) of reading (Afflerbach, 1990). Skimming may be used if readers are seeking but a brief section of text or a specific piece of information. Readers may ask questions of the text as it is processed, and they may make predictions about upcoming portions of text. Readers assign importance to different aspects of text in relation to the reading task. They use prior knowledge of text content, text structure, and author motive to focus on aspects of text that are deemed useful. Text deemed not relevant is given only cursory analysis, making the process of constructing meaning more efficient. As text is processed, readers use strategies to form a mental model of the text, moving from what is on the page to what is, ultimately, the meaning constructed in the brain of the reader (van Dijk & Kintsch, 1983). This mental model is the result of comprehended text information, inferencing strategies that provide schematic information related to the text content and structure, and embellishment that emanates from readers' past experiences.

All of the above strategies, well documented in research on traditional reading, remain important in Internet reading. For example, readers overview and search at the onset of an act of Internet reading (Tabatabai & Shore, 2005). Readers must focus on content, determine importance in relation to reading goals (Zhang & Duke, 2008), and build mental models of the Internet text that is read (Eveland & Dunwoody, 2000). In essence, readers' strategies for identifying and learning text content bear remarkable resemblance to one another in both traditional and Internet reading, although the places in hyperspace in which readers find the texts and how they arrive at a particular text (or chance upon it) vary.

Strategies for Realizing and Constructing Potential Texts to Read

The process of identifying the Internet reading strategies reported in the 32 studies and comparing them with traditional forms of reading yielded particular Internet reading strategies that do not appear to have counterparts in traditional reading. This led to the development of a new category of constructively responsive reading strategy: *realizing and constructing potential texts to read*. A list of these strategies is included in Table 9.2. The strategies at the core of a reader's act of realizing and constructing potential texts to read are necessary because in particular acts of Internet reading, the text (or texts) to be read are not a "given": they must be identified. There may be many texts to choose from, and the text that the reader ultimately reads may not be known, or present, when the reader begins reading on the Internet. Thus, strategies that assist the reader in identifying texts to read are critical. For example, when reading a book in typical print media, readers may process textual information following the reading order that the author creates: the sequential display of letters, words, phrases, paragraphs, sections, and chapters. As reading is performed *in situ*, strategic readers can determine whether to read from beginning to end, to skim, to search, or to focus on a particular part of a text. These strategic behaviors reflect the reader's specific goals as well as the context of reading, and readers' strategic choices and paths occur within a boundary of the present text, a text that is temporally and spatially fixed.

In contrast, reading on the Internet can involve the reader's exploration of uncertain information in an amorphous, virtually unbounded space (Bolter, 1998; Charney, 1987; Landow, 1992). Even when reading for school tasks, the problem space of reading on the Internet can be undefined, with the possibility of unplanned detours and distractions. While a reader may read just a single screen on the Internet without any moves to other hyperlinks, much Internet reading involves searching for, locating, comprehending, and evaluating information across known and unknown texts (Leu et al., 2004).

A further distinction between traditional and Internet reading is that readers in a complex Internet hyperspace must investigate what texts are available on the system and in what order they might process the texts. The direction and scope of the reader's path may be uncertain, even for accomplished readers. Readers have the task of using minimal information, in the form of a title, subtitle, or URL, to strategically evaluate and plan their navigation, or reading path, among hyperlinks or websites. Readers must impose criteria of relevance and quality to judge this minimal information in relation to their goals for reading (Hill & Hanafin, 1997; Zhang & Duke, 2008). Successful readers navigate hyperspace using prior knowledge. This strategic knowledge of specific paths through hyperspace to needed and preferred information sources may be informed by previous experiences with particular websites and sources (Lawless, Brown, Mills, & Mayall, 2003). Accomplished readers strategically create and apply terms for searching. They are adept at combining search words and limiting these words to enable a focused search (Guinee, Eagleton, & Hall, 2003). Once accomplished readers arrive at possible links, they choose their moves (e.g., what texts to read, and in what order) in relation to the links in a strategic, principled manner (Salmeron et al., 2005). In addition, successful readers plan, predict, monitor, and evaluate each of these strategies (Coiro & Dobler, 2007).

To realize and construct potential texts to read, readers must maintain their awareness of reading goals while performing multilayered

TABLE 9.2. Constructively Responsive Reading Comprehension Strategies Used during Internet Hypertext Reading: Realizing and Constructing Potential Texts to Read

1. Searching for relevant websites or information retrieval systems to access and overview possible target information

2. Reducing the range of possible information to be encountered by generating key words related to topic and focus of a particular task

3. Scrutinizing Internet hypertextual links to anticipate and judge the usefulness and significance of the information before accessing it, based on specific reading goals

4. Exploring and sampling goal-related information in Internet hypertexts at the initial stage of reading to establish a dynamic plan to achieve one's own goal

5. Predicting utility of a link within Internet text when confronted with more than one hypertext link

6. Generating inferences about the relevance (or goodness of fit) of at least some of the other links on the pages visited prior to main act of reading

7. Choosing and sequencing the reading order by accessing links based on the criteria of coherence among links and relevance to situational interests

8. Conducting complementary searches with modified or revised keywords in order to better clarify suitability of links and potential reading path

Note. The research reviewed that contributes to this inventory included Azevedo et al. (2004); Balcytiene, (1999); Castek et al. (2008); Charney (1987); Coiro (2003); Coiro & Dobler (2007); Duke, Schmar-Dobler, & Zhang (2006); Eveland & Dunwoody (2000); Henry (2005; 2006); Hill & Hannafin (1997); Lacroix (1999); Lawless, Brown, Mills, & Mayall (2003); Leu et al. (2008); Leu, Kinzer, Coiro, & Cammack (2004); McEneany (2000); Protopsaltis & Bouki (2005, 2006); Puntambekar & Stylianou (2005); Ricardo (1998); Rouet (1992); Rouet & Passerault (1999); Salmeron, Kintsch, & Canas (2006); Salmeron, Canas, & Fajardo (2005); Schmar (2002); Sutherland-Smith (2002); Tabatabai & Shore (2005); Tosca (2000), Tremayne & Dunwoody (2001); Wenger & Payne (1996); and Yang (1997).

inferences, searching the Web to locate relevant texts and links (Coiro & Dobler, 2007). Readers must predict the relevance of displayed hyperlinks in advance, often based on multilayered information displays, determine the most appropriate next move and link, and infer the relevance of a link, sometimes with minimal information. In addition, readers may need to preview a text offered in a link, while predicting how far it might take them toward (or from) their reading goal.

Given the task of gathering information related to a content-area class, students may begin by searching for relevant websites or information retrieval systems to access and overview possible target information. A result is the listing of abbreviated descriptions of information and their accompanying URL, as encountered in a Google search. The list may number in the thousands, or even the millions. The strategic reader scrutinizes the Internet hypertextual links to anticipate and judge the usefulness and significance of the information before accessing it, based on specific reading goals (Kuiper, Volman, & Terwel, 2005). Based on initial scrutiny of this list, the strategic reader may decide to reduce the range of possible information to be encountered by generating (or subtracting) additional key words or combinations of key words.

The strategic reader then continues to explore and sample specific links to check the suitability of information for helping achieve the reading goal. The reader must infer or predict the utility of a link within Internet text when confronted with more than one hypertext link; this is often done with relatively quick judgment using minimal information (Leu et al., 2008). Or it may be an inference based on more detailed consideration of the information found by clicking through to preview particular webpages and websites. Concurrently, the strategic reader may generate inferences about the relevance, or goodness of fit, of alternative links on the pages visited prior to the main act of reading (Lawless et al., 2003). The strategic student reader chooses the reading order by accessing links based on a criteria of coherence among links and the apparent relevance of the website or webpage to the specific situational interests (Protopsalitis, 2008). As reading continues, the reader may conduct complementary searches with modified or revised keywords to better clarify suitability of links and potential reading paths (Salmeron et al., 2005).

In summary, there is a group of strategies that appears to be unprecedented in traditional reading, one that figures centrally in constructing meaning from Internet texts. This group of strategies, *realizing and constructing potential texts to read*, is representative of accomplished readers' strategic approaches to reducing uncertainty, determining the most appropriate reading path, and managing a shifting problem space. Readers must successfully navigate the complex and sometimes unknown spaces of the Internet. These new strategies appear to be a necessary development as accomplished readers are situated in the new contexts and demands of Internet reading.

Strategies for Monitoring

In traditional reading, the reader must consistently and accurately monitor different aspects of reading on the path to constructing meaning and attaining specific goals of reading. These strategies include monitoring the meaningful processing of text, making progress toward a goal (or goals), facing the emergence of challenges to comprehension, and activating processing owing to awareness of reading difficulties (Pressley & Afflerbach, 1995). Successful readers also monitor to determine the difficulty of the text, the relationship of the readers' background knowledge to text content, and if the text content is relevant to the reading goal. Monitoring strategies, in which readers work to manage the multiple spaces and tasks of Internet reading, are critical. Internet reading demands sophisticated executive control and strategy use, and there is much to be managed. Accomplished Internet readers must monitor their navigational processes to avoid getting lost in an often-complex hyperspace. They must check to determine if their choice of text is appropriate. They must determine if their original goals for reading remain the same or change as a result of navigating the Internet environment (e.g., encountering new texts) and if incoming information changes the reading path and reading goal (Yang, 1997). Internet readers may encounter texts and construct meaning in different sequences and from a multitude of sources, requiring them to monitor the construction of meaning by predicting, selecting, and evaluating information or text content (Bolter, 1998; Charney, 1987). However, readers may be unable to choose appropriate Internet links, sites, information, and texts in a strategic and coherent manner. In such cases, the basic assumption of an available relevant text is not guaranteed. This may cause readers' disorientation in hyperspace (Yang, 1997), and failure to monitor may result in the exhaustive but nonproductive use of Internet navigation and hyperlinks (Niederhauser, Reynolds, Salmen, & Skolmoski, 2000). These processing impairments can result in ineffective comprehension.

Monitoring strategies come into play when Internet readers simultaneously conduct the tasks of managing information and comprehending text(s) (Balcytiene, 1999; Eveland & Dunwoody, 2000; Yang, 1997). On the Internet, readers comprehend text information and construct an understanding of what they read. At the same time, Internet reading requires strategic management of information. Internet texts may have unpredictable forms and may be encountered on an unpredictable schedule. In such situations, successful Internet readers reduce the range of information to be located, selecting and evaluating relevant and credible information and links, and avoiding unnecessary materials. Failure to strategically arrange the information encountered on the Internet may hinder the construction of meaning, as when readers do not adequately monitor their strategic resources to cope with the dual challenges of constructing meaning and managing the complex process of Internet reading. The resulting bottleneck of text information to learn and strategies to manage may result in unsuccessful reading on the Internet.

In summary, monitoring while reading on the Internet is central to reading success. Many of the monitoring strategies reported by Internet readers bear a close relationship to the strategic monitoring used in traditional reading. Based on the reader's particular goals, Internet reading can vary decidedly in the scale and scope of available texts and possible reader moves in relation to accessing, reading, and constructing meaning from them. In addition, Internet reading can be marked by varied degrees of uncertainty, related to what text to access and in what order, the source of the text, and how reading a particular text might actually help a reader progress toward one or more goals for reading. Reading on the Internet can introduce challenges to the manageability of reading, as readers must choose, sequence, access, read, move ahead or back, and simultaneously keep track of the goal of reading. It appears that reading on the Internet, depending on the specifics of the situation, may increase the order of magnitude of need for monitoring strategies.

Strategies for Evaluating

Strategies for evaluation in traditional reading typically include readers' evaluations of the text or author: vocabulary choices, rhetorical style, the quality of writing, the relationship between claims made in a text and evidence to support these claims may all be evaluated by readers. Accomplished readers focus on the content of text as well. Evaluative strategies are used to render judgments about texts' currency, interesting, and accuracy. Some readers bring evaluative mind-sets to acts of reading, consistently using strategies of questioning, verifying, and reflecting. Other readers appear to be acritical in relation to some (or all) of the above-mentioned aspects of text (Pressley & Afflerbach, 1995).

Evaluating texts in relation to their sources and the quality of their information is essential to Internet reading success (Bruce, 2000; Henry, 2005). The Internet is a rich resource for skilled readers who are able to analyze and evaluate materials because if offers a vast array of information that may stimulate students' motivation and interests. However, the Internet text may present obstacles for readers. Any person or group may author a text encountered on the Internet, but the authorship and sponsorship of the Internet text may be unknown. This is akin to traditional reading situations in which accomplished readers cannot ascertain the source, subtext, or purpose of a particular text.

The Internet, like any modern mass media such as radio and television, has sectors that are commercialized and privatized, and this can transform Internet users into consumers (Fabos, 2008). As with traditional text reading, a reader may mistake selling a product for sharing information. There might not be any credible source information available, or it might be the writer's plan to deliberately deceive readers. This places the reader in the difficult position of needing to make evaluations with often limited (or missing) information. Strategic readers are alert to texts that may mislead and are wary of encountering biased opinions, inaccurate information, implausible websites, or seductive information (Leu et al., 2008). Readers must have the strategies to help them evaluate information on the Web. Thus, there seems a direct connection to Internet reading and traditional reading of texts when the author, purpose, and publisher (or producer) of the text are not known, or only partially known. Related strategies to help the reader evaluate text and author are shared across Internet and traditional reading.

Internet readers must not only evaluate what they read, but also make decisions about selecting or ignoring particular texts (Rieh, 2002). Efficient readers do not try to click through every link and webpage yielded by a search: they strategically evaluate possible links, paths, and information based on their prior knowledge and goal-awareness as they construct texts to read. Readers with a healthy skepticism of texts located in certain Internet environments will read with a consistent evaluative stance, and after locating texts, judge the texts for credibility, usefulness, or reliability. These two phases of Internet reading in turn enhance effective searches and help readers both to avoid disorientation and to construct meaning. Strategic readers may employ evaluative reading strategies during the entire process of searching for, locating, comprehending, and judging Internet information (Tabatabai & Shore, 2005).

In summary, evaluative strategies are central to the successful construction of meaning from text. These strategies are employed as readers begin a reading task, and they continue to be used as readers make evaluative decisions about trustworthiness, the relation of their knowledge to the text content, the author's ability, and the suitability of information in a text for a given task. These strategies are consistent with both traditional and Internet reading. Internet reading may raise the bar for evaluative strategies: it can increase the frequency and severity of situations in which readers cannot ascertain specific sources of information, the author of a text, or the reliability of information found in text. This, of course, may make reading more challenging. The sheer volume of possible reader–text interactions on the Internet suggests that evaluation strategies may be regularly taxed.

DISCUSSION

Reading Strategies in New and Traditional Forms of Reading

There is clearly a change in the context of reading and it is therefore critical to determine if the strategies used by Internet readers are new reading strategies, if they are previously documented strategies used in new contexts, or if they are strategies that are modified from known traditional reading strategies. Based on the comparison of constructively responsive reading and reading on the Internet, we can offer a preliminary account of the commonalities between Internet reading and traditional text reading and the novel strategies and stances demanded of the Internet reader.

At the completion of our consideration of how (and if) reading strategies vary in relation to Internet and traditional texts, we detect three themes. First, we find commonality when we examine accounts of the constructively responsive reading of traditional texts and compare them with accounts of reading Internet texts. Accomplished readers report using strategies for identifying and learning text content, monitoring, and evaluating that are shared in the two distinct reading environments. The literature on intertextual reading anticipates some of this strategy use. Second, certain characteristics of Internet reading demand special applications of constructively responsive reading strategies that are previously documented and explained. Monitoring and evaluation strategies maintain core functions in Internet reading, but expert readers revise them as needed in the new reading architecture of the Internet. Third, Internet reading demands new strategies of constructively responsive readers. Readers use strategies for realizing and constructing potential texts to read to address the unique characteristics and demands of Internet reading.

We began our consideration of reading strategies in traditional and new forms of reading with an overview of the research on intertextual reading strategies. This research literature has roots that precede the widespread use of the Internet. We believe that the strategies necessary for comprehending single traditional texts and combinations of these texts help us anticipate particular Internet reading demands. It is possible to interact with the Internet in a highly disciplined, focused manner. Such an approach helps the reader locate and construct meaning from a single text. In this scenario, Internet reading bears a fair resemblance to traditional reading. However, if such single text–reader interactions are not expected, the ability to read and construct meaning intertextually is necessary. Many intertextual reading strategies are invoked in Internet reading.

Our next focus was on strategies for identifying and learning text content. We found a strong correspondence between many of the strategies reported by expert readers in traditional and Internet reading. As with readers of traditional texts, readers on the Internet regularly report strategic approaches to assigning importance to and using prior knowledge of the content and texts to inform this process. Readers infer information that is not explicitly stated in the text. Readers cycle information with strategies that help them build summaries of what they read. Successful readers use all of these strategies in relation to specific reading goals, whether reading traditional texts or Internet texts. A defining difference here is that the navigation of the space and architecture of the Internet influences readers' strategic applications.

The investigation of accomplished readers' Internet reading revealed strategies that appear to have no counterpart in traditional reading. The unique strategies that readers use in such situations can be labeled *realizing and constructing potential texts to read*. We propose this as an addition to the catalog of strategies developed by Pressley and Afflerbach (1995). Traditional reading is often bounded by the fact of a single text in proximal temporal and spatial distance. However, the Internet represents a change in the architecture of reading (Afflerbach & Cho, 2009). Internet readers must have strategies that help them successfully deal with series of links, texts, decisions, and interactions. Realizing and constructing potential texts to read are strategies whose form and function might be expected for Internet reading. Internet readers must scrutinize hypertextual links for usefulness and significance, and they must make choices about reading direction often based on minimal information. The act of accessing text changes, as readers may need to submit search terms just to reach a set of potential texts to read. With practice, Internet readers may learn strategies that help better direct searches—they must be strategic in interacting with the universe of possible texts to read to reduce uncertainty and the number of texts. They must use inferencing strategies related to the relevance and goodness of fit of particular (often underspecified) texts for a reading task.

Monitoring strategies figure greatly in any successful act of constructing meaning. There is much that is shared by the reader of traditional text and the reader of Internet text in relation to monitoring strategies. As might be anticipated, the often-nebulous space of the Internet, filled with complex problems, possible missteps, and potentially huge numbers of texts that may be accessed and read, highlights the need for accomplished monitoring. When accomplished readers report challenges to maintaining focus on reading goals because of the distractions, puzzling links, or unclear paths of the Internet, the connections to monitoring strategies developed when reading traditional texts are apparent. However, Internet reading appears to change the structure of what and how a reader monitors.

Evaluation strategies are the fourth category of our investigation. As with monitoring strategies, there is much overlap in the strategies that accomplished readers report when reading traditional and Internet texts.

Readers of both types of texts use strategies to determine the quality of information, the ability of the author, and the stated and unstated purposes of a text. Like readers of traditional texts, accomplished Internet readers evaluate the sources, reliability, and trustworthiness of the texts they encounter. While determination of these aspects of texts is by no means a given with traditional reading, the sheer volume of texts that are available on the Internet, the lowered bar to publishing that the Internet often presents, and the sometimes elusive provenance of Internet text demand the scrutiny that evaluative strategies support.

The Developing Reader and Internet Reading Strategies

Given the nature of accomplished readers' strategy use, we may anticipate the challenges that less strategic readers (or readers who are not Internet-savvy) will encounter in reading on the Internet. First, Internet environments present (con)textual features that are distinctive from print-based reading environments, including the basic physical features of the keyboard, mouse, screen, and peripherals. These allow access to the Internet and reading on the Internet, and they can influence the type, sequence, and frequency of readers' strategies for successful Internet reading. Those features remind us that the Internet is the open-ended electronic hypertext media that connects a massive amount of texts with varied types of information representation. Developing readers must build familiarity and competence in relation to these Internet-specific reading features, as well as developing the cognitive skills, strategies, engagement, and motivation that are necessary for successful traditional reading.

If competent readers are challenged by acts of Internet reading, struggling readers may encounter bottlenecks created by the reading task, Internet navigation, and increased reading demands. Internet readers may have to deal with text and information that they do not need and want. Internet search engines, such as *Yahoo!* or *Google*, provide many links and related choices for reader moves, as well as educative and informative sources when a search term is applied. Often, these include a preponderance of commercial (.com) sites that have business interests. A result is that while readers do not have the intention to search for such unnecessary documents, they must filter useless or less relevant links and webpages and select relevant sources by comparing and contrasting such texts. They must deal with information that represents a comingling of commercial interests and the public domain, of information with varying degrees of accuracy. Readers encounter diverse informational sources on the Internet, sources that may contain contradictory opinions, arguments, or facts.

Our attempts to design instruction and help students become accomplished Internet readers should be informed by both the new and the known. There are considerable parallels with traditional reading and Internet reading, and we should regularly reference the catalog of known reading strategies for traditional text as we contemplate our student readers' challenges and related instruction for Internet reading. The challenges of Internet reading can be addressed with what we know about how readers adjust to, and become fluent with, forms of reading. Changes in the architecture of reading, the magnitude of the operational problem space and accompanying demands on identifying and remembering important information, monitoring reading, and evaluating reading require our applied understanding of both traditional and Internet reading. Instruction that references these areas of potential challenge, while building on the strategies that are common to both traditional and Internet reading, should help developing readers.

Although considerably more research is needed to build a comprehensive account of Internet reading in all its variations, we believe that instruction related to both traditional and Internet reading strategies should be closely connected. Building on existing instructional strategies that help students construct meaning from traditional texts (Palincsar & Brown, 1984; Pressley et al., 1998), instruction should focus on strategies that are closely aligned in both types of reading, while attending also to the additional strategies that readers need to be accomplished readers of the Internet. These include the group of strategies that we characterize as *realizing and constructing potential texts to read*.

Future Research Directions

The strategic Internet reader is situated in a particular task-text scenario. Sensitivity to the parameters of this situation, including awareness of the reading goal, a plan to achieve the goal, determination of a primary text and subsequent texts, and a plan to manage the entire operation, guarantees complex strategy use. It also means that Internet readers may be expected to be highly idiosyncratic in how they use strategies: particular readers vary in the sequence of strategies, the simultaneous use of strategies, and the recursive nature of particular strategies they use in Internet reading. Our understanding of how Internet strategy use changes and is maintained in relation to reader and situation characteristics is an important, ongoing goal of research.

As in traditional reading, the Internet reader/task interaction is influenced by many variables, including the reader's skill and strategy ability, prior knowledge, stance, volition, motivation, and epistemology. Investigations of these influences on Internet reading are needed, as they can provide situated, individual accounts of the variety of Internet reading texts and tasks. A reader of traditional text may read a poem for the experience of reading a poem and for luxuriating in the use of language. A reader of instructions for operating a fire extinguisher may be more interested in the immediate deployment of constructed meaning to put out a fire. Internet reading also reflects wide variation. It can be predictable: saving an Internet bookmark for a newspaper's editorial page, scrolling to the bookmark and clicking through to the editorial affords the reader the enactment of a simple, straightforward act of reading. In contrast, searching in an alien domain, struggling to generate appropriate search terms, determining the most suitable links, and deploying considerable monitoring and evaluating strategies amount to a complex reading task. The lesson is that Internet reading varies as much as traditional reading in the relative simplicity or complexity of the act. Clicking through hyperlinks and scrolling to text can be much like opening the cover and turning the page, or they may be more akin to opening Pandora's Box.

CONCLUSIONS

Context matters. The attention to how context influences developing and expert readers' strategies has been a focus of Michael Pressley's work. The variation in strategies that we observe in both traditional and Internet reading reminds us of the importance of context and the necessity of strategy. Our analysis suggests that many strategies are carried over from traditional contexts to Internet contexts—and vice versa. This finding is good news for both theory and practice. However, there is a special group of strategies, one we label *realizing and constructing potential texts to read*, that appears to be unique to reading the Internet. These strategies help readers deal with the sometimes unknown and unpredictable structure, content, and interactivity that Internet reading can involve. Research that continues to investigate Internet reading in all its variety will allow for the continuing comparison of Internet strategies with those already documented as involved in traditional reading.

The finding that Internet strategies have much in common with traditional text reading is promising for strategy instruction. Efficiency is one hallmark of the successful strategy user. Those interested in strategy research should be pleased with the strong overlap of traditional and Internet reading strategies, whether the strategies are fully developed or nascent and awaiting further growth. The fact that Internet reading and traditional reading share a considerable number of strategies means that reading strategy instruction for both share a common purpose. Thus, moving from one to the other may be enhanced by attention to these shared strategies and may help prepare students for learning what we believe are new reading strategies.

The unique architecture of the Internet influences readers' choices and navigations of text. Readers who struggle with constructing meaning with traditional texts may be overwhelmed by the need to locate, anticipate, and understand texts on the Internet. Given the monitoring and evaluating strategies reported by accomplished Internet readers, it is clear that developing readers must be supported in their growth to become both metacognitive and critical consumers of Internet information. In effect, the Internet poses a considerable challenge to readers who may struggle with traditional texts.

We consider our account of similarities and differences between traditional and Internet reading strategies to be preliminary. The understanding of constructively responsive reading on the Internet will continue to develop as we investigate accomplished and developing readers as they undertake a diversity of reading tasks in the multitude of environments that are possible with the Internet. As new information is added to our understanding of Internet reading, theoretical models and related instructional programs will be refined. This refinement should contribute to the robustness of our descriptions of Internet reading and the effectiveness of related Internet reading strategy instruction.

REFERENCES

Afflerbach, P. (1990). The influence of prior knowledge on expert readers' main idea construction strategies. *Reading Research Quarterly, 25*, 31–46.

Afflerbach, P. (2001). Teaching reading self-assessment strategies. In C. C. Block & M. Pressley (Eds.), *Comprehension instruction: Research-based best practices* (pp. 9–111). New York: Guilford Press.

Afflerbach, P., & Cho, B. (2009). Identifying and describing constructively responsive comprehension strategies in new and traditional forms of reading. In S. Israel & G. Duffy (Eds.), *Handbook of research on reading comprehension* (pp. 69–90). New York: Routledge.

Afflerbach, P., & Johnston, P. (1984). On the use of verbal reports in reading research. *Journal of Reading Behavior, 16*, 30–322.

Azevedo, R., Guthrie, J. T., & Siebert, D. (2004). The role of self-regulated learning in fostering students' conceptual understanding of complex systems with hypermedia. *Journal of Educational Computing Research, 30,* 87–111.

Balcytiene, A. (1999). Exploring individual processes of knowledge construction with hypertext. *Instructional Science, 27,* 30–328.

Bolter, J. (1998). Hypertext and the question of visual literacy. In D. Reinking, M. McKenna, L. Labbo, & R. Kieffer (Eds.), *Handbook of literacy and technology: Transformations in a post-typographic world* (pp. –13). Mahwah, NJ: Erlbaum.

Braten, I., & Stromso, H. I. (2003). A longitudinal think-aloud study of spontaneous strategic processing during the reading of multiple expository texts. *Reading and Writing: An Interdisciplinary Journal, 16,* 19–218.

Brown, R., Pressley, M., Van Meter, P., & Schuder, T. (1996). A quasi-experimental validation of transactional strategies instruction with low-achieving second grade readers. *Journal of Educational Psychology, 88,* 1–37.

Bruce, B. (2000). Credibility of the Web: Why we need dialectical reading. *Journal of Philosophy of Education, 34,* 9–109.

Bruner, J. (1985). Models of the learner. *Educational Researcher, 14,* –8.

Castek, J., Leu, D. J., Coiro, J., Gort, M., Henry, L. A., & Lima, C. (2008). Developing new literacies among multilingual learners in the elementary grades. In L. Parker (Ed.), *Technology-mediated learning environments for young English learners: Connections in and out of school* (pp. 111–153). Mahwah, NJ: Erlbaum.

Charney, D. (1987). *Comprehending non-linear text: The role of discourse cues and reading strategies.* Paper presented at Hypertext '87, Chapel Hill, NC.

Coiro, J. (2003). Reading comprehension on the Internet: Expending our understanding of reading comprehension to encompass new literacies. *The Reading Teacher, 56,* 45–464.

Coiro, J., & Dobler, E. (2007). Exploring the online reading comprehension strategies used by sixth-grade skilled readers to search for and locate information on the Internet. *Reading Research Quarterly, 42,* 21–257.

Duke, N. K., Schmar-Dobler, E., Zhang, S. (2006). Comprehension and technology. In M. C. McKenna, L. D. Labbo, R. D. Kieffer, & D. Reinking (Eds.), *International handbook of literacy and technology* (Vol. 2, pp. 317–326). Mahwah, NJ: Erlbaum.

Eveland, W., & Dunwoody, S. (2000). Examining information processing on the World Wide Web using think-aloud protocols. *Mediapsychology, 2,* 21–244.

Fabos, B. (2008). The price of information. In J. Coiro, M. Knobel, C. Lankshear, & D. J. Leu (Eds.), *Handbook of research on new literacies* (pp. 83–870). New York: Erlbaum.

Guinee, K., Eagleton, M., & Hall, T. (2003). Adolescents' Internet search strategies: Drawing upon familiar cognitive paradigms when accessing electronic information sources. *Journal of Educational Computing Research, 29,* 36–374.

Hartman, D. (1995). Eight readers reading: The intertextual links of proficient readers reading multiple passages. *Reading Research Quarterly, 30,* 52–561.

Henry, L. (2005). Information search strategies on the Internet: A critical component of new literacies. *Webology, 2,* Article 9.

Henry, L. A. (2006). SEARCHing for an answer: The critical role of new literacies while reading on the Internet. *Reading Teacher, 59,* 614–627.

Hill, J. R., & Hannafin, M. J. (1997). Cognitive strategies and learning from the World Wide Web. *Educational Technology Research and Development, 45,* 3–64.

Internet World Stats. (2008). *World Internet users and populations stats.* Retrieved September 20, 2008, from *www.internetworldstats.com/stats.htm.*

Kiili, C., Laurinen, L., & Marttunen, M. (2008). Students evaluating Internet sources: From versatile evaluators to uncritical readers. *Journal of Educational Computing Research, 39,* 7–95.

Kintsch, W. (1998). *Comprehension: A paradigm for cognition.* New York: Cambridge University Press.

Kress, G. (2003). *Literacy in the new media age.* New York: Routledge.

Kuiper, E., Volman, M., & Terwel, J. (2005). The Web as an information resource in K–12 education: Strategies for supporting students in searching and processing information. *Review of Educational Research, 75,* 28–328.

Lacroix, N. (1999). Macrostructure construction and organization in the processing of multiple text passages. *Instructional Science, 27,* 221–233.

Landow, G. P. (1992). *Hypertext: The convergence of contemporary critical theory and technology.* Baltimore: Johns Hopkins University Press.

Lankshear, C., & Knobel, M. (2003). *New literacies: Changing knowledge and classroom learning.* Buckingham, UK: Open University Press.

Lawless, K., Brown, S., Mills, R., & Mayall, H. (2003). Knowledge, interest, recall and navigation: A look at hypertext processing. *Journal of Literacy Research, 35,* 91–934.

Leu, D. J., Kinzer, C. K., Coiro, J. L., & Cammack, D. W. (2004). Toward a theory of new literacies emerging from the Internet and other information and communication technologies. In R. B. Ruddell & N. J. Unrau (Eds.), *Theoretical models and processes of reading* (5th ed., pp. 157–1613). Newark, DE: International Reading Association.

Leu, D. J., Zawilinski, L., Castek, J., Banerjee, M., Housand, B., Liu, Y., et al. (2008). What is new about the new literacies of online reading comprehension? In L. Rush, J. Eakle, & A. Berger (Eds.), *Secondary school literacy: What research reveals for classroom practices* (pp. 3–68). Urbana, IL: National Council of Teachers of English.

Marsh, J. (2005). *Popular culture, new media and digital literacy in early childhood.* London: Routledge/Falmer.

McEneaney, J. E. (2000). *Navigational correlates of comprehension in hypertext.* Paper presented at Hypertext 2000, San Antonio, TX.

Niederhauser, D., Reynolds, R., Salmen, D., & Skolmoski, P. (2000). The influence of cognitive load on learning from hypertext. *Journal of Educational Computing Research, 23,* 23–255.

Palfrey, J., & Gasser, U. (2008). *Born digital: Understanding the first generation of digital natives.* New York: Basic Books.

Palincsar, A. S., & Brown, A. L. (1984). Reciprocal teaching of comprehension-fostering and comprehension-monitoring activities. *Cognition and Instruction, 1*, 117–175.

Perfetti, C. A., Rouet, J.-F., & Britt, M. A. (1999). Toward a theory of documents representation. In H. van Oostendorp & S. R. Goldman (Eds.), *The construction of mental representations during reading* (pp. 9–122). Mahwah, NJ: Erlbaum.

Pressley, M., & Afflerbach, P. (1995). *Verbal protocols of reading: The nature of constructively responsive reading.* Hillsdale, NJ: Erlbaum.

Pressley, M., El-Dinary, P. B., Gaskins, I., Schuder, T., Bergman, J., Almasi, J., et al. (1992). Beyond direct explanation: Transactional instruction of reading comprehension strategies. *Elementary School Journal, 92*, 51–555.

Pressley, M., Wharton-McDonald, R., Mistretta, J., & Echevarria, M. (1998). The nature of literacy instruction in ten grade-4/5 classrooms in upstate New York. *Scientific Studies of Reading, 2*, 15–191.

Protopsaltis, A. (2008). Reading strategies in hypertexts and factors influencing hyperlink selection. *Journal of Educational Multimedia and Hypermedia, 17*, 19–213.

Protopsaltis, A., & Bouki, V. (2005). *Towards a hypertext reading/comprehension model.* Paper presented at the SIGDOC 05, Coventry, UK.

Protopsaltis, A., & Bouki, V. (2006). Designing navigational support in hypertext systems based on navigational patterns. *Instructional Science, 33*, 451–481.

Puntambekar, S., & Stylianou, A. (2005). Designing navigation support in hypertext systems based on navigational patterns. *Instructional Science, 33*, 451–481.

Ricardo, F. J. (1998). *Stalking the paratext: Speculations on hyperlinks as a second order text.* Paper presented at Hypertext 98, Pittsburgh, PA.

Rieh, S. (2002). Judgment of information quality and cognitive authority in the Web. *Journal of the American Society for Information Science and Technology, 53*, 14–161.

Rosenblatt, L. (1938). *Literature as exploration.* New York: Appleton-Century.

Rouet, J.-F. (1992). *Cognitive processing of hyperdocuments: When does nonlinear help?* Paper presented at the ACM ECHT conference, Milano, Italy.

Rouet, J.-F., Britt, M., Mason, R., & Perfetti, C. (1996). Using multiple sources of evidence to reason about history. *Journal of Educational Psychology, 88*, 47–493.

Rouet, J.-F., Favart, M., Britt, M., & Perfetti, C. (1997). Studying and using multiple documents in history: Effects of discipline expertise. *Cognition and Instruction, 15*, 8–106.

Rouet, J.-F., & Passerault, J.-M. (1999). Analyzing learner-hypermedia interaction: An overview of online methods. *Instructional Science, 27*, 201–219.

Salmeron, L., Canas, J. J., & Fajardo, I. (2005). Are expert users always better searchers? Interaction of expertise and semantic grouping in hypertext search tasks. *Behavior and Information Technology, 24*, 471–475.

Salmeron, L., Canas, J., Kintsch, W., & Fajardo, I. (2005). Reading strategies and hypertext comprehension. *Discourse Processes, 40*, 17–191.

Salmeron, L., Kintsch, W., & Canas, J. J. (2006). Reading strategies and prior knowledge in learning from hypertext. *Memory and Cognition, 34,* 1157–1171.

Schmar, E. S. (2002). A collective case study of reading strategies used by skilled fifth graders reading on the Internet (Doctoral dissertation, Kansas State University). *Dissertation Abstracts International, 63,* 4227.

Sutherland-Smith, W. (2002). Weaving the literacy Web: Changes in reading from page to screen. *Reading Teacher, 55,* 662–669.

Tabatabai, D., & Shore, B. (2005). How experts and novices search the web. *Library and Information Science Research, 27,* 22–248.

Tosca, S. P. (2000). *A pragmatics of links.* Paper presented at Hypertext 2000, San Antonio, TX.

Tremayne, M., & Dunwoody, S. (2001). Interactivity, information processing, and learning on the World Wide Web. *Science Communication, 23,* 111–134.

Van Dijk, T., & Kintsch, W. (1983). *Strategies of discourse comprehension.* New York: Academic Press.

Wenger, M. J., & Payne, D. G. (1996). Comprehension and retention of nonlinear text: Considerations of working memory and material-appropriate processing. *American Journal of Psychology, 109,* 93–103.

Wolfe, M., & Goldman, S. (2005). Relations between adolescents' text processing and reasoning. *Cognition and Instruction, 23,* 46–502.

Yang, S. (1997). Information seeking as problem-solving using a qualitative approach to uncover the novice learners' information-seeking processes in a Perseus hypertext system. *Library and Information Science Research, 19,* 7–91.

Zhang, S., & Duke, N. K. (2008). Strategies for Internet reading with different reading purposes: A descriptive study of twelve good Internet readers. *Journal of Literacy Research, 40,* 12–162.

10

Metacognition and Strategies Instruction in Writing

Karen R. Harris
Tanya Santangelo
Steve Graham

Writing research has expanded significantly in recent decades and has produced important insights about the processes and variables that comprise and influence skillful composition. Whereas writing was historically viewed as a linear and somewhat simplistic activity, contemporary models now recognize it as cognitive, linguistic, affective, behavioral, and physical in nature and set within a larger socio-cultural context (e.g., Graham, 2006; McCutcheon, 2006; Prior, 2006). Collectively, the most influential theoretical frameworks emphasize the idea that writing is a recursive, strategic, and multidimensional process central to (1) planning what to say and how to say it, (2) translating ideas into written text, and (3) revising what has been written (e.g., Bereiter & Scardamalia, 1987; Hayes, 1996; Hayes & Flower, 1980; Zimmerman & Risemberg, 1997; for detailed reviews, see, e.g., Graham, 2006 and Harris, Graham, Brindle, & Sandmel, in press).

While composing, skillful writers devote varying degrees of attention and other cognitive resources to their writing topic, their intended audience, their compositional purpose, and their text structure (e.g., Raphael,

Englert, & Kirschner, 1989). Thus, it is not surprising that even professional authors commonly lament the complexity and difficulty associated with writing, and the even greater challenge associated with learning how to write (e.g., Graham, 2006b; McCutchen, 2006; Sitko, 1998). As Red Smith noted, "Writing is easy. All you have to do is sit down to a typewriter and open a vein."

In this chapter, we focus on the critical role of metacognition in writing. First, we define metacognition and provide an overview of its role and impact with regard to composing. Then we focus on writing instruction and illustrate how one extensively researched model of strategies instruction, Self-Regulated Strategy Development, can be used to promote writing development, including development of critical metacognitive abilities and performance.

METACOGNITION AND WRITING

Metacognition can be conceptualized as having two fundamental elements: (1) knowledge about cognition, or thinking, and (2) deliberate, conscious regulation and control of cognitive activity, which demands self-regulation (e.g., Ertmer & Newby, 1996; McCormick, 2003; Sitko, 1998; for detailed discussions, see, e.g., Harris & Graham, in press and Wong, 1999). We discuss both metacognitive knowledge and self-regulation, and their relationship to writing performance, next.

Metacognitive Knowledge

What Is Metacognitive Knowledge?

The first element of metacognition, metacognitive knowledge, includes two components: knowledge about cognition and awareness of one's own cognition. Researchers and theorists have identified three distinct, but closely related, facets of metacognitive knowledge: declarative knowledge, procedural knowledge, and conditional knowledge (McCormick, 2003; Paris, Lipson, & Wixson, 1983). Academic development and performance is influenced by and contingent upon the successful application and coordination of all three (e.g., Alexander, 1997; Pressley & Harris, 2006).

Declarative knowledge refers to the knowledge, skills, and strategies needed to effectively complete a task under one or more conditions (e.g., Hacker, 1998; Pressley & Harris, 2006; Zimmerman & Risemberg, 1997). In other words, this is "knowing what." Within the context of writing, examples of declarative knowledge include understanding the purposes for writing, the topic, needs of intended audiences, genre constraints, linguistic structures, and the higher order processes that underlie skillful composing, such as planning, drafting, and revising (e.g., Donovan & Smolkin, 2006; Lin, Monroe, & Troia, 2007; McCutchen, 2000; McCutchen, Francis, & Kerr, 1997; Saddler & Graham, 2007). Another aspect of declarative knowledge involves awareness of one's strengths and weaknesses with regard to a task, as well as other affective dimensions such as self-efficacy and motivation (e.g., Hacker, 1998; Pressley & Harris, 2006; Zimmerman & Risemberg, 1997). Thus, for composing, it is important to consider whether writers understand their levels of proficiency with respect to various forms of writing as well as various compositional processes (e.g., planning and revising), their environmental preferences, their attitudes toward writing, their levels of writing self-efficacy, and their writing motivation.

Procedural knowledge includes information about how to successfully apply the various actions or strategies comprising declarative knowledge, that is, "the repertoire of behavior available from which the learner selects the one(s) best able to help reach a particular goal" (Raphael et al., 1989, p. 347). In other words, this is "knowing how." Examples of procedural knowledge within the context of writing include an understanding of general strategies that allow for efficacious planning, text production, and revising (e.g., engaging in advanced planning activities such as creating an outline or using transitional phrases to enhance readability), as well as specific strategies that are commonly employed with particular genres (e.g., presenting details in persuasive writing). Procedural knowledge can also include information related to creating an environment that is conducive to writing (e.g., creating the right environment to compose). Although lower order skills such as spelling, grammar, punctuation, sentence construction, and handwriting have been shown to play an important role in writing development and performance (for detailed discussions, see, e.g., Graham, 2006; Graham & Harris, 2000; and McCutchen, 2006), they are typically discussed separately and conceptualized as being outside the realm of metacognitive procedural knowledge (e.g., Wong, 1999).

Conditional knowledge allows the writer to determine the appropriate conditions in which to apply procedural and declarative knowledge (e.g., McCormick, 2003; Raphael et al., 1989). In other words, this is "knowing when, where, and why." Within the context of composing, conditional knowledge enables the writer to, for example, critically consider a specific writing task, determine what skills and strategies will best scaffold achievement of the goals for that task, identify when and why to employ various compositional processes, and modify environmental conditions.

What Is the Role and Impact of Metacognitive Knowledge in Writing?

A substantial body of research offers insight about the nature and impact of metacognitive writing knowledge (e.g., Donovan & Smolkin, 2006; Graham, 2006; McCutchen, 1986, 2000; Pressley & Harris, 2006; Wong, 1999). Collectively, these studies have documented its developmental trajectory, as well as the critical role it plays with regard to writing development and performance. Specifically, the available evidence supports four propositions (Graham, 2006): (1) skilled writers are more knowledgeable about writing than less skilled writers; (2) students become increasingly knowledgeable about writing with age and schooling; (3) the level of knowledge writers bring to the composing task is related to their writing performance; and (4) instruction that enhances writers' knowledge combined with meaningful practice opportunities leads to improvements in writing output and quality. Space limitations preclude a comprehensive review of this literature; we highlight, however, a few salient findings with respect to differences between more and less skilled writers' metacognitive knowledge.

Skilled writers have a rich understanding of the essential elements and characteristics of high-quality compositions. They also have knowledge of the various higher order processes that allow one to compose proficiently (e.g., planning and revising) and, perhaps more important, they attribute successful writing to the use of effective strategies (e.g., Bereiter & Scardamalia, 1987; Graham, 2006; Lin et al., 2007; McCutchen, 2006; Saddler & Graham, 2007). In contrast, novice and struggling writers frequently lack knowledge of what constitutes good writing products and processes; their conceptualization emphasizes form (e.g., neatness and mechanics) over function (e.g., conveying ideas in an organized and engaging manner and meeting the needs of an intended audience). Revising, for instance, is viewed as synonymous with proofreading or editing, rather than making conceptual-level improvements.

A recent study by Lin et al. (2007) documented this divergent pattern. Based on interviews with typically developing writers and struggling writers in second through eighth grade, the authors found significant and meaningful differences in metacognitive writing knowledge across grades and ability levels. Older, typically developing writers demonstrated the deepest and most integrated metacognitive understanding of writing. Younger, typically developing writers and struggling writers of all ages possessed only concrete and superficial writing knowledge. Importantly, struggling writers not only started out with less metacognitive knowledge than their typically developing peers, but they evidenced a shallower rate of growth; the gap between knowledge held by typically developing and struggling writers widened as they progressed through school.

Interviews with typically developing writers and struggling writers with learning disabilities in fourth, fifth, seventh, and eighth grades in an earlier study by Graham, Schwartz, and MacArthur (1993) vividly illustrate the metacognitive knowledge discrepancies reported in Lin et al. (2007). For example, when asked "What is good writing?," sample responses from typically developing writers included "Has a beginning, middle, and end" and "Drafting it, revising it, and editing it." In contrast, struggling writers defined good writing as "It's neat, correctly formed, and stays on the baseline" and "Spelling every word right." When asked "What do good writers do?," typically developing writers were more likely to offer responses such as "They read it over and see if they have everything the way they want it," "Think of very creative ideas," and "They elaborate." In contrast, students who struggled with writing believed good writers "Check their spelling," "Use whatever paper the teacher tells them," and "Sit up straight and don't lean back in their chairs." Students' descriptions of how they would plan, write, and revise a paper further highlighted their differential knowledge of, and appreciation for, higher order compositional processes. Typically developing writers were significantly more likely to describe substantive activities and strategies such as "Think about the character I am writing about"; "Take notes and go to the library"; "Write what I am going to write about ... and number them first, second, last—whatever"; "Put my sentences in a different order"; and "Make the ending really exciting." In contrast, struggling writers emphasized mechanically focused procedures such as "Do it in ink," "Write it bigger so it takes up more space," "Try to make it neater," and "Make sure I had my date on there and name ... " (Graham et al., 1993, pp. 244–246).

Significant differences have also been found between more and less skilled writers' knowledge of the purpose and value of writing (e.g., Graham et al., 1993; Lin et al., 2007). For example, based on interviews with fourth-grade students, Saddler and Graham (2007) reported that skilled writers were more than twice as likely to articulate how writing benefited them in school. They explained, for example, it "Will help when we go to college" and "Helps the teacher understand you." Skilled writers were more than four times as likely to describe how writing could promote their future occupational success. Typical responses included "Make more money," "You might be a lawyer and have to write a persuasive story," and "If you want to be a doctor you could take special notes" (p. 241). Collectively, the data suggested that students who struggled with writing were unaware of the purposes for writing and they perceived it to have minimal personal relevance or value.

Skilled writers have a deep understanding of the attributes and structure of different genres. In contrast, novice and struggling writers often have limited understanding of writing genres, devices, and conventions (e.g., Donovan & Smolkin, 2006; Englert & Thomas, 1987; Graham & Harris, 2003). This includes some of the more sophisticated and unique forms, such as poetry or persuasive writing, as well as those which are more common, such as personal narratives and story writing. Epitomizing this lack of fundamental knowledge, a struggling writer in third grade explained the basic elements of a story include "a main character, a subject, predicate, and main idea" (Graham & Harris, 2005, p. 18). Unfortunately, this limited knowledge is often directly reflected in students' writing, as important components are frequently omitted. For instance, MacArthur and Graham (1987) reported that the handwritten, typed, and dictated compositions created by fifth- and sixth-grade students who struggled with writing typically included a main character, some information about when and/or where the story took place, and some type of action on the part of the characters. However, they rarely established a starter event, included goals for the characters, described characters' reactions, or offered a summative conclusion.

Self-Regulation

What Is Self-Regulation?

The second major element of metacognition involves consciously planning, monitoring, and evaluating cognitive activities (e.g., Ertmer & Newby, 1996; Hacker, 1998; McCormick, 2003; Sitko, 1998; Wong, 1999; for detailed discussions, see Harris & Graham, in press). Although self-regulation and strategic behavior are important components of learning in all academic domains (Alexander, 1997), they are thought to be especially potent catalysts for developing competence and promoting performance in writing (e.g., Alexander, Graham, & Harris, 1998; Graham & Harris, 2000; Pressley, 1979, 1986; Pressley, Borkowski & Schneider, 1987). As Zimmerman and Risemberg (1997) explained:

> Most students recognize that in order to become a proficient writer, they must acquire knowledge of vocabulary and grammar, however, they are far less aware of their need for high levels of self-regulation. This need stems from the fact that writing activities are usually self-planned, self-initiated, and self-sustained. Writers typically perform alone, over long periods with frequent stretches of meager results, and repeatedly revise output to fulfill personal standards of quality. These demanding personal requirements have led writers throughout history to develop varied techniques of "self-discipline" to enhance their effectiveness. (pp. 73–74)

The writing habits of a famous contemporary novelist, Irving Wallace, illustrate some of these techniques. For example, Wallace monitored his literary output by maintaining a detailed chart of his progress when writing a book, recording the number of pages written by the end of each working day (Wallace & Pear, 1977). This technique, Wallace explained, helped him establish discipline over his writing: "A chart on the wall served as such a discipline, its figures scolding me or encouraging me" (p. 65). Wallace also used a variety of strategies to help him manage the writing of his novels (Wallace, 1971; Wallace & Pear, 1977). These included making outlines, developing scenes and characters, working out the sequence of the story in his mind and then roughly on paper, and underlining story problems in need of additional work. As he began to write each novel, he carefully monitored the process, making many revisions in his plans and outlines. Once his first draft was completed, he returned to it again and again, reading the entire manuscript and revising it as he went along.

What Is the Role and Impact of Self-Regulation in Writing?

Nearly all contemporary models of skilled writing either explicitly or implicitly acknowledge the critical role of self-regulatory processes, such as those described by Wallace (e.g., Flower & Hayes, 1980; Scardamalia & Bereiter, 1986; Zimmerman & Risemberg, 1997; for detailed discussions see, e.g., Graham, 2006 and Harris et al., in press). Theorists have identified a variety of self-regulation strategies that writers use to manage the multiple facets of composing (Bereiter & Scardamalia, 1987; Graham & Harris, 1994; Zimmerman & Risemberg, 1997). These include goal setting and planning (e.g., establishing rhetorical goals and tactics to achieve them), seeking information (e.g., gathering information pertinent to the writing topic), record keeping (e.g., making notes), organizing (e.g., organizing notes or text), transforming (e.g., visualizing a character to facilitate written description), self-monitoring (e.g., checking to see if writing goals are met), reviewing records (e.g., reviewing notes or the text produced so far), self-evaluating (e.g., assessing the quality of text or proposed plans), revising (e.g., modifying text or plans for writing), self-verbalizing (e.g., saying dialogue aloud while writing or personal articulations about what needs to be done), rehearsing (e.g., trying out a scene before writing it), environmental structuring, (e.g., finding a quiet place to write), time planning (e.g., estimating and budgeting time for writing), self-consequating (e.g., going to a movie as a reward for completing a writing scene), seeking social assistance (e.g., asking another person to edit the paper), and self-selecting models (e.g., emulating the writing style or tactics of a more gifted author).

Akin to the research base on metacognitive knowledge, the extant literature supports four propositions that highlight the important role of self-regulation in writing (e.g., Graham, 2006; Graham & Harris, 2000): (1) skilled writers are more self-regulated than less skilled writers; (2) developing writers become increasingly self-regulated with age and schooling; (3) the level of self-regulation writers bring to the composing task is related to their writing performance; and (4) instruction that enhances developing and struggling writers' self-regulation combined with meaningful practice opportunities improves their writing performance. We next offer an illustrative description of the findings related to differences observed between more and less skilled writers with regard to the critical self-regulatory skills of planning and revising.

Planning is a fundamental and essential component of skillful writing that occurs before and during text production. In fact, skilled writers often devote more than two-thirds of their writing time to planning (e.g., Flower & Hayes, 1980; Gould, 1980). They typically begin planning by critically considering the task. This allows them to formulate goals and delineate conceptual-level plans that reflect crucial elements such as their rhetorical purpose, perceived audience needs, genre demands, appropriate tone, and effective linguistic style. Throughout the composition process, skilled writers frequently pause to reflect upon their developing text and draw from a robust repertoire of strategies to facilitate the generation and organization of content (e.g., Bereiter & Scardamalia, 1987; McCutcheon, 2006).

Like planning, revising is a critical and multidimensional component of skillful writing (Hayes, 2004). For skilled writers, revision is an integral, extensive, and ongoing activity that involves the coordination and management of several cognitive skills and draws upon the resources of both working and long-term memory. Guided by their overarching goals (e.g., reflecting rhetorical purpose, intended audience, and genre expectations), skillful writers iteratively increase the overall quality of their compositions by attending to both the conceptual and linguistic aspects of their texts. Skilled writers focus their attention on the macrostructure and meaning of their compositions, rather than on surface-level textual features of discrete sentences and words (McCutcheon, 2006). They adeptly identify discrepancies between the actual and intended text, and make changes that result in substantive improvements with each successive draft.

Research suggests that the planning and revising behaviors of novice and struggling writers differ significantly from those of skillful writers (e.g., Bereiter & Scardamalia, 1987; Graham, 2006b; Graham & Harris, 2000; McCutcheon, 2006; Sitko, 1998). Novice and struggling writers typically engage in little, if any, explicit planning. For example, researchers have documented the reality that struggling writers commonly devote less than one-half minute to advanced planning, regardless of their age, the writing genre, or the writing medium (e.g., handwriting, typing, or dictating), even when they are explicitly prompted to do so (e.g., MacArthur & Graham, 1987; De La Paz, 1999; De La Paz & Graham, 1997; Graham, 1990; Lane et al., 2008; Harris, Graham, & Mason, 2006). Additionally, novice and struggling writers concentrate their efforts nearly exclusively on surface-level features of their text, rather than making improvements to the conceptual aspects or global structure. For example, MacArthur and Graham (1987) found that nearly 60% of fourth- and fifth-grade struggling writers' revisions targeted spelling, punctuation, capitalization, or handwriting. Moreover, comparisons between novice and struggling writers' first and final drafts indicate their revisions have little appreciable impact on the mechanical or substantive aspects of their text (e.g., De La Paz, Swanson, & Graham, 1998; Graham, 1997; MacArthur, Graham, & Schwartz, 1991).

Collectively, novice and struggling writers' minimal use of self-regulatory processes such as planning and revising manifest as a simplistic compositional approach, frequently termed "knowledge telling" (Bereiter & Scardamalia, 1987; McCutchen, 1988). That is, they write down all information they perceive to be somewhat topic-related and use each idea, phrase, or sentence to spawn the one that follows. They rarely (if ever) critically evaluate their ideas, reorganize their text, or reflect on whether their writing is harmonious with important considerations such as the purpose of their task, the needs of their intended audience, or the demands of the genre. In contrast, with skillful approaches to writing, knowledge telling involves little metacognitive control or recursive interplay among composing processes; in essence it is writing as remembering or writing by pattern. Thus, it is probably not surprising to learn that reliance on knowledge telling typically results in the production of compositions that are extremely short, incomplete, and low in overall quality (e.g., Graham, 1990; Graham & Harris, 2000, 2003).

The following example illustrates the process and outcome of knowledge telling (in Graham & Harris, 2005). A fourth-grade struggling writer was assigned the task of writing a report on forest fires. Even after being instructed to take his time gathering information and planning his paper, he quickly glanced through one book and did not make any notes related to organization or content. Within just a few minutes, he created the following composition that included two facts he happened to remember (indicated in *italics*).

> What I know about forest fires is that they began by lightning or by somebody throwing match and forget to put it out. Sometimes because

they throw cigarettes or they forget to put the camping fire out. And I thought that forest fires were all bad for forest. What I didn't know was that *some forest fires were good for the forest* and that *Yellow Stone park was a place where lots of forest fires occurred*. (p. 131; corrected for spelling, punctuation, and capitalization miscues)

Additional insight about the knowledge telling approach in general, and the lack of proficiency with planning in particular, is found in research documenting that providing struggling writers with verbal or visual prompts leads to significant increases in compositional length and quality (e.g., De La Paz, 1999; De La Paz & Graham, 1997; Graham, Harris, MacArthur, & Schwartz, 1991). For example, Graham (1990) reported that when fourth- and sixth-grade students who struggled with writing handwrote or dictated argumentative essays, their compositions were short and incomplete. They began with a simple "yes" or "no" response to a question asking their opinion (i.e., Should students your age select their own bedtime?), offered minimal support for their premise, and on average, completed their essays in less than 6 minutes. However, when three successive verbal prompts were used to encourage them to expand their writing (e.g., "You're doing fine. Now I know this is a bit tough, but can you write some more about this?"), they generated up to four times more content, the majority of which was classified as "functional" because it represented additional reasons or elaboration to support their premise.

In summary, theoretical and empirical research conducted during the past three decades has provided many important insights regarding the metacognitive aspects of writing, as well as the metacognitive differences between more and less skilled writers. Skillful writers have an intimate familiarity with, and understanding of, diverse genre conventions. They are also able to draw upon a wealth of topical knowledge gained either through experience or research. Throughout the writing process, skilled writers are planful and reflective. They demonstrate sensitivity to the needs and perspectives of their audience, the overarching goals and purposes of their writing, and the thematic cohesion and organization of their writing. They maintain attention and demonstrate flexibility, creativity, motivation, and persistence. Finally, skilled writers exhibit extensive self-regulation by establishing goals, structuring the social and physical environment, and actively monitoring and adjusting the processes used throughout the composition process. In contrast, novice and struggling writers show significantly less metacognitive knowledge and self-regulation. They lack critical writing knowledge, such as compositional purposes, conventions, processes, and strategies. They have difficulty generating ideas and selecting topics, and evidence little planning in advance of, or during, writing. They also lack knowledge of, and proficiency with, important strategies for planning, producing, organizing, and revising text. Thus, researchers turned to investigations of writing instruction.

Writing Instruction

Graham and Harris (in press) conducted a comprehensive synthesis of extant literature focused on writing research and identified 12 evidence-based recommendations for improving writing among students in 4th through 12th grade. Based on criteria regarding the strength of the evidence and impact on writing, they included (in this order): (1) teach strategies for planning, revising, and editing writing; (2) set clear and specific goals for what writers are to accomplish in their writing product; (3) help writers learn to write more sophisticated sentences; (4) engage students in prewriting activities that help them gather and organize ideas for their compositions; (5) engage students in the process writing approach; (6) teach students strategies and procedures for summarizing reading material, as this improves their ability to concisely and accurately present information in writing; (7) incorporate instructional arrangements that allow students to work together to plan, draft, revise, and edit their compositions; (8) make it possible for students to use word processing as a tool for writing; (9) involve students in writing activities designed to sharpen their inquiry skills; (10) provide good models for each type of writing that is the focus of instruction; (11) have students monitor their writing performance or behavior; and (12) provide ample time for writing. Collectively, Graham and Harris's findings illustrate the importance of metacognition in writing. They also support the necessity of strategies instruction in writing, since that approach addresses a number of the recommendations (for detailed discussions, see, e.g., Pressley, Borkowski, & Schneider, 1987, Pressley & Harris, 2006, and Wong, Harris, Graham, & Butler, 2003).

In the remainder of this chapter, we focus on one specific model of strategies instruction, Self-Regulated Strategy Development (SRSD), as several meta-analyses have documented that this strategies instruction approach has the strongest impact on students' writing performance (see Graham, 2006; Graham & Harris, 2003, in press; Graham & Perin, 2007; Harris et al., in press). In the sections that follow, we first present a brief overview of SRSD instruction (see Graham & Harris, 2005, and Harris, Graham, Mason, & Friedlander, 2008, for detailed descriptions of the instructional process, a wide range of strategies, lessons plans, and support materials; the Association for Supervision and Curriculum Development, 2002, for a video that features the six stages of instruction being used to teach strategies in elementary and middle school classrooms; and *iris.peabody.vanderbilt.edu* for interactive tutorials). Next, we summarize the research base documenting the efficacy of SRSD, and finally, we illustrate SRSD's efficacy and continuing research needs by describing four SRSD intervention studies that targeted the critical skills of planning and revising.

Self-Regulated Strategy Development

In the area of writing, the overarching goals of SRSD can be conceptualized as fourfold: (1) help students learn and independently apply powerful writing strategies that allow for the accomplishment of specific compositional tasks, such as writing a persuasive essay; (2) ensure students acquire the procedural, declarative, and conditional knowledge needed to effectively use the strategies; (3) support students' development of self-regulation procedures that help manage the writing strategies and the task of composing; (4) enhance specific aspects of motivation, including attitude, self-efficacy, and effort.

Theoretical Perspectives and Critical Characteristics of Instruction

In the early years of research, models of strategies instruction varied in numerous ways, but over time many critical components emerged and became common across models (Pressley & Harris, 2001, 2006). These include teacher modeling and explanations; powerful task strategies; self-regulation strategies (such as self-instructions, goal setting, self-monitoring, and self-reinforcement) for effective use of task strategies; support for working and long-term memory; teacher support (scaffolding) that is gradually faded until students develop independent use and ownership of the strategies; developing an understanding of what is being learned, why it is being learned, and where it can be used; and developing attributions for effort and strategy use and other means of enhancing motivation. The nature of strategies instruction, however, is as important as its components. Good strategies instruction is based on collaboration among teachers and students; emphasizes interactive learning that requires understanding and meaningful processing; requires teachers to be enthusiastic and responsive to the instructional needs of learners varying in cognitive capacity, relevant knowledge, motivation, and other characteristics; and requires assessment of changes in affect, behavior, cognition, and metacognition (Harris, Alexander, & Graham, 2008; Harris & Graham, 1992).

Thus, SRSD includes many of the features common to other strategies instruction. At its inception in 1982, however, SRSD differed in several significant ways from other strategies instruction models (Harris,

Reid, & Graham, 2004; Harris & Graham, 1999; Wong, Harris, Graham, & Butler, 2003). While space precludes a detailed description of the evolution of SRSD (see Harris & Graham, 2008, and Harris, Santangelo, & Graham, in press, for greater detail), the majority of the early models of strategy instruction targeted normally achieving students; typically, in addition, these models were based on one main theory and development of self-regulation skills was implicitly embedded in intervention as opposed to being taught explicitly. SRSD was initially developed for students with learning disabilities and other struggling learners; these children frequently experience difficulty with self-regulation, including the ability to activate and regulate strategic behavior. For these students, development of self-regulation skills is critical to their success in school. Informed by research on expertise in the writing domain as well as social cognitive theory and motivational theory, explicit development of self-regulation strategies was integrated throughout the stages of instruction in the SRSD model (Harris et al., 2004; Harris, Graham, & Mason, 2003; Pressley & Harris, 2006).

With SRSD, students are explicitly and systematically taught writing strategies, self-regulation procedures, and relevant metacognitive knowledge, and are provided with meaningful opportunities to support their development. Furthermore, they come to understand and appreciate the importance of what they are learning, as well as where else it can be applied. SRSD instruction is scaffolded so that the responsibility for applying and recruiting the writing strategies, knowledge, skills, and self-regulation procedures gradually shifts from the teacher to the students. Throughout the learning process, students actively collaborate with the teacher and each other, and the role of student effort is emphasized and rewarded. With SRSD, the focus and process of instruction is individualized based on students' unique needs and capabilities. Instruction is further differentiated by adjusting goals, feedback, and instructional support in response to students' current levels of performance and rates of progress. Moreover, SRSD instruction is criterion- rather than time-based; students move through the instructional process at their own pace. They do not proceed to later stages of instruction until they have met criteria for doing so and instruction does not end until they demonstrate independent, efficient, and effective use of the writing and self-regulation strategies. Finally, SRSD is an ongoing process in which new strategies are introduced and previously taught strategies are upgraded over time.

SRSD Instructional Stages

Table 10.1 presents the six basic stages of instruction that are used to introduce and develop metacognitive writing knowledge, writing strategies, and self-regulation procedures in the SRSD approach. Importantly, these stages are meant to be used as a beginning framework for instruction, and can be reordered, combined, or modified in response to students' needs. They are also intended to be recursive; if a concept or component is not mastered at a certain stage, students and teachers can revisit or continue aspects of that stage as they move on to others. Although maintaining the integrity of each stage has been shown to significantly impact the degree to which struggling writers benefit from SRSD, there are instances where students may not need all six stages. For example, students who already possess robust background knowledge could skip Stage 1 or act as a resource for their peers who need that stage.

Procedures for promoting maintenance and generalization are integrated throughout the stages of instruction in the SRSD model. These include identifying opportunities to use the writing and/or self-regulation strategies in other classes or settings, discussing attempts to use the strategies at other times, reminding students to use the strategies at appropriate times, analyzing how these processes might need to be modified with other tasks and in new settings, and evaluating the success of these processes during and after instruction. It is helpful to involve others, including other teachers, parents, and other professionals (some teachers have involved, e.g., speech language professionals) as they can prompt, support, and evaluate the use of the strategies at appropriate times in other settings. Booster sessions, where the strategies are reviewed, discussed, and supported again if necessary, are very important for some of the students we have worked within terms of maintaining the strategies.

Empirical Support for SRSD

Since 1985, more than 40 studies using the SRSD model of strategies instruction in the area of writing have been reported (for a detailed review, see Graham & Harris, 2003; Graham & Harris, in press, and Harris et al., in press). Research conducted by researchers independent of Graham, Harris, and their colleagues, as well as classroom teachers, has involved students from elementary grades through high school, has featured strategies for a variety of genres. Data from these studies provide convincing evidence that SRSD is a robust and versatile instructional approach for struggling writers with and without disabilities, as well as students who do not experience writing difficulties. Following SRSD instruction, significant and meaningful improvements are typically seen in students' writing knowledge, approach to writing (e.g., use of planning and revising strategies), writing self-efficacy, and writing performance (i.e., compositional length, completeness, and quality). These

TABLE 10.1. SRSD Stages of Instruction

Develop and activate knowledge needed for writing and self-regulation.

- Read works in the genre being addressed (stories, persuasive essays, etc.), to develop declarative, procedural, and conditional knowledge (e.g., what is an *opinion?*, what are the parts of a persuasive essay, are they all here?; how do you think the author came up with this idea, what would you do?; what might the author have done to help herself come up with all of these ideas?, what might the author have done to organize the ideas? what might the author do when he gets frustrated?, etc.), appreciation of characteristics of effective writing (how did the writer grab your interest?), and other knowledge and understandings targeted for instruction. Continue development through the next two stages as needed until all key knowledge and understandings are clear.

- Discuss and explore both writing and self-regulation strategies to be learned; may begin development of self-regulation, introducing goal setting and self-monitoring.

Discuss it.

- Explore students' current writing and self-regulation abilities, their attitudes and beliefs about writing, what they are saying to themselves as they write, and how these might help or hinder them as writers.

- Graphing (self-monitoring) may be introduced using prior compositions; this may assist with goal setting; graphing prior to writing can be skipped if the student is likely to react negatively and only performance during instruction is graphed.

- Further discuss strategies to be learned: purpose, benefits, how and when they can be used or might be inappropriate (begin generalization support).

- Establish students'commitment to learn strategy and act as collaborative partner; establish role of student effort and strategy use.

Model it.

- Teacher modeling and/or collaborative modeling of writing and self-regulation strategies, resulting in appropriate model compositions.

- Analyze and discuss strategies and model's performance; make changes as needed.

- Can model self-assessment and self-recording through graphing of model compositions.

- Continue student development of self-regulation strategies across composition and other tasks and situations; discuss use here and in other settings (continue generalization support).

Memorize it.

- Though typically begun in earlier stages, require and confirm memorization of strategies, mnemonic(s), and self-instructions as appropriate.

- Continue to confirm and support memorization in following stages, make sure students have memorized the mnemonics and what they mean before independent performance.

(continued)

TABLE 10.1. (*continued*)

Support it.

- Teachers and students use writing and self-regulation strategies collaboratively to achieve success in composing, using prompts such as strategy charts, self-instruction sheets, and graphic organizers (can initially use pictures, then fade pictures in graphic organizers).

- Challenging initial goals for genre elements and characteristics of writing established collaboratively with individual students; criterion levels increased gradually until final goals met.

- Prompts, guidance, and collaboration reduced individually (graphic organizer replaced with student creating mnemonic on scratch paper) until the student can compose successfully alone.

- Self-regulation components not yet introduced may begin (typically, goal setting, self-instructions, self-monitoring, and self-reinforcement are all being used by this stage; additional forms of self-regulation, such as environmental control, use of imagery, and so on may be used as desirable).

- Discuss plans for maintenance; continue support of generalization.

Independent performance.

- Students able to use writing and self-regulation strategies independently; teachers monitor and support as necessary.

- Fading of overt self-regulation may begin (graphing may be discontinued).

- Plans for maintenance and generalization continue to be discussed and implemented.

Note. Adapted from Harris & Graham (2007). Copyright 2007 by The Guilford Press. Adapted by permission.

gains have been consistently maintained for the majority of students over time, although some students need booster sessions for long-term maintenance. Many students have also shown generalization across settings, teachers, and writing media.

Three recent meta-analyses further document the overall effectiveness of SRSD. In a meta-analysis involving 18 studies, Graham and Harris (2003) found the effect sizes for large-group studies for improvements in writing quality were 1.14 and 1.67 for struggling writers with and without learning disabilities, respectively. The average of nonoverlapping data for single-subject design studies for these two groups was above 90%. In a comprehensive meta-analysis of the writing intervention literature with students in 4th through 12th grade, Graham and Perin (2007) reported that SRSD had a strong and positive impact on the quality of students' writing, with an average weighted effect size of 1.14. In fact, SRSD yielded the highest average weighted effect size of any of the writing interventions studied. A third meta-analysis reflecting students in all grades by Graham (Graham & Harris, in press) replicated the large effect size for writing quality. In the final section of this chapter, we detail four intervention studies aimed at planning and revising that illustrate SRSD's efficacy as well as continuing research needs.

Illustrative SRSD Intervention Studies

Planning. Harris et al. (2006) examined the impact of using the SRSD model to teach pairs of second-grade struggling writers a general strategy that emphasized planning in advance and two genre-specific strategies designed to help them plan and write stories and persuasive essays. This study was unique in that it targeted students younger than those in previous studies, and it was designed to investigate whether adding a peer support component to SRSD instruction would augment students' performance, especially in terms of maintenance and generalization.

This investigation featured an experimental design; 63 struggling writers from four urban schools were randomly assigned to one of three conditions: SRSD instruction, SRSD instruction plus peer support, or control (the school's Writers' Workshop model). A struggling writer was defined using two criteria: (1) a score at or below the 25th percentile on a norm-referenced test of writing performance that measured the inclusion of specific thematic elements in a story and (2) independent verification by the classroom teacher of difficulty learning to write. In both SRSD conditions, instruction was delivered by trained graduate students and followed the model presented in Table 10.1. Instructors worked with pairs of students three times a week for 20 minutes.

Students in the SRSD conditions first learned a general strategy that emphasized planning in advance. This strategy included three steps, represented by the mnemonic POW: (1) *Pick* my ideas (i.e., decide what to write about), (2) *Organize* my notes (i.e., organize possible writing ideas into a plan), and (3) *Write* and say more (i.e., continue to modify and upgrade the plan while writing). Once students were able to independently use the POW strategy, they next learned a genre-specific strategy designed to help them carry out the second step of POW within the context of writing a story. This strategy included seven questions designed to facilitate the generation and organization of ideas for the seven basic parts of a story, represented by the mnemonic WWW, What = 2, How = 2: (1) *Who* are the main characters?, (2) *When* does the story take place?, (3) *Where* does the story take place?, (4) *What* do the main characters want to do?, (5) *What* happens when the main characters try to do it?, (6) *How* does the story end?, and (7) *How* do the main characters feel? For each question, students learned to make notes on a graphic organizer.

After students demonstrated they could successfully use POW and WWW, What = 2, How = 2 to write stories, they were taught a second genre-specific strategy that would help them carry out the second step of POW within the context of writing persuasive essays. This strategy included four statements designed to facilitate the generation and organization of content relevant to their opinion on a particular topic, represented by the mnemonic TREE: *Tell* what you believe (i.e., topic sentence), provide three or more *Reasons* (i.e., Why do I believe this?, Will my reader believe this?), *End it* (i.e., wrap it up right), and *Examine* (i.e., Do I have all of my parts?). Students generated notes and used a graphic organizer with the prompts in TREE.

Instruction in the SRSD conditions also focused on ensuring students' acquired critical writing knowledge and self-regulation strategies that would allow them to use the three writing strategies and manage the compositional tasks. For example, they learned about the purpose of stories and persuasive writing, as well as the characteristics and features of exemplary papers in each genre. They learned the importance of using "million dollar" words to make their compositions more interesting, how to "catch the reader," and the ways in which transition words can enhance readability for opinion essays. Additionally, they learned how to set goals and write complete papers (i.e., ones that included all the basic elements as well as "million dollar" words), monitor and graph their personal success in achieving these goals, and compare their preinstructional performance with their performance during instruction. Individualized self-instructions were developed to aid self-regulation of the writing process. Finally, they learned to credit their success to effort and use of the target strategies.

In the SRSD plus peer support condition, the pairs of students supported each other in strategy use outside the instruction situation. Throughout instruction, the two students discussed with the instructor other places or instances where they might use all or some of the strategies they were learning. They also considered whether and how these procedures needed to be modified for each identified situation. They were encouraged to apply the procedures they were learning to these situations, reminding and helping each other as needed. In subsequent instructional sessions, they each identified when, where, and how they applied the strategies, describing how the strategy helped them do better as well as detailing any problems encountered. They also identified any instance in which they helped their partner.

On average, students in both SRSD conditions required 6.3 hours of instruction, spanning a period of 9 to 11 weeks, to develop competence with the strategies, knowledge, and skills targeted for story writing. For persuasive writing, competence was achieved after an average of 4.0 hours of instruction occurring over a 6- to 8-week period.

The impact of SRSD on writing behavior and performance was measured by having students write in response to a series of prompts, all of which had been previously validated with regard to equivalency and age-appropriateness. Before the start of instruction, students' compositional skills were assessed in four genres (i.e., story, persuasive, personal narrative, and informative writing). After completion of instruction focused on how to plan and write a story, students' story and personal narrative writing skills were again assessed; the former measured direct instructional impact and the later was used to determine whether instructional effects transferred to a similar but uninstructed genre.

Eight weeks later, students' story-writing skills were assessed a third time to examine whether instructional effects were maintained over time. After completion of instruction focused on how to plan and write a persuasive essay, students' persuasive and informative writing skills were assessed a second time to determine direct and transfer effects. An additional persuasive writing probe was administered by the students' regular teachers to examine whether the instructional effects generalized to the classroom. For each writing assessment, four dependant variables were measured: the amount of time students devoted to planning (with the exception of the classroom generalization story writing probe), compositional length (the number of words written), overall compositional quality (rated using 8–point genre-specific holistic rating scales), and compositional completeness (inclusion of basic story elements: main characters, locale, time, main character goals, main character actions, consequences of actions, and main characters' reactions, or inclusion of basic persuasive writing elements: premise, reason, example, and conclusion).

The impact of SRSD on writing knowledge was assessed by having students individually answer three open-ended questions before and after instruction. The first question ("When you are asked to write a paper for class or for homework, what kinds of things can you do to help you plan and write your paper?") targeted knowledge of planning. The other two questions targeted knowledge of the instructed genres by asking students what they would tell a friend about the kinds of things included in a story and a persuasive essay.

The findings reported by Harris et al. (2006) were consistent with previous research documenting that SRSD instruction has a significant and meaningful impact on students' writing knowledge, writing behavior, and writing performance. In comparison with students in the schools' Writer's Workshop-only condition, students in the two SRSD conditions were more knowledgeable about how to plan a paper, as well as the basic attributes of both a good story and a persuasive essay. They spent more time planning their posttest stories, their posttest persuasive papers, and their posttest informative papers. They wrote more complete stories at posttest and maintenance; their maintenance stories were also longer and qualitatively better. They produced persuasive essays that were longer, more complete, and qualitatively better. Additionally, the persuasive papers they wrote for their classroom teacher were qualitatively better. Generalization effects further transferred to the uninstructed genres; they wrote narratives containing more story elements, and they did more advanced planning when writing informative papers. All of these differences were large, with the corresponding effect sizes ranging from 0.87–1.50.

The findings also documented the benefit of adding a peer support component to SRSD instruction, as students the SRSD plus peer support condition evidenced five important advantages. First, in contrast to the SRSD condition, students who received peer support wrote longer and qualitatively better posttest stories than did control students. Second, SRSD students who received peer support included more elements in their persuasive compositions than did students in the SRSD condition. Third, unlike students in the SRSD condition, students who received peer support wrote papers for their regular classroom teacher that contained more basic elements than ones produced by control students. Fourth, SRSD students who received peer support included more elements in their posttest narratives than did SRSD students. Finally, the informative papers produced by students in the SRSD plus peer support condition were qualitatively better than those produced by students in the control condition, a difference not seen with SRSD students. All of these differences were large (effect sizes exceeding 0.82), and collectively suggest that peer support enhanced performance in instructed genres, as well as facilitated generalization to the general classroom and the two uninstructed genres.

In a second intervention study, Lane et al. (2008) examined the effectiveness of teaching second-grade students at risk for emotional and behavioral disorders who had co-occurring writing difficulties how to plan and draft stories using the SRSD model. This investigation extended the early intervention SRSD research by targeting a new population of students and by embedding the intervention within the larger context of a schoolwide positive behavior support model. The impact of SRSD instruction was examined using a multiple baseline, across-participants design with random assignment to one of three legs and the administration of multiple probes during baseline. The sample included six second-grade students from one rural elementary school who were systematically identified as being at risk for behavioral problems and having poor writing skills.

Instruction was delivered by trained graduate students; instructors worked individually with each of their students three to four times a week for 30 minutes. Instruction targeted the general planning strategy POW, the genre-specific strategy WWW, What = 2, How = 2, as well as the accompanying knowledge and self-regulation strategies needed to apply these strategies and manage the writing tasks (as previously described by Harris et al., 2006). The SRSD model, as presented in Table 10.1, served as the framework for the instructional process, with modifications made in response to participating students' emotional and behavioral needs. These students were given more time and opportunities to master the first two stages (Develop Background Knowledge and Discuss It) and they were not introduced to self-evaluation and graphing until the Support It stage (rather than Discuss It, as is commonly done; pilot work indicated that graphing prior work earlier in instruction was a very negative experience for some students at risk for emotional and behavioral problems). Additionally, they received higher rates of verbal reinforcement, greater opportunities to respond, and concrete reinforcements (i.e., tickets) to promote engagement, active participation, and social competence (as per the school's positive behavior support plan). It took students 10 to 15 sessions over a period of 3 to 6 weeks to reach independent levels of performance with story writing.

The impact of SRSD instruction was measured by having students compose stories in response to prompts that were empirically validated to be equivalent as well as age-appropriate. Students' writing performance was assessed prior to instruction (baseline), immediately following instruction, and after a maintenance period that ranged from 1 to 11 weeks. The dependant variables measured for each assessment included advanced planning behavior and strategy use (examining notes and observing verbalizations), story length (number of words), story completeness (inclusion of basic story elements), and overall story quality (rated using a 7-point holistic quality scale).

The findings of this study were congruent with previous research showing the efficacy of SRSD instruction; the outcomes showed a clear, functional relationship between completion of instruction and strong improvements in students' writing behavior and performance. In terms of writing behavior, prior to SRSD instruction, only one student used what might be considered a relatively sophisticated advanced planning approach. He drew a picture on another piece of paper in advance of writing his three baseline stories and twice made accompanying notes. However, despite his use of those strategies, his planning approach was not very effective; his baseline stories never included more than two of the seven basic story parts. The other five students either devoted no time to advanced planning or they employed an unsophisticated approach (e.g., writing a draft of their entire story and then recopying it as a final draft, making only small changes in spelling and usage). After SRSD instruction, all the students increased their planning time as well as the sophistication of their approach. They consistently wrote down the genre-specific strategy mnemonic WWW, What = 2, How = 2 on a separate piece of paper and made notes to accompany each part.

In terms of writing performance, meaningful gains were seen in all three areas measured. First, strong improvements were seen in the completeness of students' stories. During baseline, the mean scores for basic story elements ranged from 0 to 2.86. Following instruction, however, the mean scores ranged from 6.0 to 7.0, indicating they contained most or all of the essential parts. Second, the length of students' stories increased dramatically, with the average total words rising from a range of 7.67–34.33 during baseline to a range of 34.67–113.67 after instruction. This represented 1.5– to 7–fold improvement. Third, substantial gains were seen in compositional quality. Whereas students' baseline quality scores were low (means ranging from 1.17 to 3.33), their mean scores ranged from 5 to 6 after instruction. Importantly, the improvements in compositional completeness, length, and quality were sustained (and in some instances increased) over time, as evidenced by all students' mean maintenance scores exceeding those from baseline.

Revising. Graham (1997) examined the impact of teaching a revising strategy using the SRSD model on fifth- and sixth-grade students who experienced difficulty writing. In addition to investigating the efficacy of the revising strategy, this study provided insight regarding the contribution of difficulties with self-regulatory aspects of revising, because the strategy ensured the separate elements of the revising process would be systematically coordinated and executed and it limited the number of evaluative and tactical options for each revision. The sample consisted of 12 students with learning disabilities. Evidence of their difficulties with writing was documented by their performance on norm-referenced writing measures and feedback from their teachers.

During the normal revising condition, students were asked to write a story. Two days later, they were asked to read their story carefully and revise it "to make it better." During the SRSD revising condition, students first wrote a story (for baseline comparative purposes) and then were subsequently taught a revising strategy (a modified version of that used by Scardamalia & Bereiter, 1983). Instruction was delivered by a trained graduate student and followed the SRSD model presented in Table 10.1. This revising strategy is applied on a sentence-by-sentence basis, and involves three primary stages represented by the mnemonic CDO: Compare (i.e., detect mismatches between the author's intentions and the actual written text), Diagnose (i.e., determine the cause of such mismatches), and Operate (i.e., decide what types of changes are needed and carry them out). During the first stage, Compare, students read each sentence from their text and selected from one of seven possible evaluations that were each printed on a blue index card (i.e., "This doesn't sound right," "This is not what I wanted to say," "This is not useful to my paper," "This is good," "People may not understand this part," "People won't be interested in this part," and "People won't buy this part"). During the second stage, Diagnose, students explained orally how the evaluation applied. Finally, during the last stage, Operate, students chose from one of five directives that were each printed on a blue index card (i.e., "Leave it the same," "Say more," "Leave this part out," "Change the wording," and "Cross out and say it a different way") and then made the corresponding textual revision.

To evaluate instructional impact, each student wrote and revised two stories in response to a previously validated picture prompt; the assignment of pictures was counterbalanced so the pairing of each picture and the writing–revising condition occurred with equal frequency. Each composition was evaluated for three dependent variables: revisions, length, and quality. Revisions were scored as the number of changes between the first and second draft for each condition and further identified and categorized according to one of four syntactic levels: surface (e.g., capitalization, spelling), word, phrase, or T-unit (i.e., a main clause plus any subordinate clauses). They were further coded by the type of operation (i.e., addition, deletion, substitution, or rearrangement), whether they were meaning-preserving or meaning-changing, and by impact (i.e., rated as better, no change, or lower). Length was determined by counting the total number of written words. Quality was assessed two ways: the level of improvement between the first and second draft (rated from 1, the second paper was better than the first, to –1, the second paper was worse than the first), and the overall quality of the second draft (using an 8-point holistic rating scale). Additionally, students were individually interviewed at the end of the study to obtain their perceptions of the instructional procedures and the revising strategy.

The findings demonstrated that simplifying and coordinating the revising process reduced students' difficulties with revising. Comparative analysis between students' revising under normal conditions and their revising using CDO revealed that strategy use increased the amount of time students devoted to writing, the number of substantive changes that were made to their compositions, and the overall quality of their revisions. Specifically, when students used the CDO strategy, there was an increase in the number of nonsurface (i.e., word, phrase, and T-unit changes) meaning-preserving revisions and nonsurface revisions that resulted in textual improvements. This effect was most pronounced for changes involving longer text segments; students were three times more likely to make T-unit changes that improved their compositions when using CDO than they were under normal revising conditions. Further, 10 of the 12 participants (83%) indicated that CDO was beneficial because it made the process of revising easier and facilitated their ability to improve their stories. Typical reflections on using the strategy included, "Well, you have the steps for revising and it's easier to use than no steps"; "Reminds me to look over to see if it sounds right"; "Gave me a choice of how I wanted to change it or make it different"; "Helped me make it an interesting story, and change things, and not miss much" (Graham, 1997, p. 227).

However, although students' made more individual revisions that were rated better when using CDO, there was not a statistically significant difference between the two conditions in the number of nonsurface meaning-changing revisions, the length or overall quality of students' final drafts, or the changes in quality from first to final draft. Regardless of the revising condition, the quality of students' revised stories was low, as evidenced by an average score of 2.75 on the holistic rating scale. Collectively, the data suggested that the CDO revising strategy resulted in local but not global effects on text quality: "Many problems of revision remained when students used the CDO procedure" (Graham, 1997, p. 231). Thus, Graham concluded that the study offered partial support for the hypothesized contribution of self-regulation to students' revising difficulties; self-regulation, however, was not the only factor that limited students' ability to revise effectively. It was also inhibited by a lack of metacognitive knowledge and limited proficiency with basic writing skills. Specifically, even when using CDO, students continued to emphasize form over substance, demonstrated little sensitivity to the needs of prospective readers, had difficulty detecting and diagnosing problems, and were often unable to successfully execute an intended change.

A study by De La Paz et al. (1998) was designed to replicate and extend Graham's (1997) investigation from narrative to expository text and from elementary to middle school. Postulating that the effects of self-regulation may not have been pronounced because CDO focused students' attention too intensively on issues of local aspects of their text, the authors modified the strategy and teaching procedures accordingly. The sample included 12 eighth-grade students with learning disabilities who experienced difficulty with writing. Instruction focused on improving revising within the context of persuasive essays, as opposed to stories as in Graham (1997), because the task was more pertinent and relevant to middle school students.

As in the Graham study (1997), students' revising under normal conditions was documented by having them initially compose a first draft and then subsequently asking them to read it carefully and revise it to "make it better." However, in this investigation, students received a typed copy of their first draft and were explicitly told not to worry about correcting errors involving spelling, punctuation, and capitalization. Additionally, they were asked to cycle through their paper a second time and make additional revisions.

In the CDO condition, students first wrote a baseline essay using the procedures featured with normal revising. They were then taught to use a modified version of the CDO strategy featured in Graham (1997) that utilized slightly different evaluative and directive options and included two revising cycles, one focused on the overall representation and structure of the paper and the second involving specific segments of text. During the first cycle, students *Compared* and *Diagnosed* problems with the overall structure and content of their essays. This was achieved by having them read through their entire essay and select any of four evaluations that were listed individually on white index cards (i.e., "Ignores the obvious point against my idea," "Too few ideas," "Part of the essay doesn't belong with the rest," and "Part of the essay is not in the right order"). They then *Operated* by selecting one of four directives listed individually on blue index cards (i.e., "Rewrite," "Delete," "Add," and "Move") and executing the change. If more than one initial evaluation was selected, each was addressed in turn. During the second revising cycle, students were directed to reread their paper and highlight any areas that still needed to be addressed (*Compare*). For each section of highlighted text, they next *Diagnosed* the problems by selecting one of six evaluations listed individually on yellow index cards (i.e., "This one doesn't sound right"; "This is not what I intended to say"; This is an incomplete idea"; This is a weak idea"; "This part is not clear"; and "The problem is _____") and then *Operated* by selecting one of the four directives listed on the blue index cards.

Instruction was delivered to each student individually by one of the authors, and followed the SRSD model presented in Table 10.1. The data analysis procedures mirrored those of Graham (1997); instructional impact was evaluated by comparing students revising under normal conditions with their revising using CDO and interviewing them to obtain perceptions of the strategy's impact.

As in the Graham study (1997), students' evaluations of the CDO revising routine were positive, with all but one (90%) indicating that the strategy made revising easier. Illustrative responses to the interview questions included "Helped me find mistakes and repair things," "Some sentences didn't fit, so it helped me move them around," "It made me think more about what I should put in, take out, and rewrite," "Cards help you see mistakes," and "It let me know when to make corrections and what to do to make it better." Even the student who did not endorse the use of CDO (he thought it took too much time) indicated its use improved his essay: "It might be boring, but it does work." The use of CDO also had a positive effect on students' revising behavior. When compared to the normal revising condition, students made nearly 1.5 times more nonsurface revisions with CDO. This finding held true for both meaning-preserving and meaning-changing revisions; students engaged in an average of three additional revisions for each type. A statistically significant difference was also seen in the degree to which students focused on larger units of text; T-unit revisions were seven times more likely with CDO. Students also made twice as many nonsurface revisions that improved the quality of the text when using CDO, as compared to the normal revising condition. Importantly, unlike the findings reported by Graham (1997), in this investigation CDO revising had a greater impact on the overall quality of students' text, as compared to normal revising. With CDO, 67% of students' essays improved from the first to the final draft, whereas only 17% of the papers became better with normal revising.

Collectively the findings from De La Paz et al. (1998) provided stronger support for the hypothesized contribution of self-regulation to students' revising difficulties than those reported by Graham (1997); the use of CDO lead to more improvements in students' revising behavior and quality than in Graham's investigation. The authors attributed the enhanced impact to increasing the number of revising cycles with CDO from one to two, and utilizing evaluative statements focused on both global and local textual concerns. However, although the instructional impact was more robust than that reported in Graham (1997), an examination of students' revisions indicated "there was considerable room for improvement when students made evaluative or tactical decisions" (De La Paz et al., 1998, p. 458). Thus, the findings also emphasize that self-regulation is an important, but not the sole, element that underlies successful revision.

CONCLUSION

In this chapter, we explored the critical role of metacognition in writing. We then focused on what we have learned from research in strategies instruction, and specifically on cognitive strategies instruction in writing. We explored the current state of the art in strategies instruction in writing and the characteristics of one approach, SRSD in writing. Finally, illustrative studies and future research needs were presented. While there is a rich history of theory and research in the areas of metacognition, writing, and strategies instruction, much remains to be addressed in the future.

REFERENCES

Alexander, P. (1997). Mapping the multidimensional nature of domain learning: The interplay of cognitive, motivational, and strategic forces. In M. Maeher & P. Pintrich (Eds.), *Advances in motivation and achievement* (Vol. 4, pp. 213–250). Greenwich, CT: JAI Press.

Alexander, P. A., Graham, S., & Harris, K. R. (1998). A perspective on strategy research: Progress and prospects. *Educational Psychology Review, 10*, 129–154.

Association for Supervision and Curriculum Development (Producer). (2002). *Teaching students with learning disabilities: Using learning strategies* (Video). (Available from the Association for Supervision and Curriculum Development, 1703 North Beauregard Street, Alexandria, VA 22311–1714)

Bereiter, C., & Scardamalia, M. (1987). *The psychology of written composition.* Hillsdale, NJ: Erlbaum.

De La Paz, S. (1999). Self-regulated strategy instruction in regular education settings: Improving outcomes for students with and without learning disabilities. *Learning Disabilities Research and Practice, 14*, 92–106.

De La Paz, S., & Graham, S. (1997). Effects of dictation and advanced planning instruction on the composing of students with writing and learning problems. *Journal of Educational Psychology, 89*, 203–222.

De La Paz, S., Swanson, P. N., & Graham, S. (1998). The contribution of executive control to the revising of students with writing and learning difficulties. *Journal of Educational Psychology, 90*, 448–460.

Donovan, C. A., & Smolkin, L. B. (2006). Children's understanding of genre and writing development. In C. A. MacArthur, S. Graham, & J. Fitzgerald (Eds.), *Handbook of writing research* (pp. 131–143). New York: Guilford Press.

Englert, C., & Thomas, C. (1987). Sensitivity to text structure in reading and writing: A comparison between learning disabled and non-learning disabled students. *Learning Disability Quarterly, 10*, 93–105.

Ertmer, P. A., & Newby, T. J. (1996). The expert learner: Strategic, self-regulated, and reflective. *Instructional Science, 24*, 1–24.

Flower, L. S., & Hayes, J. R. (1980). The dynamics of composing: Making plans and juggling constraints. In L. W. Gregg & E. R. Steinberg (Eds.), *Cognitive processes in writing* (pp. 31–50). Hillsdale, NJ: Erlbaum.

Gould, J. (1980). Experiments on composing letters: Some facts, some myths, and some observations. In L. Gregg & E. Steinberg (Eds.), *Cognitive processes in writing* (pp. 97–127). Hillsdale, NJ: Erlbaum.

Graham, S. (1990). The role of production factors in learning disabled students' compositions. *Journal of Educational Psychology, 82*, 781–791.

Graham, S. (1997). Executive control in the revising of students with learning and writing difficulties. *Journal of Educational Psychology, 89*, 223–234.

Graham, S. (2006). Writing. In P. Alexander & P. Winne (Eds.), *Handbook of educational psychology* (2nd ed., pp. 457–478). Mahwah, NJ: Erlbaum.

Graham, S., & Harris, K. R. (1994). The role and development of self-regulation in the writing process. In D. Schunk & B. Zimmerman (Eds.), *Self-regula-*

tion of learning and performance: Issues and educational applications (pp. 203–228). New York: Erlbaum.

Graham, S., & Harris, K. R. (2000). The role of self-regulation and transcription skills in writing and writing development. *Educational Psychologist, 35,* 3–12.

Graham, S., & Harris, K. R. (2003). Students with learning disabilities and the process of writing: A meta-analysis of SRSD studies. In H. L. Swanson, K. R. Harris, & S. Graham, (Eds.), *Handbook of learning disabilities* (pp. 323–344). New York: Guilford Press.

Graham, S., & Harris, K. R. (2005). *Writing better. Effective strategies for teaching students with learning difficulties.* Baltimore: Brookes.

Graham, S., & Harris, K. R. (in press). Evidence-based writing practices: Drawing recommendations from multiple sources. *British Journal of Educational Psychology.*

Graham, S., Harris, K. R., MacArthur, C. A., & Schwartz, S. (1991). Writing and writing instruction with students with learning disabilities: A review of a program of research. *Learning Disability Quarterly, 14,* 89–114.

Graham, S., & Perin, D. (2007). *Writing Next: Effective strategies to improve writing of adolescents in middle and high schools—A report to the Carnegie Corporation of New York.* Washington, DC: Alliance for Excellent Education.

Graham, S., Schwartz, S. S., & MacArthur, C. A. (1993). Knowledge of writing and the composing process, attitude toward writing, and self-efficacy for students with and without learning disabilities. *Journal of Learning Disabilities, 26,* 237–249.

Hacker, D. J. (1998). Definitions and empirical foundations. In D. J. Hacker, J. Dunlosky, & A. C. Graesser (Eds.), *Metacognition in educational theory and practice* (pp. 1–23). Mahwah, NJ: Erlbaum.

Harris, K. R., Alexander, P., & Graham, S. (2008). Michael Pressley's contributions to the history and future of strategy research. *Educational Psychology, 43,* 86–96.

Harris, K. R., & Graham, S. (1992). Selfregulated strategy development: A part of the writing process. In M. Pressley, K. R. Harris, & J. Guthrie (Eds.), *Promoting academic competence and literacy in school* (pp. 277309). New York: Academic Press.

Harris, K. R., & Graham, S. (1999). Programmatic intervention research: Illustrations from the evolution of self-regulated strategy development. *Learning Disability Quarterly, 22,* 251–262.

Harris, K. R., & Graham, S. (2007). Marconi invented the radio so people who can't afford TVs can hear the news: Research on teaching powerful composition strategies we have and research we need. In M. Pressley, A. K. Billman, K. H. Perry, K. E. Reffitt, & J. M. Reynolds (Eds.), *Shaping literacy achievement: Research we have, research we need* (pp. 175–196). New York: Guilford Press.

Harris, K. R., & Graham, S. (in press). Self-regulated strategy development in writing: Premises, evolution, and future. *British Journal of Educational Psychology.*

Harris, K. R., Graham, S., Brindle, M., & Sandmel, K. (in press). Metacognition and children's writing. In D. J. Hacker, J. Dunlosky, & A. C. Graesser (Eds.), *Handbook of metacognition in education.* Mahwah, NJ: Erlbaum.

Harris, K. R., Graham, S., & Mason, L. (2003). Selfregulated strategy development in the classroom: Part of a balanced approach to writing instruction for students with disabilities. *Focus on Exceptional Children, 35,* 116.

Harris, K. R., Graham, S., & Mason, L. (2006). Improving the writing performance, knowledge, and motivation of struggling writers in second grade: The effects of self-regulated strategy development with and without peer support. *American Educational Research Journal, 43,* 295–340.

Harris, K. R., Graham, S., Mason, L., & Friedlander, B. (2008). *Powerful writing strategies for all students.* Baltimore: Brookes.

Harris, K. R., Reid, R., & Graham, S. (2004). Self-regulation among students with LD and ADHD. In B. Wong (Ed.), *Learning about learning disabilities* (3rd ed., pp. 167–195). Orlando, FL: Academic Press.

Harris, K. R., Santangelo, T., & Graham, S. (2008). Self-regulated strategy development in writing: Going beyond NLEs to a more balanced approach. *Instructional Sciences, 36,* 395–408.

Hayes, J. (1996). A new framework for understanding cognition and affect in writing. In M. Levy & S. Ransdell (Eds.), *The science of writing: Theories, methods, individual differences, and applications* (pp. 1–27). Mahwah, NJ: Erlbaum.

Hayes, J. (2004). What triggers revision? In L. Allal, L. Chanquoy, & P. Largy (Eds.), *Studies in writing: Vol. 13. Revision: Cognitive and instructional processes* (pp. 9–20). Norwell, MA: Kluwer.

Hayes, J., & Flower, L. (1980). Identifying the organization of writing processes. In L. Gregg & E. Steinberg (Eds.), *Cognitive processes in writing* (pp. 3–30). Hillsdale, NJ: Erlbaum.

Lane, K. L., Harris, K. R., Graham, S., Weisenbach, J. L., Brindle, M., & Morphy, P. (2008). The effects of self-regulated strategy development on the writing performance of second-grade students with behavioral and writing difficulties. *Journal of Special Education, 41,* 234–253.

Lin, S. C., Monroe, B. W., & Troia, G. A. (2007). Development of writing knowledge in grades 2–8: A comparison of typically developing writers and their struggling peers. *Reading and Writing Quarterly, 23,* 207–230.

MacArthur, C. A., & Graham, S. (1987). Learning disabled students' composing under three methods of text production: Handwriting, word processing, and dictation. *Journal of Special Education, 21,* 22–42.

MacArthur, C. A., Graham, S., & Schwartz, S. (1991). Knowledge of revision and revising behavior among students with learning disabilities. *Learning Disability Quarterly, 14,* 61–74.

McCormick, C. B. (2003). Metacognition and learning. In W. M. Reynolds & G. E. Miller (Eds.), *Handbook of psychology: Vol. 1. Educational psychology* (Vol. 7, pp. 79–102). New York: Wiley.

McCutchen, D. (1986). Domain knowledge and linguistic knowledge in the development of writing ability. *Journal of Memory and Language, 25,* 431–444.

McCutchen, D. (1988). "Functional automaticity" in children's writing: A problem of metacognitive control. *Written Communication, 5,* 306–324.

McCutchen, D. (2000). Knowledge, processing, and working memory: Implications for a theory of writing. *Educational Psychologist 89,* 667–676.

McCutchen, D. (2006). Cognitive factors in the development of children's writing. In C. A. MacArthur, S. Graham, & J. Fitzgerald (Eds.), *Handbook of writing research* (pp. 115–130). New York: Guilford Press.

McCutchen, D., Francis, M., & Kerr, S. (1997). Revising for meaning: Effects of knowledge and strategy. *Journal of Educational Psychology, 89,* 667–676.

Paris, S. G., Lipson, M. Y., & Wixson, K. K. (1983). Becoming a strategic reader. *Contemporary Educational Psychology, 8,* 293–316.

Pressley, M. (1979). Increasing children's self-control through cognitive interventions. *Review of Educational Research, 49,* 319–370.

Pressley, M. (1986). The relevance of the good strategy user model to the teaching of mathematics. *Educational Psychologist, 21,* 139–161.

Pressley, M., Borkowski, J. G., & Schneider, W. (1987). Cognitive strategies: Good strategies users coordinate meta-cognition and knowledge. In R. Vasta & G. Whitehurst (Eds.), *Annals of child development* (Vol. 4, pp. 89–129). Greenwich, CT: JAI Press.

Pressley, M., & Harris, K. R. (2001). Teaching cognitive strategies for reading, writing, and problem solving. In A. L. Costa (Ed.), *Developing minds: A resource book for teaching thinking* (3rd ed., pp. 466471). Alexandria, VA: Association for Supervision and Curriculum Development.

Pressley, M., & Harris, K. R. (2006). Cognitive strategies instruction: From basic research to classroom instruction. In P. A. Alexander & P. Winne (Eds.), *Handbook of educational psychology* (2nd ed., pp. 265–286). New York: Macmillan.

Prior, P. (2006). A sociocultural theory of writing. In C. A. MacArthur, S. Graham, & J. Fitzgerald (Eds.), *Handbook of writing research* (pp. 54–66). New York: Guilford Press.

Raphael, T. E., Englert, C. S., & Kirschner, B. W. (1989). Students' metacognitive knowledge and writing. *Research in the Teaching of English, 23,* 343–379.

Saddler, B., & Graham, S. (2007). The relationship between writing knowledge and writing performance among more and less skilled writers. *Reading and Writing Quarterly, 23,* 231–247.

Scardamalia, M., & Bereiter, C. (1983). The development of evaluative, diagnostic, and remedial capabilities in children's composing. In M. Martlow (Ed.), *The psychology of written language: Development and educational perspectives* (pp. 67–95). London: Wiley.

Scardamalia, M., & Bereiter, C. (1986). Written composition. In M. Wittrock (Ed.), *Handbook of research on teaching* (3rd ed., pp. 778–803). New York: Macmillan.

Sitko, B. M. (1998). Knowing how to write: Metacognition in writing instruction. In D. J. Hacker, J. Dunlosky, & A. C. Graesser (Eds.), *Metacognition in educational theory and practice* (pp. 93–116). Hillsdale, NJ: Erlbaum.

Wallace, I. (1971). *The writing of one novel.* Richmond Hill, Ontario: Simon & Schuster.

Wallace, I., & Pear, J. (1977). Self-control techniques of famous novelist. *Journal of Applied Behavioral Analysis, 10,* 515–525.

Wong, B. (1999). Metacognition in writing. In R. Gallimore, L. P. Bernheimer, D. L. MacMillan, D. L. Speece, & S. Vaughn (Eds.), *Developmental perspectives on children with high-incidence disabilities* (pp. 183–198). Mahwah, NJ: Erlbaum.

Wong, B. Y. L., Harris, K. R., Graham, S., & Butler, D. L. (2003). Cognitive strategies instruction research in learning disabilities. In H. L. Swanson, K. R. Harris, & S. Graham (Eds.), *Handbook of learning disabilities* (pp. 323344). New York: Guilford Press.

Zimmerman, B. J., & Risemberg, R. (1997). Becoming a self-regulated writing: A social cognitive perspective. *Contemporary Educational Psychology, 22,* 73–101.

11

Metacognition, Intelligence, and Academic Performance

Cesare Cornoldi

Metacognition is one important facet of human intelligence but it is also the aspect of intelligence that can be more easily promoted by education. The present chapter examines this issue on the basis of a cognitive model of intelligence. The model is presented in the first section, followed by an examination of the implications of the model for education and academic learning and a description of the place of metacognition in the model. In the final section, I present some data supporting the model, discuss group differences in intellectual functioning, and offer some educational implications of the model, in particular with reference to metacognition. Throughout the entire chapter, data and examples are focused on different categories of exceptional children.

THE CONTRIBUTION OF COGNITIVE SCIENCE TO THE STUDY AND EDUCATION OF HUMAN INTELLIGENCE

It is by no means easy to talk about intelligence and its education, both because of the richness and heterogeneity of theoretical and method-ological approaches and because of the vague and slippery nature of the intelligence construct. Nonetheless, in the past 30 years new elements have emerged that allow us to approach the issue in a different way (for reviews, see Wilhelm & Engle, 2005). Mostly these elements are directly related to cognitive psychology and, more generally, to the cognitive neurosciences and the growing interest in the area of individual differences.

More specifically, what has clearly emerged in the last few years is how cognitive psychology has given "psychological" contents to an entity that had, until then, mostly been inferred through measurement testing and through presumed biological correlates. In particular, the psychometric approach had an important place in the history of research on intelligence, in the creation of measuring tools, and for its ability to identify critical issues. From a pure theoretical standpoint, the different positions within psychometrics were not particularly sophisticated and have given rise to the classical debate: "Is it possible to talk about intelligence as a single entity or are there many forms of intelligence?" From an educational point of view, psychometric theories proposed a core entity (the "g factor") that had a statistical, but not a psychological, identification, and by consequence could not represent a target for education.

By giving a psychological identity to intelligence, cognitive psychology has provided education with an object and a method, which remained unidentifiable to the extent to which intelligence was defined on the basis of a statistical extrapolation or a neurological correlate. However, different cognitive theories have focused on different, although partially overlapping, cognitive constructs, like processing speed, attention, working memory, learning capacity, executive functions, and metacognition.

In a series of papers (e.g., Cornoldi, 2006, 2007; Cornoldi & Vecchi, 2003) I have developed a framework for the comprehension of issues related to the study of intelligence. The theoretical analysis begins with the contributions of psychometrics, psychopathology, classical educational projects, and psychobiology, but then moves on to the ambitious goal of going beyond these approaches. I argued that the contributions of neuroscience are critical to the identification of the basic factors essential to cognitive functioning, and of the compatibility between a psychological theory of intelligence and its neural substrates. In this respect, evidence is increasingly showing the importance of biological (genetic) factors (e.g., Plomin, De Fries, Craig, & McGuffin, 2003) and favors the idea that the so-called executive processes, mainly related to cognitive control and associated with the functioning of prefrontal areas, are critically involved in intellectual functioning (Duncan, 2005). However, psychobiological studies typically focus on the basic structure of intelligence (BSI; associated with performance on neuropsychological tests) which must be distinguished from the use of BSI (UI; associated with success in everyday life activities). The framework sketched in the present chapter assumes that BSI is a powerful, but not the sole predictor of UI. A key assumption of the approach is that psychological dimensions are continuous (Cornoldi & Vecchi, 2003). The assumption of continuity also applies to the distinction between BSI and UI. Pure BSI is a hypothetical construct because intelligence is always expressed in its use, but is better approximated by classical neuropsychological and IQ tests.

Concerning the basic aspects of intelligence, a hierarchical theory of intelligence seems to represent a good compromise, overcoming the limitations of both the unitary and the multiple approach. However, there is a need for a psychological theory of basic intelligence capable of going beyond the simple statistical analysis of intelligence and actually instilling a psychological content in the processes assumed to be located at the top of the hierarchical BSI. Different cognitive constructs, candidates mostly considered critical for explaining the central aspects of BSI, were contrasted (Cornoldi, 2007), using empirical evidence and the capacity of explaining exceptionality as criteria, and in particular the differences between groups assumed a priori to have a lower level of intelligence (animals vs. humans, young children vs. mature children, typically developing children vs. mentally impaired children with an associated genetic syndrome). More specifically, a number of assumptions were made, that is, that human beings' intelligence matures with age (with a specific decline in the elderly), that from a phylogenetic perspective human beings represent the highest form of intelligence, and that certain genetic conditions are associated with cognitive difficulties. Certain criteria were highlighted which, although not perfect, have solid foundations. A theory of intelligence must thereby be capable of accounting for the ontogeny, phylogeny, and psychopathology of this phenomenon while also being compatible with data emerging from biology, neuroscience, and genetics. Table 11.1 offers a synthesis of the analyses made by Cornoldi (2007) in order to compare the capacity of different cognitive constructs in explaining BSI specificities that can be found in different groups of individuals. No construct seems completely adequate, nor is clear evidence available for each slot, but working memory best fits with the overall pattern of data.

Intelligence and Atypical Development

As anticipated, the study of psychopathological profiles associated with cognitive deficits, emerging in the context of failures to life adaptation, offers the possibility of testing the theoretical constructs lying at the heart of our view of intelligence, both considering BSI and UI. In the developmental field, different disorders may offer important information for the development of a theory of intelligence. In particular, the presence of specific disorders, as is particularly evident in learning disabilities (e.g.,

TABLE 11.1. Capacity of Different Constructs of Explaining the Basic Structure of Intelligence with Reference to Differences between Humans and Animals (A), Typical Development (TD), Mental Retardation (MR), Learning Disabilities (LD), Aging Impairment (AI), Giftedness (G), Biological Evidence (BE)

	A	TD	MR	LD	AI	G	BE
Speed of processing	–	*	*	–	**	*	*
Executive functions	**	*	*	*	**	**	
Learning capacity	–	–	*	–	**	*	–
Temporary memory	–	**	*	–	*	*	
Working memory control	*	**	**	*	**	**	**
Metacognition	**	**	*	–	*	**	–

Note. A, differences between humans and animals; TD, typical development; MR, mental retardation; LD, learning disabilities; AI, aging impairment; G, giftedness; BE, biological evidence; **, strong evidence in favor; *, evidence in favor; –, contrasting evidence. Data from Cornoldi (2007).

developmental dyslexia) and in some neuropsychological dissociations, shows that intelligence cannot be considered as unitary, but rather articulated in a series of semi-independent abilities. However, the fact that these abilities do not have the same critical importance and overlap to different degrees supports the existence of an interconnected hierarchical intelligence system. Finally, the fact that some children, despite good BSI, fail in an impressive series of relevant everyday situations, or that, despite having equal levels of IQ, have different manifestations of intelligence, shows that BSI must be distinguished from UI.

Therefore, the present framework highlights the weakness of both the unitary and the multiple views of intelligence and includes a hierarchical organization that recognizes the existence of various forms of intelligence of differing levels of importance. However, in order to decide between different cognitive constructs candidates used to define the core of basic intelligence, as many criteria as possible must be taken into consideration. As Table 11.1 suggests, the construct of working memory control is the most adequate for explaining BSI. Indeed, the other candidates reveal some weaknesses with respect to some criteria. For example, speed of processing cannot explain why individuals with low intelligence may have high rapidity; on the contrary, individuals with specific failures, but relatively good (elderly), or average intelligence (e.g., individuals with learning disabilities), or even with high intelligence (e.g., gifted), may not have a speed corresponding to their level of intelligence.

When considering the three connected constructs of attention, temporary memory, and working memory control, the present view assumes that the most adequate explanation of intelligence must both consider the functions of temporary maintenance and of attentional control. Indeed, for many years evidence has supported the claim that working memory is a critical factor of intelligence (e.g., Kyllonen & Christal, 1990). This conclusion has remained open to criticism. For example, the meta-analysis of Ackerman, Beier, and Boyle (2005) found an effect size corresponding to a medium correlation between IQ and working memory. However, this analysis did not consider the multiple facets of intelligence and the hierarchical organization of working memory. In fact, it is not realistic to assume that a single relatively simple cognitive system is able to explain all the manifestations of human intelligence. Thus, in the present framework, controlled working memory is not considered to overlap with intelligence, but rather to best predict the most central facets of the basic structure of intelligence. Furthermore, converging evidence shows that working memory can be distinguished in different aspects, in particular in the relatively passive processes involved in the simple maintenance of information and in active controlled processes involved in the manipulation of maintained information (e.g., Cornoldi & Vecchi, 2003; Kane & Engle, 2002; Lanfranchi, Cornoldi, & Vianello, 2004). BSI seems more directly related with active rather than with passive processes.

The Continuous Hierarchical Organization of Working Memory and Intelligence

The distinction between simple maintenance processes and active controlled processes has usually been considered to be dichotomous. However, a hierarchical theory of basic intelligence based on the construct of working memory implies the need for a hierarchical model of working memory. Given the recognition that working memory (i.e., the ability to temporarily maintain and process a series of information and/or procedures) is an essential interpretative tool for the understanding of intelligence, the analysis of the hierarchical organization of working memory can be useful in understanding the hierarchical organization of intelligence. In this respect, the continuity model of working memory (Cornoldi, 1995; Cornoldi & Vecchi, 2003) seems appropriate for describing the cognitive basis of intelligence. The model assumes that working memory operations can be distinguished according to two main orthogonal dimensions, that is, content (e.g., verbal vs. numerical vs. visual vs. spatial) and active control; active control in the (vertical) dimension may vary along a continuum, moving from very passive maintenance processes (e.g., tapped by simple short-term recognition tasks) through to moderately active tasks still loading on the nature of the processed content (e.g., backward word span, reading span tasks), to very active tasks (e.g., dual working memory tasks).

The application of the continuity model to the structure of intelligence may offer a cognitive description of classical hierarchical views of intelligence. For example, Vernon's (1961) approach to intelligence considered some aspects of cognitive functioning to be more central than others. This position was revised by subsequent psychometric analyses and approaches (see, e.g., the radix models; Marshalek, Loman, & Snow, 1983).

It is interesting to notice that, according to these views, different aspects of learning were located at different hierarchical levels. For example, Vernon (1961) and Marshalek and colleagues (1983) located reading comprehension and arithmetic reasoning at more central levels than reading decoding and arithmetic calculation. The same conclusion is reached by the present approach. Consistent with this view and the working memory control approach, reading comprehension and arithmetic calculation are strongly associated with working memory operations requiring a high level of control, whereas the other skills are associated with low control working memory operations (see Cornoldi, Carretti, & De Beni, 2001) (see Figure 11.1). Furthermore, achievement attainments are not only distinguished on the basis of the degree of control, but also on the basis of the type of content—for example, verbal, numerical, visual. Indeed, in the present approach, a single basic academic ability, for example, reading decoding, is distinguished from another basic ability, for example, knowledge of arithmetic facts, with reference to the content dimension, and is distinguished from a more controlled ability, for example, reading comprehension, with reference to the active control dimension.

BSI and UI

The description of academic abilities based on a working memory model does not take into account the observation that academic abilities rely on the basic structures of intelligence, but cannot be identified with them, as they represent a form of intelligence in use largely affected by experience and education. UI cannot be identified, nor is it totally explained, by the basic structure of intelligence; otherwise the concept would be useless. As already mentioned, there is evidence that the products of intelligence can deviate from what could be predicted by the levels of basic intelligence. Older people and people with high intellectual talent can perform at an intellectual level that other people with the same basic skills cannot. The same individual, under different conditions, can produce different intel-

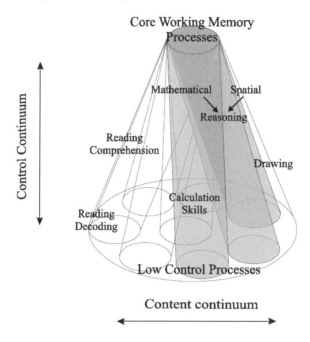

FIGURE 11.1 Cognitive components mainly involved, within a hierarchical structure of intelligence, with different academic competencies.

lectual results (Mueller & Dweck, 1998). A question to be answered is why certain people with highly developed cognitive faculties are unable to exploit their talents while others with rather less developed faculties are able to do so quite successfully. Furthermore, although basic intelligence is biologically rooted and modestly modifiable (Plomin, De Fries, Craig, & McGuffin, 2003), there is evidence that genius and other aspects of intellectual development can be affected by experience, education, and emotional–motivational variables.

To account for the relationship between BSI and UI, Cornoldi (2007) presents a model (see Figure 11.2; Table 11.2 offers a synthesis of the main points of the model), where the cone, representing the hierarchical organization of the BSI, is described as being affected at different levels by three main categories of variables: experience, culture-values-motivations and emotional metacognition. Experience is a necessary condition for the development of intelligence and offers direct stimulation for the development of low level skills. Indeed, lower level skills are mainly content-dependent processes that are supported by content knowledge and repeated exposure. The second component is represented

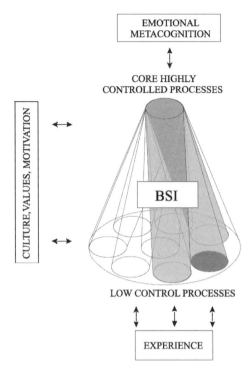

FIGURE 11.2. A contextualized model of intelligence based on metacognition and working memory control: the interaction between the basic structure of intelligence (BSI) and the three factors affecting the use of intelligence.

by a domain including culture, values, and motivation. In fact, a part of experience is socially and culturally mediated (Ceci, 1996; Vygotsky, 1978) and is acquired not only through education, but also through the immersion of an individual in a social community characterized by a particular cultural context. In this way not only knowledge is transmitted, but also an individual's values and motivation are modulated. This second component can influence intelligence at different hierarchical levels, depending on the particular case. For example, culture may influence the child's motivation to develop a great expertise in a specific skill, but can also motivate him to increase his general skills. The third component is represented by (hot) metacognition, that is, metacognition also including motivational-emotional aspects, as will be illustrated in the following paragraphs. Research on metacognition emphasizes how representations of the mind, strategies, and metacognitive control processes can actually influence the ways in which the basic structures are used. Thus, metacog-

TABLE 11.2. Assumptions of the Metacognitive Working Memory Theory of Intelligence

1. Intelligence in use in the real world is different from and is the consequence of basic intelligence in interaction with emotional metacognition, culture, and experience. A theory of intelligence in use must be able to explain the nature of intelligence expressions, from failures to genius productions.

2. Basic intelligence, as inferred from traditional IQ tests and other neuropsychological measures, is biologically rooted, mainly located in the prefrontal lobes.

3. Basic intelligence is adequately described by a hierarchical theory better than by the unitary and the multiple ones.

4. A theory of basic intelligence, in order to have psychological and educational implications, must give psychological meaning to its hierarchical structure.

5. A theory of basic intelligence must be able to explain exceptionality, for example differences between typically developing individuals and (a) younger children, (b) mentally retarded individuals with genetic syndromes, (c) animals, (d) gifted individuals.

6. Between the different cognitive constructs hypothesized to describe the core of human intelligence (speed, learning capacity, short-term memory, controlled attention, etc.) working memory control appears to be the most powerful and the most adequate for describing the hierarchical organization of intelligence.

7. A hierarchical model of basic intelligence founded on the notion of working memory control assumes that the functions at the low control level are less critical for intellectual functioning and are in direct interaction with experience, whereas the highest levels are the most critical and are in direct interaction with emotional and cognitive awareness of mind functioning. Culture-mediated values and experiences interact at all the levels of the hierarchical system.

Note. Data from Cornoldi (2007).

nition guides the strategic and effective use of cognitive abilities while a correct cultural-motivational stance supports and reinforces the manifestation of intelligence.

On the basis of a model of intelligence including a basic component and three associated components, it is possible to make inferences concerning how intelligence can be enhanced through education. Indeed, education can affect the three associated components more easily than the BSI. Concerning the interactions between the three components and the BSI, practice and experience can enhance specific lower level abilities; positive cultural and motivational influences can affect competence in using basic cognitive structures at different levels, according to the type of accent given by the context; finally, effective metacognition is especially critical in affecting the central control processes of working memory. Consequently, if an educational effort is focused on the most central aspects of intelligence, high control working memory processes, modestly modifiable, and metacognition, more deeply modifiable, become critical.

THE ROLE OF METACOGNITION

As discussed earlier, the role of metacognition in intellectual functioning (Hertzog & Robinson, 2004) can be better disambiguated by considering both the distinction between BSI and UI and by the fact that metacognition may imply many different aspects (Schneider, 1998). As is evident from the large body of literature produced in the field and from the various positions offered in this volume, the concept of metacognition is rather broad and can be articulated in various ways. However, a largely shared approach (e.g., Schneider & Pressley, 1989) makes a distinction between knowledge about mind functioning (we will call it "metacognitive knowledge") and metacognitive procedures (for a conceptual discussion, see Schneider, 1998). These two components have been studied and considered either as substantially independent or strongly interconnected. Furthermore, metacognitive knowledge may be considered as a by-product of cognitive competence (e.g., Begg, Duft, Lalonde, Melnick, & Sanvito, 1989) or as a factor that has an important influence on cognitive performance via the metacognitive procedures. According to a strong metacognitive view (Cornoldi, 1998), an individual's metacognitive knowledge is a complex system including attitudes, knowledge, and emotions concerning mind functioning, in general, and more specifically his or her own mind. Furthermore, metacognitive knowledge affects the selection and use of specific strategies and control processes, and this function affects performance.

To account for different facets of metacognitive knowledge, Cornoldi (1987) introduced the concept of *metacognitive attitude*, which concerns an emotionally positive subject's attitude towards his or her mind and the possibility of understanding and using it effectively. The *metacognitive attitude* (Cornoldi, 1998) is a general tendency of a person to develop reflection about the nature of his or her own cognitive activity and to think about the possibility of extending and using this reflection. Cornoldi (1998) made a distinction between general metacognitive knowledge, specific metacognitive knowledge, and metacognitive attitude. He assumed that the tendency to think about a task (producing a metacognitive conceptualization of the task) and to use metacognitive knowledge (both preexisting and developed when facing the task) is affected by the metacognitive attitude. As metacognitive attitude develops with age, also the relationship between metacognitive knowledge and its application to the completion of tasks (if not automatized) develops with age, as confirmed by the fact that the correlation between specific metacognitive knowledge and cognitive behavior increases with age (see Schneider & Pressley, 1989).

Emotional Components of Metacognition

Both the metacognitive attitude and general metacognitive knowledge (e.g., general ideas about cognitive functioning, naïve theories of intelligence, intellectual self-esteem, self-attribution) represent a mixture of cognitive and emotional aspects. In particular, the role of self-attribution has been repeatedly documented. Indeed, an effort attribution, that is, a self-attribution for the effects of effort on performance, represents a critical aspect of metacognitive knowledge and of the metacognitive attitude (in its implications for the tendency to reflect on the task and on the use of cognitively expensive strategies). For example, a method used for studying the child's self-attribution is based on questionnaires. The child is invited to give an explanation of why he failed or was successful in a particular engaging task and may choose between different factors either internal (effort, ability) or external (luck, received help, task facility). It has been shown (e.g., Pearl, Bryan, & Donahue, 1980) that children with learning difficulties also tend to give fewer effort explanations for the outcomes of their actions, especially concerning failures. The direction of this relationship could be questioned on the basis of the consideration that more successful individuals have better opportunities for developing a greater confidence in their effort. However, it has been shown that a modification of the attributional state plays a critical role in influencing the effects of a treatment (Borkowski, Carr, Rellinger, & Pressley, 1990).

The Impact of Metacognitive Knowledge on Metacognitive Procedures and on Performance

As has already been discussed, it has been suggested that reflection cannot penetrate a series of cognitive processes (Fodor, 1983) or may be an epiphenomenon produced by the cognitive process itself (Begg et al., 1989; Kaufmann, 1996). On the contrary, in the present view, metacognition affects cognitive behavior through its influence on metacognitive procedures. For example, memory performance is affected by the specific strategies and processes the individual has decided to use, in a more or less aware way, and this decision has been affected by the subject's attitude and his metacognitive knowledge. However, this position assumes that the relationship between metacognitive knowledge and cognitive behavior is far from perfect, as the actual behavior will be influenced by a series of contextual and task constraints and by other subject's characteristics.

The relationship between different aspects of metacognitive knowledge and metacogntive procedures related to self-regulation can be exemplified by a study that established the role of metacognitive factors on academic achievement of students in our university (Cornoldi, De Beni, & Fioritto, 2003). A group of 240 randomly selected students attending the second year in different faculties of the University of Padua, and assumed to represent the population of the undergraduate students at this university, were administered a series of questionnaires which respectively assessed four main metacognitive knowledge variables: the student's attitude toward the modifiability of his or her own intelligence (implicit theory) with its associated belief on the role of effort (effort attribution), his or her perception of self-efficacy (self-efficacy), and knowledge and use of study strategies (strategies). A fifth questionnaire concerned the adequate use of metacognitive procedures (self-regulation) and a final questionnaire collected information on the student's academic achievement. In order to test our model of the factors producing self-regulation we looked for the best structural equation describing the pattern of relationships between the overall variables measured. This was done using the LISREL program. We tested a series of models which described different patterns, proceeding toward the best description. Figure 11.3 shows how the final empirical model (Figure 11.3a) substantially corresponded to the hypothesized pattern of relationships between the variables (Figure 11.3b). The obtained indexes were rather satisfactory.

GROUP DIFFERENCES IN INTELLECTUAL FUNCTIONING AND EDUCATIONAL IMPLICATIONS

The intelligence model proposed here can be used in trying to understand the differences between groups and the most adequate types of educational approaches. Superior performances are not the focus of the present chapter, nor were they tested by our research, but will be considered briefly as they well represent the differences between the outcomes mainly due to the BSI and those outcomes due to the critical intervening role of the three associated variables (see Figure 11.4). In fact, giftedness is typically considered with reference to high performance in IQ tests and has been shown (e.g., Johnson, Im-Bolter, & Pascual Leone, 2003; Swanson, 2006) to be highly related with the performance in high-control working memory tasks. On the contrary, biographical studies and some experimental evidence show that the attainments of people, unanimously considered as geniuses, are the result of a mixture of basic abilities, creativity, and metacognitive, emotional, motivational, and cultural influences (Runco, 1999). In a similar vein, talent can be considered

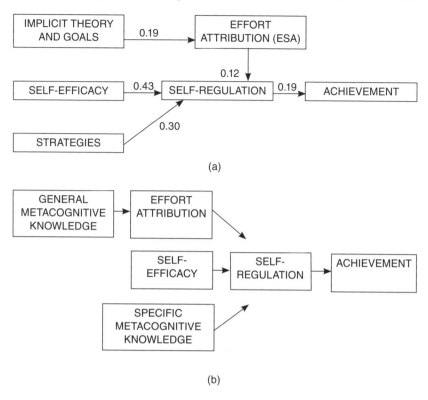

FIGURE 11.3. Example of interaction between different aspects of emotional metacognition affecting cognitive performance: (a) empirical data and (b) theoretical framework. Adapted from Cornoldi, De Beni, and Fioritto, (2003). Copyright 2003 by Emerald Group Publishing Ltd. Adapted by permission.

as a specific, probably innate, exceptional ability, whereas expertise in a particular field is probably inspired by an innate talent, but is mainly the result of an interaction between motivation, culture, and prolonged experience and practice. Finally, the superior performances reached by the so-called idiot savants could be the product of interaction between specific competence in a very low control skill and repeated specific experience (with the support of specific motivation).

Figure 11.5 describes the application of the model to the case of developmental disabilities. This application is partly the consequence of the model presented in Figure 11.1 and can be used for understanding which areas of the working memory system are mainly involved in children's weaknesses. Children specifically failing in different areas of

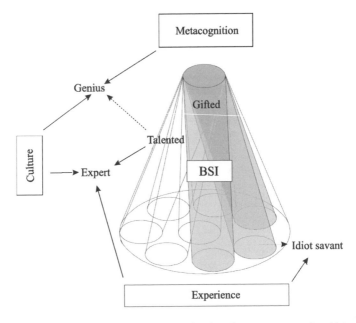

FIGURE 11.4. Components critically involved within a contextualized hierarchical model of intelligence in different types of exceptionality.

academic achievement are located in the position of the intelligence cone corresponding to the position occupied by the corresponding ability, as also confirmed by the specific working memory deficits presented by these groups (see Cornoldi & Vecchi, 2003). For example, dyslexic children are located in correspondence with low-control verbal processes; dyscalculic children are located at a relatively low level in correspondence with a different position of the content continuum. All these children are able to take advantage of specific practice in the area of weakness. Children with visuospatial (nonverbal) learning disabilities represent a rather heterogeneous group defined by the presence of specific learning difficulties in association with high verbal abilities and poor spatial abilities and can have difficulties in the visuospatial part of the working memory cone, but at different levels of the control continuum (Cornoldi & Vecchi, 2003).

Effects of Metacognitive Training: Low-Level versus High-Level School Abilities

An assumption of the present approach is that metacognition is closer to the high-control processes than to the low-control ones, and a modification in the metacognitive state will affect the latter to a lesser extent. For

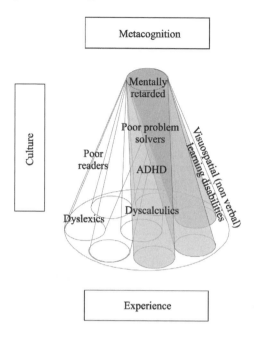

FIGURE 11.5. Typical cognitive failures within a hierarchical basic structure of intelligence in different developmental disabilities.

example, in the area of basic learning skills, it is assumed that metacognition has a greater influence on controlled processes of reading comprehension, writing expression, and problem solving, than on basic processes of reading decoding, orthography, and calculation. Decoding, orthography, and calculation are progressively automatized, offering further evidence in favor of the modest penetrability of these processes. In fact, automatization is a typical feature of low-control processes. However, a partial automatization through repeated practice also applies to high-control processes. Indeed, low- and high-control processes remain distinguishable even at equal levels of practice, as it obviously is in the case of reading which, at certain levels of learning, simultaneously involves lower and higher control skills, that is, decoding and comprehension. In general, the approach assumes that even at early stages of learning, decoding, orthography, and calculation are more affected by specific cognitive processes than by metacognition, whereas metacognition is directly involved in text comprehension, expressive writing, and problem solving both at low and at high levels of expertise. In fact, there is substantial evidence that people with good text comprehension skills also have higher metacognition (Cornoldi & Oakhill, 1997). The evidence concerning expressive writing (e.g., Re & Cornoldi, in preparation), study skills (e.g., Meneghetti, De Beni, & Cornoldi, 2007), and problem solving (e.g., Lucangeli & Cornoldi, 1997) is less extensive, but is still in the same direction and shows that children who are more competent in academic abilities also have higher metacognition.

From an intervention point of view, the most interesting evidence concerns the effects of metacognitive training on reading, writing, and mathematics. Considering the particular case of children with reading difficulties, it is interesting to note that the effects of training may be greater for reading comprehension than for reading decoding (Swanson & Sachse, 2000). More specifically, effective programs on reading comprehension include a series of metacognitive elements.

A study that directly tested the hypothesis that metacognitive training affects higher level reading and mathematics (comprehension and problem solving), but not lower level reading and mathematics (decoding and calculation), was conducted by Lucangeli, Galderisi, and Cornoldi (1995, Study 2). In the study, 111 children, third to fifth graders, mainly with learning difficulties, were divided into a control group trained according to a traditional approach (based on practice and language skills) and an experimental group that underwent a reading metacognitive program, developing knowledge about reading, reading strategies, reading sensitivity to different texts, and monitoring skills. At the end of the program, the metacognitive group was better than the other group on a measure of reading comprehension but the two groups had a similar performance on a reading decoding test. It is interesting to notice that similar results can also be found with a metacognitive program focused on a different area. Indeed, the results were replicated by Cornoldi and Lucangeli (1996) in a study examining the effects of a metacognitive program aimed at improving children's study skills. Also in this case, the metacognitive group outperformed the other group in the controlled learning areas but not in the low-control learning areas. In a further study Lucangeli, Cornoldi, and Tellarini (1998) examined the effects of a metacognitive program focused on mathematics (enhancing metacognitive knowledge, attitude, and procedures) on primary school children. In one study (Study 2) 30 trained children outperformed the control group in logical thinking and problem solving, but not in arithmetic and geometrical information.

Effects of Metacognitive Training: Generalizability

Another prediction concerning metacognitive training concerns its capacity to produce generalization effects. It is well known that training focused on a specific ability, and based on repeated practice, often fails to produce skills that are generalizable to similar skills and contexts. In the case of metacognition, it has been shown that individuals with higher meta-cognition are better at transferring learned strategies to new contexts (e.g., Cavanaugh & Borkowski, 1980). This effect is consistent with the assumption that metacognition affects central cognitive functions that rely, to a lesser extent than low-control processes, on the specific content domain.

In the previously cited research by Lucangeli et al. (1995), the first study showed that children who were trained in metacognitive knowl-edge were better in transferring a learned strategy to a new context. In the study, both the metacognitive group and a control group were trained in the use of the alphabetical strategy, consisting in the orderly scanning of the alphabet to get a phonological cue for retrieving information. At the end of the training, the two groups obtained a similar performance in a task requiring the use of the strategy. However, when the task request was modified and thus required an adaptation of the strategy, the meta-cognitive group outperformed the control group. In their second study, Lucangeli et al. (1995) supported the generalization hypothesis in two ways. First it was shown that the group that underwent the reading meta-cognitive program was not only better than the other group in reading comprehension, but also in problem solving, whereas the two groups were similar not only in decoding but also in calculation. The same study included another group that used a metacognitive program which did not have a direct relationship, with either reading or with mathemat-ics. In fact, this third group was administered a metacognitive program focused on knowledge about memory, actually the same program used in the first study. Results were even more exciting than for the other condi-tions, because the children who had worked on metamemory were bet-ter in reading and problem solving than the children who had practiced their reading and problem solving. Also the other previously mentioned study on mathematical metacognitive training (Lucangeli et al., 1998) produced a similar outcome: Indeed, the metacognitive group outper-formed the control group not only in controlled mathematics but also in reading comprehension.

CONCLUSIONS

The present chapter offers an overview of an approach to human intel-ligence that shows how basic cognitive structures, biologically deeply rooted, can be described and how they are affected by other variables more susceptible to modifications due to education. It is argued that controlled working memory represents the core component of basic intelligence: the relationship between intelligence and working memory increases in correspondence with increases in the degree of attentional control of working memory, thus taking into account the hierarchical structure of intelligence.

In fact, working memory also better explains some crucial differences between groups assumed to have different intellectual abilities. In particular, individuals with mental retardation function poorly in central components both of intelligence and working memory. On the contrary, individuals with specific learning disabilities function poorly in more peripheral working memory and intelligence components. Furthermore, controlled working memory is a key construct for understanding the biological bases of intelligence associated with the development of executive functions, and there is evidence that controlled working memory training may affect fluid intelligence, probably modifying the subject's ability to use controlled processes.

In fact, basic intelligence is affected, in its use, by three main variables: experience, culture, and metacognition. Metacognition is the most critical variable as it affects the core components of intelligence. In the chapter evidence collected in our laboratory was presented to show the efficacy of metacognitive programs in improving higher level academic skills (reading comprehension and problem solving), but not lower level skills (reading decoding and arithmetic). The fact that a metacognitive approach produced important transfer effects constitutes further evidence of its role on more central, less domain-dependent effects.

In conclusion, the debate concerning the modifiability of human intelligence can be solved by distinguishing between a biologically rooted basic intelligence, somewhat modifiable, that is strictly associated with working memory, and components that make basic intelligence applicable to real-life situations. Of these components, metacognition appears particularly critical because it affects the most central aspects of basic intelligence and may directly contribute to a better capacity to control working memory operations. Another important reason for paying particular attention to the educational implications of metacognition is that usual life events and traditional cultural and educational efforts do not necessarily guarantee the development of metacognition.

REFERENCES

Ackerman, P. L., Beier, M. E., & Boyle, M. O. (2005). Working memory and intelligence: The same or different constructs? *Psychological Bulletin, 131,* 30–60.

Begg, I., Duft, S., Lalonde, P., Melnick, R., & Sanvito, J. (1989). Memory predictions are based on ease of processing. *Journal of Memory and Language, 28,* 610–632.

Borkowski, J. G., Carr, M., Rellinger, E., & Pressley, M. (1990). Self-regulated cognition: Interdependence of metacognition, attributions, and self-esteem. In B. F. Jones & L. Idol (Eds.), *Dimensions of thinking and cognitive instruction* (pp. 53–92). Hillsdale, NJ: Erlbaum.

Cavanaugh, J. C., & Borkowski, J. G. (1980). Searching for metamemory–memory connections: A developmental study. *Developmental Psychology, 16,* 441–453.

Ceci, S. J. (1996). *On intelligence: A bioecological treatise.* Cambridge, MA: Harvard University Press.

Cornoldi, C. (1987). Origins of intentional strategic memory in the child. In B. Inhelder, D. De Caprona, & A. Cornu-Wells (Eds.), *Piaget today* (pp. 183–201). Hillsdale, NJ: Erlbaum.

Cornoldi, C. (1995). La memoria di lavoro visuo-spaziale. In F. Marucci (Ed.), *Le immagini mentali* (pp. 145–181). Rome: La Nuova Italia Scientifica.

Cornoldi, C. (1998). The impact of metacognitive reflection on cognitive control. In G. Mazzoni & T. O. Nelson (Eds.), *Metacognition and cognitive neuropsychology* (pp. 139–159). Mahwah, NJ: Erlbaum.

Cornoldi, C. (2006). The contribution of cognitive psychology to the study of human intelligence. *European Journal of Cognitive Psychology, 18,* 1–17.

Cornoldi, C. (2007). *L'intelligenza.* Bologna: Il Mulino.

Cornoldi, C., Carretti, B., & De Beni, R. (2001). How the pattern of deficits in groups of learning-disabled individuals help to understand the organization of working memory. *Issues in Education, 7,* 71–78.

Cornoldi, C., De Beni, R., & Fioritto, M. C. (2003). The assessment of self-regulation in college students with and without academic difficulties. *Advances in Learning and Behavioral Disabilities, 16,* 231–242.

Cornoldi, C., & Lucangeli, D. (1996, July 18–22). *The effects of a metacognitive study skills program on reading and mathematical skills.* Paper presented at the Memory Conference, SARMAC Symposium, Abano Terme, Italy.

Cornoldi, C., & Oakhill, J. (Eds.). (1996). *Reading comprehension difficulties: Processes and intervention.* Mahwah, NJ: Erlbaum.

Cornoldi, C., & Vecchi, T. (2003). *Visuospatial working memory and individual differences.* Hove, UK: Psychology Press.

Duncan, J. (2005). Frontal lobe function and general intelligence: Why it matters. *Cortex, 41,* 215–217.

Fodor, J. A. (1983). *The modularity of mind.* Cambridge, MA: MIT Press.

Hertzog, C., & Robinson, A. E. (2004). Metacognition and Intelligence. In O. Wilhelm & R. W. Engle (Eds.), *Handbook of understanding and measuring intelligence* (pp. 101–123). Thousand Oaks, CA: Sage.

Johnson, J., Im-Bolter, N., & Pascual-Leone, J. (2003). Development of mental attention in gifted and mainstream children: The role of mental capacity, inhibition, and speed of processing. *Child Development, 74,* 1594–1614.

Kane, M. J., & Engle, R. W. (2002). The role of prefrontal cortex in working memory capacity, executive attention, and general fluid intelligence: An individual-differences prospective. *Psychonomic Bulletin and Review, 9,* 637–671.

Kaufmann, G. (1996). The many faces of mental images. In C. Cornoldi, R. H.

Logie, M. A. Brandimonte, G. Kaufmann, & D. Reisberg (Eds.), *Stretching the imagination* (pp. 77–118). New York: Oxford University Press.

Kyllonen, P. C., & Christal, R. E. (1990). Reasoning ability is little more than working memory capacity? *Intelligence, 14,* 389–433.

Lanfranchi, S., Cornoldi, C., & Vianello, R. (2004). Verbal and visuo-spatial deficits in children with Down sindrome. *American Journal on Mental Retardation, 6,* 456–466.

Lucangeli, D., & Cornoldi, C. (1997). Mathematics and metacognition: What is the nature of the relationship? *Mathematical Cognition, 3,* 121–139.

Lucangeli, D., Cornoldi, C., & Tellarini, M. (1998). Metacognition and learning disabilities in mathematics. *Advances in Learning and Behavioral Disabilities, 12,* 219–244.

Lucangeli, D., Galderisi, D., & Cornoldi, C. (1995). Specific and general transfer effects following metamemory training. *Learning Disabilities: Research and Practice, 10,* 11–21.

Marshalek, B., Lohman, D. F., & Snow, R. E. (1983). The complexity continuum in the radex and hierarchical models of intelligence. *Intelligence, 7,* 107–127.

Meneghetti, C., De Beni, R., & Cornoldi, C. (2007). Strategic knowledge and consistency in students with good and poor study skills. *European Journal of Cognitive Psychology, 19,* 628–649.

Mueller, C. M., & Dweck, C. S. (1998). Praise for intelligence can undermine children's motivation and performance. *Journal of Personality and Social Psychology, 75,* 33–52.

Pearl, R., Bryan, T., & Donahue, M. (1980). Learning disabled children's attributions for cognitive behaviors and failure. *Learning Disability Quarterly, 3,* 3–9.

Plomin, R., De Fries, J. C., Craig, I. W., & McGuffin, P. (Eds.). (2003). *Behavioral genetics in the postgenomic era.* Washington, DC: American Psychological Association.

Re, A. M., & Cornoldi, C. (in preparation). *Metacognition and expressive writing in ADHD.*

Runco, M. A. (1999). A longitudinal study of exceptional giftedness and creativity. *Creativity Research Journal, 12,* 161–169.

Schneider, W. (1998). The development of procedural metamemory in childhood and adolescence. In G. Mazzoni & T. O. Nelson (Eds.), *Metacognition and cognitive neuropsychology* (pp. 1–21). Mahwah, NJ: Erlbaum.

Schneider, W., & Pressley, M. (1989). *Memory development between 2 and 20.* New York: Springer-Verlag.

Swanson, H. L. (2006). Cognitive processes that underlie mathematical precociousness in young children. *Journal of Experimental Child Psychology, 93,* 239–264.

Swanson, H. L., & Sachse, L. (2000). A meta-analysis of single-subject-design intervention research for students with LD. *Journal of Learning Disabilities, 33,* 114–136.

Vernon, P. E. (1961). *The structure of human abilities.* London: Methuen.

Vygotsky, L. S. (1978). *Mind in society: The development of higher psychological processes.* Cambridge, MA: Harvard University Press.

Wilhelm, O., & Engle, R. W. (Eds.). (2005). *Handbook of understanding and measuring intelligence.* Thousand Oaks, CA: Sage.

Part IV

CONCLUSION

12

Common Themes and Future Challenges

Harriet Salatas Waters
Wolfgang Schneider

This volume was designed to acknowledge the progress we have made in understanding metacognition, strategy development, and its impact on instruction across domains, while highlighting common findings and perspectives. Although the researchers have pursued the interplay between metacognition and strategy use in quite different domains, the chapters converge around a number of common issues that seem likely to be central in future strategy development research. These issues, in spite of differing methodological approaches and content areas, or because of them, are highlighted by bringing these chapters together in one volume.

As many of the researchers acknowledge, key questions that have guided the strategy development field from its inception have only been partially answered, even after several decades of research. The core question "What develops?" has been replaced with a more complex set of questions that focus on the interplay between content knowledge, metacognition, and strategy use. Furthermore, although all of these topics have been investigated over the years, which ones have received greater attention has changed as the strategy development field has broadened into different knowledge domains and into applied settings. One of the most striking features of the chapters included in this volume is the increasing prominence of metacognition. Our own interpretation is that this change has in part been driven by the move into math and science areas and the corresponding importance of explanation and reflection on ongoing problem solving. In addition, the move into the classroom has forced the issue of transfer to the fore and, with that, more sophisticated discussions of the role of metacognitive knowledge in promoting transfer in academic settings.

The shift toward metacognition encourages us all to regroup to some degree and examine strategy acquisition within a more metacognitive mind-set. We have selected a number of themes that emerged from our reading of the chapters that are likely to be central in future discussions of metacognition and strategy use. We list them below for our readers and offer them as guides for future research.

GOAL-DIRECTED ACTIVITY

Understanding goal-directed strategy use was a key question from the early days of memory development (Flavell, 1971). But with studies showing differing degrees of what seemed to be deliberate strategy use and innumerable ways of prompting more or less strategy use in children, what was goal-directed became somewhat obscured. Researchers argued that the notion of intentionality was difficult to pin down (e.g., Wellman, 1977, 1988), and further, that metacognitive assessments did not necessarily link what children "said" to what they did.

The current chapters indicate, however, that there has been a reemergence of the importance of understanding goal-directed strategy use from the more traditional memory paradigms to interventions in classroom environments. Waters and Kunnmann explore early childhood in which deliberate strategy use has been questionable and challenged repeatedly over the years. They argue that young children can be goal-directed in their strategy use under the appropriate conditions and that a transfer of strategies can be achieved. Ornstein, Grammer, and Coffman's work in the classroom also argues for the possibility of goal-directed strategy use in young children. Although the mechanisms by which "high mnemonic" teachers prompt strategy use in their students still needs further investigation, the results are unambiguous. Young students exposed to teachers who use metacognitive language in the classroom show broad-based and enduring strategy use, even as they leave their teacher's classroom and progress through the elementary school grades.

The Ornstein et al. work is particularly exciting because it provides a link between early school years and the later goal-directed strategy use shown by older students engaged in scientific problem solving (e.g., Kuhn,

Mayer). It opens the door for a more continuous progression toward goal-directed strategy use, with the possibility of establishing building blocks in early elementary school ready to be adapted to the academic challenges of later school years. There is no doubt that the work on scientific reasoning demonstrates the importance of framing questions and implementing strategies to answer those questions, that is, goal-directed activity.

The science literature, however, only provides a partial view of the importance of goal-directed strategy use in later school years. The chapters on reading, writing, and academic performance in the last section of this volume grapple with "cognitive engagement" in reading (Afflerbach and Cho), effective management of writing strategies (Harris, Santangelo, and Graham), and "intelligence in use" in characterizing individual differences (Cornoldi). These and many of the other chapters address different ways to prompt greater engagement and depth of understanding in students, all in the service of more deliberate strategy use to meet the goals of academic performance. This remains a key question at the intersect of developmental and educational psychology.

INTERPLAY BETWEEN METACOGNITIVE KNOWLEDGE AND SELF-MONITORING

As Schneider notes in his chapter, the early discussions of metacognition had the seeds of further category differentiation of what constitutes metacognition. "What we know about our own cognitive processes" was quickly divided into two basic groupings, declarative metacognitive knowledge and procedural metacognitive knowledge. Although different researchers have introduced nuances over the years that have led to even greater differentiation, for our comments, the two groupings suffice.

As Werner (1957) noted so many years ago, differentiation prompts integration. The field is now clearly in an "integration" phase. The researchers in our volume are very much concerned about the ramifications of how and why declarative and procedural knowledge interact. The theoretical complexity of this interaction has already been noted (e.g., the good information-processing model; Pressley, Borkowski, & Schneider, 1989), but much remains to do on the details of this interaction and how it is expressed in different contexts. Moreover, interrelations between subcategories within the declarative and procedural knowledge components need closer investigation. For instance, it is still unclear how the monitoring and control aspects of procedural knowledge interact in different age groups. Undoubtedly, one of the most striking themes of the current volume concerns researchers' interest in how declarative metacognitive knowledge and procedural knowledge (self-monitoring) inter-relate within different domains, different individuals, different cultures, and in different contexts (laboratory vs. classroom).

A number of the chapters are particularly representative of this inter-est. Carr's discussion of the interplay between metacognitive knowledge and self-monitoring within the field of math strategies and achievement is both informative and sets the stage for further investigation. As with many of the other researchers, her focus is on instruction and interven-tion within the classroom, with an eye toward adapting instructional techniques to meet the needs of different children, some of whom may be struggling with academic demands. Similar analyses can be found in the writing chapter by Harris et al, and that of the reading strategies chapter by Afflerbach and Cho. In the former chapter we learn how both metacognitive knowledge and self-regulation skills can be integrated into an effective writing program for both normally achieving students and those with learning difficulties. In the latter chapter comparisons of Inter-net reading and more traditional reading formats highlight even more the importance of the interplay between metacognitive knowledge and self-monitoring. Finally, the Cornoldi chapter expands the discussion to include the effects of content areas, experience, culture, and values. The reader can't help but be impressed by the progress that all of this research represents. At the same time there is a great deal more to be done to change educational implications into educational realities for both low-functioning and high-functioning children.

TYPES OF KNOWLEDGE

Further differentiation did not stop with "metacognition." More recent analyses of scientific problem solving also address the range of knowl-edge that comes into play as an individual attempts to solve scientific reasoning problems. As Mayer points out in his chapter, the necessary knowledge ranges from specific facts to conceptual knowledge to strate-gies and metastrategies that guide problem solutions and accompanying monitoring. The key of course is for students to effectively coordinate all of these types of knowledge to help build understanding and adaptively use that understanding to guide problem solving. Once again, differentia-tion focuses our research efforts on integration and coordination.

Waters and Waters also weigh in by investigating the interplay between domain-general and domain-specific knowledge as child and adult bird experts deal with the cognitive demands of various problem-solving tasks. Although their findings are primarily demonstrations of how these individuals perform across tasks, the differences argue for a complex interplay between task demands, age, education, and degree of expertise. Waters and Waters introduce the idea of knowledge utilization to explain some of the differences and argue that there is diversity in both knowledge utilization and overall knowledge among individuals. They suggest that future research should explore factors that influence effective knowledge utilization and encourage science educators to foster more flexible knowledge use by varying student activities in the classroom. If we add to this the advantages of self-explanation (Siegler) and interactive multimedia lessons (Mayer) to the mix, we introduce the dimension of depth of understanding within different types of knowledge. All of this points to further investigations on the interaction between knowledge, reasoning strategies, and performance inside and outside of the classroom.

INDIVIDUAL DIFFERENCES
AND THE SHIFT TO MICROGENETIC DESIGNS

Another striking feature of the chapters included in this volume is the interest in individual differences. Our contributors are of common mind that there are different paths to competence and that individuals may need differing types of support depending on what they bring to the task of learning. A number of the chapters examine educational interventions that impact children with learning difficulties and many include longitudinal designs that enable researchers to track different developmental paths over time. Schneider reports that progression toward consistent strategy use may be abrupt or more incremental, and that how close or far apart the assessments are will impact on the patterns identified. Ornstein and his collaborators show different trajectories toward more competent strategy use over the early grades of elementary school depending on whether children were exposed early to a teacher who relied on metacognitive-rich language in her or his lessons.

Given the early reliance on cross-sectional designs in the basic strategy development literature, this is a significant change in methodology. Not only have longitudinal designs provided new insights in the heterogeneity of development, but they give us an opportunity to fine-tune our educational interventions. Perhaps this is most apparent in the studies that use microgenetic analyses. For example, Kuhn and Pease were able to tease apart the effects of higher level partners versus lower level partners on joint problem solving over several months of computer-based scientific inquiry problems. Siegler and Lin used microgenetic analyses to pin down how exactly self-explanation facilitates learning at different ages and with different cognitive tasks. The richness of the data enabled the authors to draw fairly specific conclusions about the how and why of the positive effects of self-explanation. For example, they report that variability of initial reasoning is positively linked to adopting a more sophisticated solution on subsequent trials. Only microgenetic analyses can track these nuances in individual patterns of development.

THE MOVE INTO THE CLASSROOM

Our readers with more established interests in educational applications might chuckle when they encounter this "theme" because they have been there already for many years. But the chapters included in this volume accentuate the fact that the division between basic and applied research has always been artificial. Not only Michael Pressley, but many of the contributors in this volume, have devoted their careers in making the point that research on cognitive development is not only of great relevance for understanding children's progress in school, but that understanding cognitive development requires examining cognitive development in the real world.

In particular, many of the chapters report findings from the classroom that offer an opportunity to reconsider some of the assumptions that have arisen out of laboratory-based research. For example, the Ornstein et al. research on the impact of teachers' mnemonic style on children's long-term strategy use in both experimental and more typically school-based memory tasks could only be done "in the classroom." But its findings are significant not only because we learn how teachers' language use can influence strategy development, but because they challenge the traditional view that metacognition's relationship with strategy use is somewhat tenuous in early childhood. Siegler and Lin's results on the positive effects of self-explanations with younger children concur, as do the memory strategy results of Waters and Kunnmann.

Another example of the importance of classroom research in changing our views of cognitive development are the findings presented in several chapters that deal with computer–student interactions. As noted earlier, one of the key themes of this volume is goal-direct activity. Learning in the contemporary classroom moves our students from sitting at their desks to actively engaging with computers for an increasing range of learning goals. And with that move, we seem to be rediscovering how important goal-directed strategy use is for broad-based cognitive development that enables students to adaptively and effectively generalize to new situations. More such research is likely on the horizon and our appreciation of the learner's adeptness at meeting the learning challenges of our changing classrooms is likely to increase. It may be that as we demand more goal-directed strategy use from our students, students will respond in kind.

PEER SUPPORT

The final theme is the importance of social context in learning. Social cultural perspectives have become more prominent in the field in recent years, with researchers investigating children's learning in interactions with adults and with peers. Of some note in the current set of chapters is the emphasis on peer support for strategy development in a number of domains including math strategy development, scientific reasoning, and writing skills. There is of course a practical side to this development, that is, why not use peers as a resource as well as teachers and other instructional resources?

But the findings suggest that peer interaction can be a powerful force for development. Carr, for example, describes numerous studies that show that metacognitive instruction combined with cooperative learning enhances mathematics learning. This research nicely confirms findings from previous studies showing that metacognitive training can exert powerful effects on children's school learning (e.g., Palincsar & Brown, 1984). Kuhn and Pease emphasize that cognition is fundamentally and most often a social activity that takes place in a social context. They demonstrate that working on scientific inquiry problems with a partner over several months enhances fifth graders' scientific reasoning, noting that social interaction helps students recognize the weaknesses of less effective strategies. Harris et al. describe the advantages of adding a peer support component to writing instruction with young writers who are struggling. Finally, the Siegler and Lin work on self-explanations points out that explaining the solutions of others is more potent than explaining one's own solutions. Talking to peers is likely to prove a direct path to rule-based understanding and effective generalization of strategies for a wide range of students, young and old, high and low achieving.

SUMMARY

In offering some key themes that emerge from reading the chapters included in this volume, we have concluded that the scales have tipped decidedly toward the importance of metacognition in understanding strategy development and in developing new and more effective interventions. Researchers are filling in the details on how metacognitive knowledge and self-monitoring interact as students take on the tasks of reading, writing, math, and science problem solving. The line between basic and applied research has all but disappeared, allowing researchers to benefit from the advances on both sides of the "line." Future research is likely to reflect greater integration of common interests as research focuses even more on individual differences and educational interventions.

REFERENCES

Flavell, J. H. (1971). First discussant's comments: What is memory development the development of? *Human Development, 14,* 272–278.

Palincsar, A. S., & Brown, A. L. (1984). Reciprocal teaching of comprehension-fostering and comprehension-monitoring activities. *Cognition and Instruction, 1,* 117–175.

Pressley, M., Borkowski, J. G., & Schneider, W. (1989). Good information processing: What it is and what education can do to promote it. *International Journal of Educational Research, 13,* 866–878.

Wellman, H. M. (1977). The early development of intentional memory behavior. *Human Development, 20,* 86–101.

Wellman, H. M. (1988). The early development of memory strategies. In F. E. Weinert & M. Perlmutter (Eds.), *Memory development: Universal changes and individual differences* (pp. 73–100). Hillsdale, NJ: Erlbaum.

Werner, H. (1957). The concept of development from a comparative and organismic point of view. In D. B. Harris (Ed.), *The concept of development: An issue in study of human development* (pp. 125–148). Minneapolis: University of Minnesota Press.

Author Index

Page numbers followed by an *f* or *t* indicate figures or tables.

Subject Index

Page numbers followed by an *f*, *n*, or *t* indicate figures, notes, or tables.